本教材获湖北省政府第八届高校教学研究成果奖

The Art of English Public Speaking

(The 3rd Edition)

英语演讲艺术

（第3版）

刘诺亚　付华军 ➔ 著

华中科技大学出版社
http://www.hustp.com
中国·武汉

内 容 提 要

作者将十余年来收集珍藏的影视演讲资料倾心奉献！本书宗旨：老师快乐地教，学生快乐地学！本书摒弃了国内传统教材例证和演讲材料过于严肃正式、过于冗长、用词生僻、难度过大、枯燥沉闷的缺点，以大量的影视英语演讲视频和文字材料作为例证，贯穿全书。每章后还为课堂内外提供了"一分钟演讲"训练话题，都是近年来国内热点话题和大型演讲比赛的题目。本书可供英语专业和非英语专业学生作为教材使用，也是英语爱好者享受英语文化的精神食粮和练习听力、口语的良师益友。

图书在版编目(CIP)数据

英语演讲艺术/刘诺亚,付华军著. —3 版. —武汉：华中科技大学出版社,2018.9 (2021.1重印)
ISBN 978-7-5680-4429-5

Ⅰ.①英… Ⅱ.①刘… ②付… Ⅲ.①英语-演讲-语言艺术 Ⅳ.①H311.9

中国版本图书馆 CIP 数据核字(2018)第 221017 号

英语演讲艺术（第 3 版）   刘诺亚 付华军 著
Yingyu Yanjiang Yishu (Di 3 Ban)

策划编辑：刘 平
责任编辑：刘 平
封面设计：刘诺亚
责任校对：李 琴
责任监印：周治超
出版发行：华中科技大学出版社（中国·武汉） 电话：(027)81321913
     武汉市东湖新技术开发区华工科技园 邮编：430223
录 排：华中科技大学惠友文印中心
印 刷：武汉开心印印刷有限公司
开 本：787mm×1092mm 1/16
印 张：17 插页：1
字 数：410 千字
版 次：2021 年 1 月第 3 版第 7 次印刷
定 价：48.00 元

本书若有印装质量问题，请向出版社营销中心调换
全国免费服务热线：400-6679-118 竭诚为您服务
版权所有 侵权必究

《英语演讲艺术》是作者在十多年的英语演讲教学和竞赛培训实践中,经过不断总结经验和心得体会,反复修改完成的。该书内容系统全面,从演讲的概念和重要性到演讲稿各环节的准备,从演讲者的语言、声音到体态语技巧,从演讲中的幽默到演讲与修辞的关系,从特殊场合的演讲到演讲比赛,等等。我自己也研究过法庭的演说艺术,并且研读了国内不少关于演讲的教材、专著和文章,但是相比之下,阅读这本书稿时,我更能感受到一种扑面而来的清新而独特的气息。

首先,这本书时尚新潮,别具一格。与其他教材相比,它最大的特色和亮点就是突破传统,以影视演讲作品为分析和学习的主要例证,这在国内英语演讲教学和研究领域填补了一项空白,开拓了新方向。语言学习不能脱离文化,影视作品中体现出来的生动有趣的各种文化场景和真实活泼的语言引人入胜,令人乐此不疲。我相信让人耳目一新、短小精悍的影视演讲更能让人感受语言与文化的魅力,享受英语学习带来的快乐、自信和成就感,更能激发学习者的欲望,让学习过程和氛围轻松活泼。引人注意的是书中最新的例子更新到了2011年的美国MTV音乐奖、2012年发行的电影作品和2012年美国电影金球奖和奥斯卡颁奖典礼上的演讲。同时,书中使用了大量多样化的影视演讲文字和视频资料,可以看出作者对英语影视文化比如片名、剧情、演员、角色、年份等等信息了如指掌,如数家珍,对其研究和运用的广度和深度令人佩服。

其次是创新性和前沿性。该书是国内第一本详细探讨英语演讲中的幽默问题的教材;结合影视英语演讲范例,涉及幽默的定义、幽默在演讲中的功能、使用方法和误区。在"英语演讲与修辞"一章中,作者所引用的例证大多也是发布在新闻媒体和电影中的演讲片段。在"特殊场合英语演讲"一章中,作者列出多达21种英语文化特殊场合的演讲,这是前所未有的。同样,所用的例子几乎全是影视中的英语演讲。就语言层面来说,影视作品的优点是:它们为我们展示了风格多样、文体各异的语言特色。严肃场合中用词正式、句式和篇章结构严谨的例子,如《空军一号》里,美国总统的演讲铿锵有力,一气呵成,用词、句式都是高阶段英语学习者的典范材料。其中一句结构精致的"Real peace is not just the absence of conflict; it's the presence of justice."能引起我们强烈的共鸣。有的例子让我们也体会到了非正式场合口语化、生活化的语言魅力,少数演讲中甚至出现了粗俗的俚语和禁忌语,比如在一次课堂辩论演讲中,一个女生用了"haul my ass to the kitchen"来表达"屁颠屁颠地奔向厨房"之意。对英语学习者来说，了解学习这种语言的重要性和必要性在于，这才是英美人在生活中实际使用的、真正的、活的、地道的语言，而且是我们在课堂上和课本上学不到的语言。

再次是可读性和实用性。本书语言浅显易懂，深入浅出，理论紧密联系实践，而且图文并茂，例证生动。本书还有很多方便教学者和学习者的人性化的地方，比如：对重难点生词提供汉语注释，提供配套的视频、音频光盘，每章后提供"一分钟演讲"的训练话题，还有作者自选自译、非常实用且针对性强的名人名言集，等等。作者的辛劳勤恳及良苦用心，可见一斑。

最后是通用性。本书既可供英语专业和非英语专业学生作为教材使用，也是英语爱好者享受英语文化熏陶的精神食粮和练习听力、口语的良师益友。

华中科技大学出版社的刘平编辑是很有眼光的。相信这本书出版后一定会受到广大师生和读者的欢迎。

是为序。

2012.4.27

（原华中师范大学外国语学院院长、博士生导师）
二〇一二年阳春于抑扬斋

前　言

　　演讲作为一种口语传播活动,从古希腊开始便在人类文明的经济、政治、军事、文化、生活等领域中发挥着重要的作用。对现代人来说,较高的演讲能力更是成功交际的必要手段。随着英语学习者对国际交流场合中英语沟通技能的重要性认识逐步加深,对培养和提高演讲技能的兴趣和需求越来越强烈,也随着英语交流技能在大学生综合素质中的重要性更加突显,越来越多的大学开设了英语演讲课,并逐步从英语专业课堂走出来,作为公共选修课步入大众视野,受到了广大非英语专业学生的欢迎。放眼全国,各级各类英语演讲比赛在学校和社会各行各业如火如荼地举行,包括 CCTV 和 *China Daily* 在内的主流媒体主办的全国大型英语演讲比赛进一步推动了英语演讲的火热发展态势。在过去的十多年里,我一直给英语专业学生主讲"英语演讲学"这门课,与此同时,辅导大学生参加各类大型比赛,并多次参与英语演讲教学培训研讨会。2011 年,开始在全校范围开设"影视中的英语演讲艺术"公共选修课,报名学习的人数大大超过了一个班的预期,多达 130 人,也见证了同学们的学习热情和对知识的渴求。

　　新世纪对具有创新能力的高素质人才的需求,迫使我们必须更新教育观念,树立创新意识,对教学内容与课程体系不断进行改革完善。在目前的大学英语课堂学习中存在诸多问题,其一是不重视口语表达和交流。即使有"说"的练习,也只是为了练语言而练语言,语言交际能力训练仍然处于表面状态。在语言的实际运用中,我们不能仅仅停留在语言的基本技能训练和基础知识学习这一层面。就英语演讲来说,还需要提高批判性思维和综合分析能力,借助非语言手段来辅助、感染和增强语言的说服力和社会交际能力。因此,英语演讲对学习者的综合技能和素质的要求给我们带来了新的挑战,也提供了新的机遇。

　　作为一门国内新兴的课程,英语演讲课在课程设置、培养方案、教材等方面还存在着很多不足,需要在各方面加强研究,吸收营养,来促进英语演讲教学的健康快速发展。最重要的首先是教材问题。虽然英语演讲的普及和对英语演讲的进一步研究为我们提供了越来越多的资源,但市面上合适的教材相对不足,演讲资源仍然匮乏。在多年的演讲教学中,笔者使用了好几种版本的演讲学教材,大多不尽如人意。在开设演讲学课程的大学或学院(对象不管是英语专业还是非英语专业的学生,是选修课还是必修课)一般都是以每学期 36 学时,即每周 2 学时的进度来安排课程计划,但是从市面上已经出版的几种教材来看,有的内容过于繁杂,有的内容过少,深度、宽度不够,有的编排体例不利于课堂学习。

演讲教材中例证材料单一陈旧和课堂教学模式老化也是一个大问题。从现有的演讲教材来看，绝大多数例证采用的是名人演讲和政论演讲。这些演讲的艺术技巧和语言魅力确实是我们学习的典范，但它们几乎都千篇一律，过于严肃正式，过于冗长，用词生僻，咬文嚼字，致使课堂气氛沉闷。这样的课堂让学生又回到了讲生词、学语法的传统学习模式中去，很容易导致他们疲惫和厌倦。而优秀影视作品中的演讲精巧短小，活泼生动，是语言学习的好素材，让学习者乐于学，愿意学。演讲课既是一门学习者提高个人素质、语言技能和沟通能力的课程，更是一门学习者享受快乐、提高自信的课程。它应该把学生从枯燥乏味的英语课堂中解脱出来，从为备考而学习的压力中解放出来，让他们不是为了学英语而学习，而是因为喜欢英语而学习。只有学生能快乐地学，教师能快乐地教，才能真正体现英语演讲课的魅力和价值。

为了突出自身的教学理念和特点，也正如 David Hume 所说，"一个演讲教学者应当主要以范例来演示"(Stephen Lucas, 2011)，从 2006 年开始，我把收集的影视演讲视频和文字材料大量引入课堂教学中作为讲解范例，深受学生欢迎。这也是编写本书的初衷。

《英语演讲艺术》的主要特色是：

(1) 讲究实用，重点突出，语言力求简洁易懂，避免啰唆和烦琐。

(2) 不罗列艰深难懂的理论和堆砌生涩的词汇，注重讲授方法和技巧，同时指出实践中的误区和陷阱。这些都尽量用条目的形式，清晰易懂地列出，而不采用大段连篇累牍的文字叙述。

(3) 书中所涉及的演讲范例以影视演讲作品为主，少量引用了国内外其他场合的优秀演讲。

(4) 为方便教师在课堂上组织和指导学生进行有针对性的演讲训练，每章后面都布置了"一分钟演讲"的题目，多为近来社会和校园热点话题。

本书不仅可以作为英语专业和非英语专业大学生课堂内外学习的教材，也是英语爱好者的良师益友和趣味学习伴侣。

在撰写过程中，我参考和引用了一些专著和教材的内容以及一些国内外演讲范文和材料，在此对相关作者及著作权人一并表示感谢。

因笔者水平有限，时间仓促，肯定还存在不足和谬误之处，恳请专家学者和使用本书的老师同人和同学们提出宝贵的批评和建议，以期将来修订和完善。

作　者
2012 年 5 月
于荆楚理工学院

第 3 版修订说明

《英语演讲艺术》(第 3 版)延续第 1、2 版以影视英语演讲为范例的基本特色和十个章节的框架结构。根据广大师生与读者的反馈建议和意见,本次修订做了如下改进。

(1) 第九章《特殊场合的演讲》做了全面修订,包括增删文字内容,更换演讲实例等;本章的修订融合了作者另一本教材《英美影视演讲欣赏》的主要内容,以达到把两书合二为一的目的。

(2) 更正和补充了部分文字错漏,增删了部分内容,包括全面更换第二章"演讲稿的准备"中的部分内容。

(3) 修订、增加了几十条中英文对照名人名言。

(4) 更换了版式,改进了版面,使阅读体验更舒适。

本教材作为教研项目"英语演讲教材建设"的一部分,获得了荆楚理工学院教研成果一等奖和湖北省政府第八届高校教学研究优秀成果三等奖。感谢荆楚理工学院副校长刘建清教授对本项目建设的关心和指导,感谢荆楚理工学院外国语学院领导和同行的支持以及团队成员的付出。这次修订也是广大师生与读者继续关爱和支持的结果,感谢使用本书的读者和同人,欢迎和期待朋友们继续提出批评和修改意见,以便下次再版时改进。

作 者

2018 年 6 月 1 日

第 2 版修订说明

　　《英语演讲艺术》(第 2 版)保持了以影视演讲为范例的特色,主要更换了部分不完整或不很适合的演讲材料,增添了部分最新影视作品中的演讲文字材料和相应的视频材料,包括一段南非前总统曼德拉在一次庭审中的自我辩护演说、几段民权运动领袖马丁·路德·金在多次集会中的演说、第 57 届格莱美音乐颁奖中奥巴马总统的一段电视演讲、第 88 届奥斯卡颁奖典礼上莱昂纳多·迪卡普里奥的获奖演讲,等等;更正和补充了书中部分文字错误和缺漏,删去和补充了部分章节的内容,增加了几十条名人名言英汉对照条目等。特别感谢我校外教 John Rodriguez 先生为全书做了文字校对工作;感谢我的演讲课程教学团队成员们的帮助和付出,特别感谢吴晓凤老师、蒯冲老师、田媛媛老师、黄音频老师和周静老师;感谢使用本书的读者和同人,并欢迎和期望朋友们继续提出批评和修改意见,以便本书再版时改进。

作　者
2016 年 3 月

Contents

Chapter 1　Public Speaking—An Overview(公众演讲:综述) ……………… (1)
　1.1　Introducing Public Speaking ………………………………………… (1)
　1.2　Importance of Public Speaking ……………………………………… (5)
　1.3　Features of English Speeches in Films ……………………………… (10)
　1.4　The Importance of Learning Public Speaking from Films ………… (18)

Chapter 2　Preparing a Public Speech(演讲稿的准备) ………………… (20)
　2.1　Selecting Our Topic …………………………………………………… (20)
　2.2　Supporting What We Have to Say …………………………………… (30)
　2.3　Organizing the Body of Our Speech ………………………………… (44)
　2.4　Beginning of Our Speech ……………………………………………… (58)
　2.5　Ending of Our Speech ………………………………………………… (70)
　2.6　Outlining Our Speech ………………………………………………… (81)
　2.7　Rehearsing Our Speech ……………………………………………… (86)

Chapter 3　Varieties of Public Speaking(演讲的种类) ………………… (88)
　3.1　Speaking Informatively ……………………………………………… (88)
　3.2　Speaking Persuasively ………………………………………………… (94)
　3.3　Speaking from Manuscript …………………………………………… (100)
　3.4　Speaking from Memory ……………………………………………… (101)
　3.5　Speaking Extemporaneously ………………………………………… (101)
　3.6　Speaking Impromptu ………………………………………………… (102)
　3.7　Answering Questions ………………………………………………… (104)

Chapter 4　Language in Delivery(演讲的语言因素) …………………… (108)
　4.1　Conquering Speaking Anxieties ……………………………………… (108)
　4.2　Rhetoric and Public Speaking ………………………………………… (111)
　4.3　Public Speaking and Daily Conversation …………………………… (129)

Chapter 5　Vocal Factors in Delivery(演讲的声音因素) ……………… (132)
　5.1　A Perfect World of Sound …………………………………………… (132)
　5.2　Pronunciation: Say the Words Correctly …………………………… (133)

5.3　Articulation: Speak Clearly ……………………………………… (134)
　　5.4　Volume: We Must Be Heard …………………………………… (136)
　　5.5　Pitch & Intonation: Make Our Voice Varied …………………… (137)
　　5.6　Tone: Be Consistent with the Subject Matter ………………… (138)
　　5.7　Rate: Don't Speak Too Fast …………………………………… (138)
　　5.8　Pause: Let It Sink in …………………………………………… (139)
　　5.9　Timbre(音色) …………………………………………………… (142)
　　5.10　Register(音域) ………………………………………………… (142)
Chapter 6　Body Language in Delivery(演讲的体态语因素) ……… (143)
　　6.1　Body Language and Nonverbal Communication ……………… (143)
　　6.2　Functions of Nonverbal Factors ………………………………… (146)
　　6.3　Managing Our Body Language ………………………………… (147)
Chapter 7　Using Humor in Delivery(演讲中的幽默) ……………… (153)
　　7.1　The Importance of Humor in Our Speech ……………………… (153)
　　7.2　How to Be Humorous in Public Speaking ……………………… (159)
　　7.3　The Pitfalls of Using Humor in Public Speaking ……………… (164)
　　7.4　Enjoy a Speech …………………………………………………… (166)
Chapter 8　Tools and Aids in Delivery(演讲中的辅助工具和手段) … (168)
　　8.1　Using Tools to Aid Our Speech ………………………………… (168)
　　8.2　Advice on Handling Aids and Tools …………………………… (172)
Chapter 9　Speaking on Special Occasions(特殊场合的演讲) …… (175)
　　9.1　Introducing & Presenting ……………………………………… (176)
　　9.2　Award Giving …………………………………………………… (179)
　　9.3　Award Receiving ………………………………………………… (180)
　　9.4　Toasting ………………………………………………………… (183)
　　9.5　Tribute …………………………………………………………… (185)
　　9.6　Eulogy …………………………………………………………… (186)
　　9.7　Debating ………………………………………………………… (188)
　　9.8　Press Conference ………………………………………………… (189)
　　9.9　School Opening & Valedictory Speech ………………………… (191)
　　9.10　Election Campaign …………………………………………… (194)
　　9.11　Inauguration Address ………………………………………… (195)
　　9.12　Business Presentation ………………………………………… (196)
　　9.13　Opening & Closing Ceremony ………………………………… (200)
　　9.14　Sermon ………………………………………………………… (204)
　　9.15　Farewell ………………………………………………………… (207)
　　9.16　Class Speech …………………………………………………… (209)
　　9.17　Court Opening & Summation ………………………………… (212)

  9.18 Wedding Hosting ……………………………………………………… (214)
Chapter 10 English Speaking Competitions(英语演讲比赛) ………………… (218)
  10.1 English Speech Evaluation ……………………………………………… (218)
  10.2 Topic-Assigned Speech …………………………………………………… (224)
  10.3 Unprepared Speech ………………………………………………………… (225)
  10.4 The Q & A Session ………………………………………………………… (228)
  10.5 Debating …………………………………………………………………… (231)
Selected Maxims & Mottos(最好的格言警句精选) …………………………………… (239)
References ……………………………………………………………………………… (258)

Chapter 1

••• Public Speaking—An Overview •••
公众演讲：综述

Every time we have to speak, we are auditioning for leadership. —James Humes
每次开口讲话都是对我们领导能力的一次面试。□ 詹姆斯·休姆斯

You can have brilliant ideas, but if you can't get them across, your ideas won't get you anywhere.
—Lee Iacocca
你可以有很多优秀的思想,但如果不会表达,那也是徒劳。□ 李·艾科卡

• 本章要点 •

● 公众演讲的定义
● 公众演讲的重要性
● 影视作品英语演讲的特点
● 学习影视作品英语演讲的意义

Introducing Public Speaking

1.1.1 Definition of public speaking

Imagine the following situations: a new member introduces himself to others upon joining a club; a job applicant presents himself in front of a panel of interviewers; a student gives a presentation in a classroom; a teacher speaks to the class; a master hosts a ceremony; a corporate manager runs a staff meeting; a guest introduces an award winner who then subsequently gives an acceptance speech; the head of a nation addresses the media or the citizens on some issue... All these occasions engage us in a certain form of social event—Public Speaking, which, to be exact, is often mistaken as a public speech. What is the difference? A public speech is a more general term which may refer to either the written form or the oral form of a speech, but public speaking, more often than not, applies to only the oral form of speech on a public occasion.

From a literal perspective, public speaking refers to a social act in a public place, both verbally and nonverbally, to expound a theme or express one's views, emotions and ideas on a specific topic, with the purpose of passing on information, or achieving propaganda and agitation. So in this sense, and first of all, public speaking is a form of communication and of exchange of ideas.

From a rhetorical view, public speaking is the art of ruling the minds of men by acting both verbally (expressing in spoken words) and nonverbally (expressing in ways other than using spoken words). Aristotle (384 BC—322 BC) discussed the relationship between speaking and rhetoric in his iconic *Rhetoric*. According to him, rhetoric is the faculty of discovering in the particular case all the available means of persuasion. It is the process of developing a persuasive argument, and oratory (public speaking) is the process of delivering that argument. (Clark, D. L., 1957). Aristotle produces his classic theory of *mastering* of the art in three areas that calls for the power of logical reasoning (logos), a knowledge of character (ethos), and a knowledge of the emotions (pathos).

Technically speaking, public speaking is a social science of public propaganda, which, in theology, is called Homiletics—the branch of theology that deals with sermons and homilies, or simply the art of preaching. With a term oratory to define the art and the practical methodology to deliver it, combining moral ethics, social politics and literary art, a public speaking process involves seven elements:

- Speaker, the message bearer;
- Message itself;
- Audience, the message receiver;
- Channel: the manners of delivery;
- Context: the settings of the event;
- Interference from the setting and the audience;
- Feedback loop: how the speaker and listener interact.

This is a system of talking, expressing and communicating, which indicates the nature of a public speaking process.

(*The Great Dictator*, 1940)

"I'm sorry but I don't want to be an Emperor—that's not my business—I don't want to rule or conquer anyone. I should like to help everyone if possible, Jew, gentile(非犹太人), black man, white. We all want to help one another. Human beings are like that.

We want to live by each other's happiness, not by each other's misery. We don't want to hate and despise(鄙视) one another. In this world there is room for everyone and the good earth is rich and can provide for everyone. The way of life can be free and beautiful. But we have lost the way. Greed has poisoned men's souls—has barricaded(阻碍) the world with hate; has goose-stepped(走正步,挺进) us into misery and bloodshed. We have developed speed but we have shut ourselves in: machinery that gives abundance has left us in want(匮乏). Our knowledge has made us cynical(愤世嫉俗的), our cleverness hard and unkind. We think too much and feel too little. More than machinery we need humanity; more than cleverness we need kindness and gentleness.

Without these qualities, life will be violent and all will be lost. The aeroplane and the radio have brought us closer together. The very nature of these inventions cries out for (迫切需要) the goodness in men, cries out for universal brotherhood for the unity of us all. Even now my voice is reaching millions throughout the world, millions of despairing men, women and little children, victims of a system that makes men torture and imprison innocent people. To those who can hear me I say 'Do not despair'.

The misery that is now upon us is but the passing of greed, the bitterness of men who fear the way of human progress, the hate of men will pass and dictators die and the power they took from the people, will return to the people and so long as men die, liberty will never perish...

Soldiers—don't give yourselves to brutes(暴徒), men who despise you and enslave you—who regiment(控制) your lives, tell you what to do, what to think and what to feel, who drill(训练) you, diet you, treat you like cattle, use you as cannon fodder(炮灰). Don't give yourselves to these unnatural men, machine men, with machine minds and machine hearts. You are not machines. You are not cattle. You are men. You have the love of humanity in your hearts. You don't hate—only the unloved hate, the unloved and the unnatural. Soldiers—don't fight for slavery, fight for liberty.

In the seventeenth chapter of Saint Luke(圣经:《路加福音》), it is written 'the kingdom of God is within man'—not one man, nor a group of men—but in all men—in you, the people.

You the people have the power, the power to create machines, the power to create happiness. You the people have the power to make life free and beautiful, to make this life a wonderful adventure. Then in the name of democracy, let's use that power—let us all unite. Let us fight for a new world, a decent world that will give men a chance to work that will give you the future and old age and security. By the promise of these *things, brutes have risen to power, but they lie. They do not fulfill their promise, they never will. Dictators(独裁者) free themselves but they enslave the people. Now let us fight to fulfill that promise. Let us fight to free the world, to do away with national barriers, to do away with greed, with hate and intolerance. Let us fight for a world of reason, a world where science and progress will lead to all men's happiness. Soldiers—in the name of democracy, let us all unite!"*

This is a classic speech, involving not only speaking, but also acting; not only verbally, but also nonverbally, made by the hairdresser played by Charlie Chaplin in *The Great Dictator* (1940). It exemplifies all the elements in a communication process: the speaker—the hairdresser; the audience—the Nazi troops and the whole world; the message—"let us all unite to build a new world"; the channel—delivery method and lastly; the feedback—the stirred emotion of the audience. We can feel the power in the end, where the inspiration would have chilled all the dictators to the spine. It was said that the impromptu part of the speech was improvised by Chaplin himself, beginning with a little flatness and even uneasiness, but gradually it climaxes to the height of eloquence and vehemence, and ends in a quiet tone, igniting hope among people who are languishing in the shackles of the dictators. It deserves to be categorized among the top ten speeches in movie history.

1.1.2 Tradition of public speaking

Public speaking in the west dates back to 4,500 years ago, when the oldest known handbook on effective speech was written on papyrus in ancient Egypt where the pharos considered speaking a more powerful weapon than fighting. In ancient Rome and Greece, where eloquence was highly esteemed, a person who could mount to a higher ground to speak in public was awed as the leader of the congregation. Speaking was also a weapon in social and political argument and struggle, with a large number of noted speakers of the times appearing, such as Socrates, Plato, Aristotle in Greece and Quintilian, Cicero in Rome. In 467 BC, a Greek started enrolling students and teaching them the art of speaking, which was then called rhetoric. Aristotle's (384 BC—322 BC) *Rhetoric*, composed during the third century B.C., is still considered the most authoritative masterpiece on speaking. (Stephen Lucas, 2007) The ancient Roman and Greek civilizations, with their openness and democracy, and more importantly, with the aid of debating and speaking, have boosted the development of democratic politics and spread it around the world.

China also shares its part of the same long history of public speaking tradition. As early as the times of Spring & Autumn and Warring States, there emerged a great many diplomats such as Su Qin, Zhang Yi, Tang Sui, Lin Xiangru, who engaged themselves in the strenuous work of persuading, lobbying, arguing and political strategizing in their struggle for the welfare of the people and the survival and prosperity of their nation. And in folk culture, we have enjoyed stories of such eloquent legends as Yan Zi (as in the folklore of Yan Zi commissioned to Chu Kingdom) in the Spring & Autumn Period, Mao Sui (as in the folklore of Mao Sui who volunteered his service) in the Qin Dynasty, Dongfang Shuo in the Han Dynasty, Zhu Geliang in the Three Kingdom period, Ji Xiaolan in the Qing Dynasty, and so on. Their wisdom, intelligence, bravery and more importantly, their eloquence, has earned them everlasting reputation and respect in Chinese history.

Importance of Public Speaking

1.2.1 Public speaking is a form of empowerment

Public speaking is the language of power and leadership. The following two remarks have told it all: "Every time we have to speak, we are auditioning for leadership." "Talkers have always ruled. They will continue to rule. The smart thing is to join them."

Developing excellent communication skills is absolutely essential to effective leadership. A leader must be able to share knowledge and ideas to transmit a sense of urgency and enthusiasm to others. If a leader can't get a message across clearly and motivate others to act on it, then having a message doesn't even matter, just as the Greek leader Pericles said more than 2,500 years ago, which is still true today, that one who forms a judgment on any point but cannot explain it might as well never have thought at all on the subject.

In Chinese, a saying goes that one word can cause the nation to prosper, and can also make it perish. The earliest record of public speaking practices in China can be traced back to the *Book of History* (*Shangshu*), and the *Intrigues of the Warring States* (*Zhan'guo Ce*), in which stories recorded and proved how an oratorical official (minister of the court) can help the nation survive and prosper.

In the western world, the art of speaking has played a vital role in civic life. We have Plato, Aristotle, and Cicero etc. in the ancient times. Modern times have witnessed such great names as Mahatma Gandhi, Franklin Roosevelt, Winston Churchill, Nelson Mandela, Ronald Reagan, Martin Luther King, Bill Clinton and Barrack Obama, and so on and so forth. "I Have a Dream" is a 17-minute speech, in which Martin Luther King called for racial equality and an end to discrimination. The speech, from the steps of the Lincoln Memorial during the "March on Washington for Jobs and Freedom" on August 28, 1963, was a defining moment of the American Civil Rights Movement. It was ranked the top American speech of the 20th century by a 1999 poll of scholars of public address.

Delivering to over 200,000 civil rights supporters, the speaker had the power, the ability, and the capacity to transform those steps on the Lincoln Memorial into a monumental area that will forever be recognized. By speaking the way he did, Martin Luther King informed, educated, and inspired the people throughout America and the world. King's speech caught the mood and moved the crowd and rose above mere oratory and the matchless eloquence. In the wake of the speech and March, King was named Man of the Year by *TIME* magazine for 1963, and in 1964, he was the youngest person ever awarded the Nobel Peace Prize. His undying "I Have a Dream" will always resound in the sky of all mankind history. This is the power of speech.

Another great speech, "The Torch Has Been Passed to the New Generation", delivered by 35th US President John F. Kennedy in his inaugural address on January 20, 1961, is widely acclaimed to be among the best presidential inauguration speeches in American history. Here are the most lauded sentences selected from it:

"Let the word go forth... that the torch has been passed to a new generation of Americans."

"Let every nation know... that we shall pay any price, bear any burden, meet any hardship, support any friend, oppose any foe, to assure the survival and the success of liberty."

"The world is very different now. For man holds in his mortal hands(凡夫之手) the power to abolish(消除) all forms of human poverty and all forms of human life."

"Let us never negotiate out of fear. But let us never fear to negotiate."

"Ask not what your country can do for you — ask what you can do for your country."

"For only when our arms are sufficient beyond doubt can we be certain beyond doubt that they will never be employed."

"All this will not be finished in the first 100 days. Nor will it be finished in the first 1,000 days, nor in the life of this Administration, nor even perhaps in our lifetime on this planet. But let us begin."

Enjoying a high esteem as the best president among American people, Kennedy expressed in this speech both his earnestness for world peace and heartfelt appeal for building a new world. The power of the speech, with its imposing majesty and stirring luxury, has influenced generations of American people as well as people in the world.

In the movie *Invictus* (2011, Morgan Freeman), newly-elected South African president Nelson Mandela, the first black president in Africa ever, works on his first day only to find that the offices are empty and the white-colored employees in the president's office are packing to leave. Please look at how Mr. Mandela convinces them to stay.

(*Invictus*, 2009)

> "Good morning. How are you feeling this morning? It's good to see you. Thank you for coming on such a short notice. Some of you may know who I am. I could not help noticing the empty offices as I came to work this morning and all of the packing boxes.
>
> Now, of course, if you want to leave, that is your right. And if you feel in your heart that you cannot work with your new government, then it is better that you do leave. Right away. But if you are packing up because you fear that your language or the color of your skin or who you worked for before disqualifies (使失去资格) you from working here, I'm here to tell you: have no such fear. What is verby is verby (荷兰语:过去): the past is the past. We look to the future now. We need your help. We want your help. If you would like to stay, you would be doing your country a great service. All I ask is that you do your work to the best of your abilities and with good heart. I promise to do the same. If we can manage that, our country will be a shining light in the world."

From this speech, we see how a great man uses simple but heart-felt language to move and convince people, and meanwhile, we see the power of speech coming from a man of high character and noble spirit.

In modern China, such names as Sun Yat-sen, Mao Zedong, Zhou Enlai, Deng Xiaoping have been remembered not only for their roles in changing the course of history in China as well as the world, but also for their undying great voices resounding over and over again in millions of people's hearts.

An even more recent example is the successful bidding for the 2008 Olympics in Beijing. The then-incumbent Vice-Premier Li Lanqing spoke in front of the IOC in English and the famous woman activist Yang Lan also played an important role in presenting China with her beautiful English.

(Yang Lan addressing the IOC presenting China)

"Mr. President, Ladies and Gentlemen, Good afternoon!

Before I introduce our cultural programs, let me tell you one thing first about 2008. You're going to have a great time in Beijing.

Many people are fascinated by China's sports legend in history. For example, back to Song Dynasty, which was the 11th century, people in our country started to play a game called Cuju, which is regarded as the origin of ancient football. The game was so popular that women were also participating. So now, you would probably understand why our women's football team does so well today.

There are a lot more wonderful and exciting events waiting for you in the New Beijing, a modern metropolis(大都市) with 3,000 years of cultural treasures woven into the urban tapestry(织锦). Along with the iconic(标志性的) imagery of the Forbidden City, the Temple of Heaven and the Great Wall, the city also offers an endless mixture of theatres, museums, discos, all kinds of restaurants and shopping malls which will amaze you and delight you.

But beyond all that, this is a city of millions of friendly people who love to meet people from around the world. They believe if the 2008 Olympic Games is held in Beijing, it will help to enhance the harmony between our culture and the diverse cultures of the world, and guarantee their gratitude will pour out in open expressions of affection for you and the great Movement that you guide.

Within our cultural programs, education and communication will receive the highest priority. We seek to create an intellectual and sporting legacy by broadening the understanding of the Olympic Ideals throughout the country.

Cultural events will unfold(开展) each year, from 2005 to 2008. We will stage multi-disciplined cultural programs, including concerts, exhibitions, art competitions and camps, which will involve young people from around the world. During the Olympics, these activities will also be held in the Olympic Village and in the city for the

Public Speaking—An Overview 公众演讲：综述

benefit of the athletes.

Our Ceremonies will give China's greatest — and the world's greatest artists a chance to celebrate the common aspiration（向往）*of humanity and the unique heritage of Chinese culture and that of the Olympic Movement.*

With a concept inspired by the famed Silk Road, our Torch Relay will break new ground（新创举）*, traveling from Olympia through some of the oldest civilizations known to man—Greek, Roman, Egyptian, Byzantine*（拜占庭）*, Mesopotamian*（美索不达米亚）*, Persian*（波斯）*, Arabian, Indian and Chinese. Carrying the message "Share the Peace, Share the Olympics", the eternal flame will reach new heights as it crosses the Himalayas*（喜马拉雅山）*over the world's highest summit—Mount Qomolangma*（珠穆朗玛峰）*, which is known to many of you as Mt. Everest. In China, the torch will pass through Tibet, cross Yangtze and Yellow rivers, travel the Great Wall and visit Hong Kong, Macau, Taiwan and the 56 ethnic communities who make up our society. On its journey, the flame will be seen by and inspire more human beings than any previous relay.*

I am afraid I cannot give you the full picture of our cultural programs within such a short period of time. Before I end, let me share with you one story. Seven hundred years ago, amazed by his incredible descriptions of a far away land of great beauty, people asked Marco Polo whether his stories about China were true. And Marco answered: What I have told you was not even half of what I saw. Actually, what we have shown you here today is only a fraction（小部分）*of the Beijing that awaits you.*

Ladies and gentlemen, I believe Beijing will prove to be a land of wonders to all of you, to athletes, spectators and the worldwide television audience alike. Come and join us. Thank you, Mr. President. Thank you all. Now I'd like to give the floor back to Mr. He."

Just as many scholars have commented, no matter how strong China's position was at the time, the Games would not have come to Beijing without the confident and eloquent speeches of the Chinese delegation on that historic afternoon in Moscow.

Some students might say those are heroes and famous people. How should we be concerned with speaking since we don't all want to become such powerful people as those? Well, we could look at the situations listed at the beginning of this chapter again, and we will prove to be wrong in that assumption. The fact that in the US all students are required to take public speaking as a compulsory course bespeaks its important role in our life and career.

1.2.2 Public speaking is a soft skill

Lee Iacocca says, "You can have brilliant ideas, but if you can't get them across, your ideas won't get you anywhere." In our era of hair trigger balances, precision of communication is important, more important than ever. A false or misunderstood word may create as much disaster as a sudden reckless act. By soft skill, we mean how we present our personal values and images in dealing with people around us. These include interpersonal skills, team spirit, social grace and negotiation skills and so on.

Our success in persuading others lies in the effectiveness of oral communication skills. "In the future, access to work will depend predominantly on the individual's interpersonal skills, skills at networking and digital literacy, ability to successfully engage in critical decision making and problem solving and the ability to organize and sustain flexible life and career contexts." (Roux, 2002) CEO of Worthington Industries John McConnell (2004) also said, "Take all the speech courses and communication courses you can, because the world turns on communication."

1.2.3　What benefits can public speaking bring to students?

☆ Language competence. Public speaking training can greatly improve our all-round language ability, i. e. verbally, a fluent, eloquent speaker, and nonverbally, a composed and effective speaker.
☆ Academic benefits. Throughout our academic days in schools, there will be numerous occasions where we have to present us orally in front of the teacher and our classmates. The training on both language and image will definitely benefit us in our academic performance.
☆ Professional benefits. We will find in our future career how crucial a communication and presentation ability is for us to excel in our job interview and in work performance evaluation, and to have a sound interpersonal relationship in our working environment. Our image to participate confidently, the ability to think quickly, clearly and analytically, to organize and run a team effectively, etc. can quickly improve our chance to be appreciated, hired, and promoted in a working place.
☆ Social benefits. A healthy mind is housed in a healthy body. A person with good communication skills and interpersonal relationship will always live a sounder life than those who lack for these skills. Creating a world conducive to us with good friendship, mutual-understanding, harmony and peace will surely benefit us greatly in our life.

We see the points above that effective oral communication skills benefit us on many levels, academically, professionally and socially.

Features of English Speeches in Films

There are a large number of public speaking scenes in films, and the occasions, styles and forms vary greatly from one to another. The viewers can enjoy not only the roller coaster tension, the overwhelming emotion and on-the-edge-of-seat suspension of the plot, but also the colorful culture and the heart-felt enthusiastic speeches. Throughout the history of English films, dating back from the black and white movies in America to modern days, we can see numerous great speeches in them, many of which deserve the attention of English learners and can be considered the ideal learning material for us. In general, there are four characteristics of speeches in movies.

1.3.1 Movie speeches as an integral part complete the plot

A speech in a movie usually happens in three places, at the beginning, middle and end. The speech at the beginning is often comparatively short and serves as the introduction to the plot; and in the middle, as a transition and an additional ingredient to aid the story development. And the speech in the end is usually longer and more emotionally-compelling, which enhances the image of the character and lifts the theme.

In general, there are four roles of a speech in a movie.

1) Having a dual audience

The speech is made to both the audience in the movie and the viewers of the movie, with the latter especially intended as the target listeners by the director of the movie in order to advocate his/her ideas, i.e. the director puts into the mouth of the character the words of the director himself/herself.

2) Speaking with a double identity

Sometimes, the speaker in the film is not only the character himself/herself in the story, but also the advocate of the movie makers, and conveys the message for and on behalf of them.

3) Creating and promoting characters and images

A character is created and promoted appealing to the viewers with his/her personal charm and charisma, through the character's speech as well as his/her appearance and body language.

4) Playing up the atmosphere

The speech happens usually at the key point or climax of the plot, putting both the audiences and the viewers into an exaggerated provocation of emotion and atmosphere.

5) Pushing the plot development

In a movie, a speech or a few speeches serve as transitions to the plot's development, and usually at the end of a movie, the climax is reached where an additional and important speech is made.

Let's cite the movie *Selma* (2014) as an example. It's a chronicle of Martin Luther King's campaign to secure equal voting rights via an epic march from Selma to Montgomery, Alabama in 1965. The unforgettable true story chronicles the tumultuous three-month period in 1965, when Dr. Martin Luther King, Jr. led a dangerous campaign in the face of violent opposition. The epic march from Selma to Montgomery culminated in

President Johnson signing the Voting Rights Act of 1965, one of the most significant victories for the civil rights movement. In this movie, Selma, the viewers learn from the story of how the revered leader and visionary Dr. Martin Luther King, Jr. and his brothers and sisters in the movement prompted change that forever altered history. There are, in general, four complete speeches in this movie, each of which plays a critical role in the development of the storyline and the construction of the movie.

The first speech happens when the story begins, providing the background for the whole campaign: Dr. King receives the Nobel Prize for Peace, and at the same time, four black girls lose their innocent young lives instantly and unknowingly in an attempted set-up blast.

(*Selma*, 2014)

"Boycotting(抵制)the buses in Montgomery(亚拉巴马州州府), segregation(种族隔离)in Birmingham(伯明翰,亚拉巴马州中部城市), now, voting in Selma(亚拉巴马州的一个市). One struggle ends just to go right to the next and the next. If you think of it that way, it's a hard road. But I don't think of it that way. I think of these efforts as one effort. And that one effort is for our life, our life as a community, our life as a nation. For our lives, we can do this. We must do this! We see children become victims of one of the most vicious crimes ever perpetrated(犯罪,作恶)against humanity within the walls of their own church! They are sainted(变成圣人,即死去)now. They are the sainted ones in this quest(寻求)for freedom. And they speak to us still. They say to us, to all of us, all colors and creeds(教义,信条)that we must do this. They say to us that it is unacceptable for more than 50% of Selma to be Negroes and yet less than 2% of Negroes here being able to vote and determine their own destiny as human beings. They say to us that the local white leadership use their power to keep us from the ballot(选票)box and keep us voiceless. As long as I am unable to exercise my constitutional(宪法的)right to vote, I do not have command of my own life. I cannot determine my own destiny for it is determined for me by people who would rather see me suffer than succeed. Those that have gone before us say, 'No more!' 'No more!' That means protest, that means march(游行), that means disturb the peace, that means jail, that means risk! And that is hard!

We will not wait any longer! Give us the vote! That's right, no more. We're not asking. We're demanding. Give us the vote!"

In this speech, firstly, Dr. King points out that the fight and request will not stop, and then tells why, because the loss of the four girls' young lives has said it all. Note the underlined "they". The speaker uses "they" as the voice calling out to them.

With the protest going on and escalating, more people are brutalized and even beaten to death. At the culmination of the march and protest, another young man's life is lost, beaten to death by the policemen. Here is the second speech made by Dr. King in a church congregation.

(*Selma*, 2014)

"*Who murdered Jimmie Lee Jackson? We know a state trooper*(州警)*, acting on the orders of George Wallace*(亚拉巴马州州长)*, pointed the gun and pulled the trigger*(扳机)*. But how many other fingers were on that trigger? Who murdered Jimmie Lee Jackson? Every white law man who abuses the law to terrorize, every white politician who feeds on prejudice and hatred, every white preacher*(教士)*who preaches the Bible and stays silent before his white congregation*(教众)*. Who murdered Jimmie Lee Jackson? Every Negro man and woman who stands by without joining this fight as their brothers and sisters are humiliated*(受辱)*, brutalized*(遭暴打)*, and ripped*(撕掉)*from this earth!*

When I heard President Kennedy had been shot and killed, when I heard just yesterday that Malcolm X(另一个黑人民权领袖)*, who stood in this very church just three weeks ago, had been shot and killed, I turned to my wife Coretta and said the same thing I often say when one of our leaders is struck down, "our lives are not fully lived if we're not willing to die for those we love and for what we believe." But today, Jimmie, we're doing the living and you have done the dying, dear brother. We'll not let your sacrifice pass in vain, dear brother. We'll not let it go! We'll finish what you were after! We'll get what you were denied! We will vote and we will put these men out of office! We will take their power! We will win what you were slaughtered for!* (Yeah! Yeah!)

We're going back to Washington. We're going to demand to see the President. And I'm going to tell him that Jimmie was murdered by an administration that spends millions of dollars every day to sacrifice life in the name of liberty in Vietnam, yet lacks the moral will and moral courage to defend the lives of its own people here in America! We will not let it go! And if he does not act, we will act! We will act! We will do it for all of our lost ones! All of those, like Jimmie Lee Jackson who have gone too soon, taken by hate(被仇恨所杀)!"

There are three parts clearly structured in the second speech: first, pointing out who are the real murderers responsible for the death of Jimmie Lee Jackson. Secondly, taking a vow that his life will not be lost in vain and his legacy will be carried on. At last, lashing out at the US government and pledging to fight for full liberty.

This speech serves as a transition in the development of the storyline, pushing the plot where the movement is stepping up once again in such immensity that the government of the US begins to take this issue seriously. Hence, we have the next speech by the President.

(*Selma*, 2014)

"*I speak tonight for the dignity of man and the destiny of democracy(民主). At times, history and fate meet at a single time in a single place. So it was last week in Selma, Alabama. There, long suffering men and women peacefully protested the denial of their rights as Americans. Rarely in anytime does an issue lay bare(赤裸地暴露)the secret heart of America itself. The issue for equal rights for the American Negro is that issue. For this issue, many of them were brutally assaulted(袭击). There is no Negro problem. There is no Southern problem. There is only an American problem. The constitution says that no person shall be kept from voting because of his race or color. To correct the denial of this fundamental(根本的)right, this Wednesday, I will send to Congress a law designed to eliminate(消除)these illegal barriers(障碍). The bill will strike down(删去)voting restrictions(限制)in all elections, federal, state and local. And we shall do this. We shall overcome.*"

President Johnson's speech proves another turning point and the culmination in the whole storyline as well as the result of the movement led by Dr. King. The speech also reveals the regret and apology of the government and the ultimate victory of this movement, at the same time, the significance of this result in the progress of human rights movement in American history.

(*Selma*, 2014)

"We heard them say we'd never make it(赶到)here. We heard them say they'd stop us, if it was the last thing they did. We heard them say we don't deserve to be here. But today, we stand as Americans. We are here, and we ain't(aren't 的口语式) gonna(going to 的口语式)let nobody turn us around. This mighty march, which will be counted as one of the greatest demonstrations of protest and progress, ends here in the capital of Alabama for a vital purpose. We have not fought only for the right to sit where we please, and go to school where we please; we do not only strive here today to vote as we please, but with our commitment, we give birth each day to a new energy that is stronger than our strongest opposition. And we embrace(拥抱)this new energy so boldly, embody(展示)it so fervently(激情地), that its reflection illuminates(照亮)a great darkness. Our society has distorted(扭曲)how we are, from slavery to the Reconstruction(指南北内战后重建), to the precipice(悬崖,险境)at which we now stand. We have seen powerful white men rule the world, while offering poor white men a vicious lie as placation(安抚), and when the poor white men's children wail(哭喊)with a hunger that cannot be satisfied, he feeds them that same vicious lie, a lie whispering to hem that regardless of their lot(命运)in life, they can at least be triumphant(胜利的)in the knowledge that their whiteness makes them superior to blackness. But we know the truth. We know the truth, and we will go forward to that truth, to freedom. We will not be stopped. We will march for our rights. We will march to demand treatments as full citizens. We will march until the viciousness and the darkness gives way to(为……让路)the light of righteousness(正义). No man, no myth, no malaise(心神不安)will stop this movement. We forbid it. For we know that it is this darkness that murders the best in us and the best of us, whether Jimmie Lee Jackson or James Reeb, or four blameless girls struck down before they had even begun. You may ask, when will we be free of this darkness? I say to you today, my *brothers and sisters, despite the pain, despite the tears, our freedom will be soon upon us, for 'truth crushed to earth will rise again'. When will we be free? Soon and very soon, because you will reap*(收获)*what you sow*(播种). *When will we be free? Soon and very soon, because no lie can live forever. When will we be free? Soon and very soon, because 'Mine eyes have seen the glory of the coming of the Lord. He is trampling*(踩踏)*out the vintage*(葡萄酒庄园)*where the grapes of wrath*(愤怒)*are stored. He hath loosed the fateful lightning of his terrible swift sword. His truth is marching on. Glory! Hallelujah! Glory! Hallelujah! Glory! Hallelujah*(赞美上帝的颂歌)*! His truth is marching on!'"* (引自美国内战期间一首歌曲 "*The Battle Hymn of the Republic*"《共和之战歌》)

The fourth and last speech comes at the end of the movie as the climax of the story. In this speech, Dr. King is not only sharing the victory and pride with his fellow men, but also warns that there is still a long road to go for black Americans. He calls on his people not to stop fighting until they earn their due justice and rights as full citizens. In the end, he quotes a part from the hymn written and sung in the Civil War times, encouraging and inspiring them with promise and hope.

From the four speeches appreciation above in Selma, we can see how important speeches are arranged in a movie: they not only work as the hinge and the thread controlling and connecting the parts of a whole movie, but also push the development of the plot, create and promote the image of characters. And more importantly, the viewers can enjoy the power and exquisiteness of the finely-crafted speeches.

1.3.2　Most speeches are brief and condensed

Speeches are often placed in a time-limited frame as we shall see later in this book. No speeches in movies will be sinfully long, lasting usually no more than 5 minutes. For example:

(*We Bought a Zoo*, 2011)

"Well, I want to say it has been an amazing experience here. Each of you, I've come to know in some small way. But the financial climate being what it is, I think none of us *thought we'd, well... I don't know how to say this. I've been adventure addict（入迷的人）my whole life, with no big regard for cost. With... well, with no regard for cost. Basically, I was just an observer and a writer. But this is my first real adventure. And I just want to say that, it's been the best one of all because it's personal. And thanks to my Katherine, the money came through（解决）. So I don't know what you've heard, but I am able to say, though I don't have a lot, I do have enough to get us by. And if you stick with me, I will give this everything. But I will need everything from you and we are going to reopen this zoo. It's the best job in the world. And it's gonna take everything to make it work. So, don't... don't give up on our adventure. Our adventure is just beginning."*

In this short speech, the speaker explains that financial shortage will not deter him from reopening the zoo, and he asks his staff to stand by and stick with him. The speech starts with "adventure", and ends with "adventure", very well organized in a short speech of only one minute. It happens in the middle of the story and serves several functions as follows: transition, pushing the plot development, as well as the character's image enhancement.

1.3.3 Movie speeches are graphical, real, and spontaneous

Compared with speech materials that are recorded in only soundtracks or written forms, speeches in movies are more dramatic, vivid and appealing, and especially so when the learners are accompanied with the plot development and affected by the characters.

1.3.4 The speeches are not only about speaking, but also acting

We all know a good presentation needs somewhat acting from the speaker. The speeches are usually elaborately acted out by the characters in movies, so the settings, the audience, the speaker's body language as well as the interaction between the speaker and the audience look more realistic.

1.3.5 The speeches are loaded with cultural materials

The benefit is more obvious when we appreciate the speech and watch the video clips at the same time. English spoken in different accents, intonations and styles is the textbook of what real English is like in the real cultural backdrop. Rich cultural elements in English movies are a great source of learning material for students. The speeches that happen in various scenes provide us a kaleidoscope of the native speakers' life.

To sum up, speeches from movies and TVs are a great source for English learners. Meanwhile, the internet has granted us unlimited access, and what's more, who can resist the charm of watching a nice movie and learning English at the same time?

1.4 The Importance of Learning Public Speaking from Films

Speaking is a social activity, a high level of verbal communication process. To speak with a purpose of passing on information and imposing ideas needs not only eloquence, thinking and analyzing abilities, but other well-round abilities as well. Watching film speeches and learning English from them is a great approach in the following senses.

1.4.1 Real English learning experience

The authenticity of the speaker, the language, and the body language is undoubtedly the ideal material for English learners. The immense range of English styles provides us a great relish of the beauty of the language: there is not only use of formal words and elaborately structured sentences in speeches on formal occasions, but also informal and even crude language in speeches on informal occasions, where there is even some vulgarity and obscenity, which we wouldn't mind much, for it's real language in real life. Our life would be boring if it's filled with people who utter only rigid words and serious long sentences. Equally, classes would be boring and tiresome if we study speeches made of only obsolete words and complicated sentences.

1.4.2 Good materials for us to imitate

With most of the speeches made of familiar words and phrases and short sentences, they are short enough for students to recite and imitate, and for teachers to organize and assess the students' performance in class activities, and also ideal ways to bring out the students' acting potential. It's a great experience for both learning and teaching in class.

1.4.3 Real time cultural experience

Gillian Brown(2003) said that communication is a risky business, for it involves not only language, but also the essence of the culture. Cultural discrepancies and conflicts often lead to a failure of communication. One can never learn a language well without being immersed and exposed into its culture. For one thing, the American and English sense of humor could be tough for us to appreciate sometimes. With the guidance of the storyline and the plot, we enjoy the authentic elements of a speaking act: the audience, the setting, and emotional involvement, and most importantly, the social and cultural immersion of the native countries.

1.4.4 Great fun to learn English from movies

Almost all good English speakers have experienced and enjoyed watching English movies, and can't resist the fun of learning English in this way; on the other hand, after all, not every one of us has the opportunity to go abroad and learn the language in the real context, so learning English from movies has greatly made up for the loss and regret.

Topics for One-Minute Speech Practice

1. Do you think people can learn as much on the Internet as they can by reading books? Which method do you prefer?
2. Hand written letters are going to vanish in the future. What do you think of the statement?
3. What problems does technology bring us?
4. What do you think of campus love?
5. Should college students be allowed to choose their own teachers?
6. Should college students concentrate more on study or on social activities?
7. What is your view on PDA (Public Display of Affection) on campus, such as kissing and hugging?
8. What would be your major consideration in choosing a job? Why?
9. If I were President of this University.
10. Competition and Cooperation.

Preparing a Public Speech
演讲稿的准备

Regardless of the changes in technology, the market for well-crafted messages will always have an audience. —Steve Burnett
不管科技如何变化，精心准备的信息推销从不缺乏听众。□ 斯蒂夫·博内特

90% of how well the talk will go is determined before the speaker steps on the platform. —Somers White
演讲成功与否百分之九十取决于演讲者上台前的准备。□ 萨默斯·怀特

● 本章要点 ●

- 如何分析听众和选题
- 如何组织和展开支撑材料
- 如何规划整体结构
- 如何开头
- 如何结尾
- 如何列提纲和排练

Selecting Our Topic

The very first step for us to prepare our speech is to decide the topic and purpose of our speech. We can begin by brainstorming, i.e. searching for potential ideas from all directions: the classes or the major we are taking; our past and present work or study experience; our hobbies; personal experience or current events that are happening at home and abroad. In this process of careful planning, we must consider the following factors in a speech: analyzing the audience, settling our purpose, deciding on the title and thesis statement.

2.1.1 Analyzing the audience

The audience is the reason we make a speech. How effective our speech will be, first of all, depends on their interest, attitude and attention span towards our speech, so in the speech preparing process, analyzing the audience's background and understanding their need will be an indispensible part in deciding our purpose, topic, style and even supporting details.

The key issues regarding the audience on an effective preparation of our speech are: their knowledge about the topic, their needs for a communication style, and their attention.

1) The audience's knowledge and demand

The audience's age, gender, belief and education background will affect their listening ability, attitude and willingness to understand or accept what we want to say. Otherwise, we are running the risk of boring the audiences, offending them or even insulting them.

2) The audience's need for a communication style

The audience expect not only what to hear from the speaker, but also how the message is to be conveyed. Whether the speech is informative, persuasive or entertaining will decide to a large extent on how we select a subject, develop a central idea, and choose the theme, examples and other supporting details as well as our rhetorical devices in the speech.

3) How can we hold their attention in the process?

For a persuasive speech, it is always a big challenge to persuade and influence the audience if there are discrepancies between the speaker and the audience in historical, social, cultural and even political views and stances. We can analyze them in three groups: those who agree and support, those who are neutral and undecided, and those who are in opposition, disagreement and even hostility.

a. For those who agree and support

Logically, in a persuasive speech, there is no need for us to go on with the topic and the theme if the audience shares our idea with consent, so there seems to be no controversy or disagreement and the part of persuasion effort seems unnecessary. But still in this case, we need to repeat and strengthen our stance so they have a deeper resonance and clearer understanding, and therefore, a more steadfast support. In some sense, they need to be inspired and boosted in their morale, and what's more, some other wavering audiences will become more convinced. In giving the great speech *I Have a Dream*, most of Martin Luther King's congregating audiences were black standing on his side fighting for freedom and equality in American society. What the speaker has achieved not only wins their support, but also boils their blood, especially in the ending part of his speech.

In the movie *Independence Day* (1996, Bill Pullman), the President character gives an inspiring speech to stir up the audience's patriotism and resolve to defend their nation from alien invasion.

(*Independence Day*, 1996)

"Good morning. In less than an hour, aircrafts from here will join others from around the world. And you will be launching the largest aerial battle(空战)in this history of mankind. Mankind huh, that word should have new meaning for all of us today. We can't be consumed(毁灭)by our petty differences anymore. We will be united in our common interests. Perhaps its fate that today is the 4th of July and you will once again be fighting for our freedom, not from tyranny(独裁), oppression(压迫), or persecution(迫害)—but from annihilation(灭绝).

We're fighting for our right to live, to exist. And should we win the day, the 4th of July will no longer be known as an American holiday, but as the day when the world declared in one voice: We will not go quietly into the night! We will not vanish without a fight! We're going to live on! We're going to survive! Today, we celebrate our Independence Day!"

In this speech, the President extends the concept of mankind and Fourth of July with its overwhelming power to inspire American people and people all over the world to fight for freedom and survival. These two examples tell us that a great speech grabs the attention of the audience who will then go along with the speakers common aspirations for justice and noble cause.

b. For those who are neutral and undecided

In a persuasive speech, these are our potential supporters and ally. What we have to do is arouse their interest, to convince them by showing how the topic is related to their interests. To do that, we need to know what their doubts and objections are. In the movie *Erin Brockovich*, the legal counsel representing the villagers who suffer from a chemical company's pollution is advising and convincing them, in a meeting, to go for a binding arbitration(有约束力的仲裁), which means the judge has the final judgment with binding force on the parties involved in a case, at the time, which is considered the only sound approach favorable for them, but because of the absence of a jury(陪审团)in court in a binding arbitration case and consequently, the uncertainty of the prospect, many of the audiences are wavering and undecided, and some of them, feeling betrayed, are even furious with the proposal, rising from their seats and ready to take off. At the moment, the counsel tries to convince them that the only reason for this choice is that they can't afford to wait for a verdict(裁决)for an indefinite length of time of 10 or 20 years or even longer, and that they have no other alternatives but to accept it or else there is no chance for anyone. At last, he says,

(*Erin Brockovich*, 2000)

"*Those who are about to leave please I'd like you to keep this date in mind*: 1978. *That's the year of the Love Canal controversy*(争端), *and those people are still waiting for their money. Think about where you will be in 15 or 20 years.*"(Hearing this, the leaving people stop and come back to their seats. Then the counsel(代理律师)continues) "*Look, everyone. Is this a big decision? Absolutely. But I do not believe, I wouldn't say this otherwise and I wouldn't say this is a sell-out*(出卖). *This is the best shot*(机会)*of getting everyone some money. You and I both know. There are people in this room who can't afford to wait, who need to take the chance. Are you going to make them wait?*"

In this case, the counsel hits the most vulnerable spot of the audience, and capitalizes on it to achieve his purpose successfully.

c. For those who are in opposition, disagreement and even hostility

For these hardened audiences, it sometimes takes a miracle to change their views and stances. There are basically two factors for their position.

One is lack of adequate knowledge of the given topic or background, hence, different perspective on the issue. For example, to some westerners, the birth control policy in China is beyond their comprehension. Whether to have children or not or how many children to have is entirely their own business and any government intervention and legal constraint is unthinkable. But they don't quite catch up with the fact that the adoption of this policy resulted from the national condition in China, which prompted the serious issues of economic development, natural resources and environment sustainability.

For another, the audiences' rooted political, cultural and religious values have formed their firm stances and views already, which is never easy to change. In this sense, it is imperative that we become a culturally effective speaker. Culturally effective speakers develop the capacity to appreciate other cultures and acquire the necessary skills to speak effectively to people with diverse ethnic backgrounds. Again, some westerners' religious tradition and dogma would never allow them to accept birth control and abortion, which is even more sinful in their eyes. Christianity advocates that life has already begun since fertilization. Therefore, abortion equals to an act of murder. A speaker who talks about birth control in front of them will certainly meet opposition from the audience. In the movie *Elizabeth* I, Queen Elizabeth speaks in front of the parliament members, convincing them to accept the idea of unity of religion. She speaks to a throng of various die-hard Catholics, Protestants and other religious believers who hold a woman-hating and cynical attitude towards her. She talks to them from her heart,

(*Elizabeth*, 1998)

"*If there is no uniformity of religious belief here, then there can only be fragmentation*(分裂), *disputes and quarrels. Surely, my lords, it is better to have a single church of England, a single church of England, with a Common Prayer Book*(公祷书), *and a common purpose. I ask you to pass this Act of Uniformity*(信仰统一法令), *not for myself, but for my people, who are my only care* ... *I have no desire to make windows to men's souls. I simply ask, can any man, in truth, serve two masters, and be faithful to both?* ... *Each of you must vote according to your conscience. But remember this: in your hands, upon this moment, lies the future happiness of my people and the peace of this realm*(国家). *Let that be upon your conscience also.*"

Queen Elizabeth convinces the audience with her sincerity. To some extent, for those hostile, cynical and hateful audiences, sincerity and honesty is more important than a skill package in the speech.

d. The last factor that can affect the audiences' reaction to the speech is the audience's attitude toward the speaker

This attitude is basically determined by how credible, qualified, authoritative and trustworthy the speaker is in the perception of the audience. The boss addressing the employees who have been told to leave will certainly face the hostility and distrust from the audience. And a speaker with bad moral sense and reputation will encounter the same attitude from the audience. In the movie *Crossing Over*, an Iraqi Muslim immigrant girl student in class is giving a speech in front of her American peers defending the terrorists' act in 9/11. We can imagine what reaction would come from the audience to the speaker: hostility, disbelief, hatred, and even disgust when hearing her speak in this way.

(*Crossing Over*, 2009)

"*The men involved in this terrorist attack have been vilified（诬蔑）, demonized（妖魔化）and condemned（谴责）by the western world. But we never want to talk about the 9/11 Jihadists（圣战分子）as real people. The media and our leaders are quick to label them as terrorists, monsters and murderers. But shouldn't we try to understand them as human beings? Everyone calls them cowards for murdering helpless passengers and causing the death of thousands of innocent lives. But cowards do not knowingly sacrifice themselves for a greater cause（事业）. You may not agree with their cause, but I do not think their actions were either cowardly or irrational. I feel, like the oppressed Palestinian people or the Iraqi citizens under occupation in their own homeland, that they found themselves without a voice. And the only way for them to be heard is to scream with the might（力量）of tons of steel and the thunderous jet engines behind them upon impact（撞击）. Their voices were heard. You may not like what they have to say, or how they got their messages across, but for the first time, we heard it.*"

In this speech, the girl student cries out for an understanding of the terrorists as human beings, and points out the cause of their inhumane act: the loss of their homeland and repression of their freedom without a voice under the occupation of the western invaders. This argument or stance, of course, will meet strong opposition from the American audiences.

2.1.2 Settling our purpose

Establishing our purpose helps us focus on our research work for the topic and theme. Generally speaking, there are three purposes in a speech: to inform, to persuade and to entertain.

1) Speaking to inform

To put it simply, an informative speaker is a teacher. He/she provides information/knowledge concerning a particular fact or circumstance, in resemblance to the work of explanatory and expository in writing. The main objective is not to entertain, or to persuade but to describe, inform and explain, so that the audience gets the knowledge about some object, process, events, concepts or issues.

2) Speaking to persuade

If we are speaking to change the audiences' attitude, to accept our view or to be motivated to take some action, then we are speaking to persuade, which, in its literal sense, means to impress, to convince and to actuate the audience, as a politician speaks in an election campaign, a lawyer speaks to defend or accuse in a court, a business executive promotes an idea or sells a product.

3) Speaking to entertain

The intention of speaking to entertain is to provide pleasure or amusement. This happens usually in a context of public gathering or a performance event, where the speaker tries to make the audience laugh, relax and feel light-hearted. Most people think of entertaining speeches given only by comedians or on special performing occasions, but humor is not the only means to be used in a speech to entertain. We need not be funny when we want to entertain the audience, but with a personal anecdote or just a story which might be moving or poignant, we can still entertain the audience.

Thus, to sum up, we should decide in this step, on our purpose in speaking, either to inform, to persuade or entertain. If we are showing our foreign guests how to make dumplings, if our history teacher asks us to give an oral report of a book we've read, we are speaking to inform; and if we try to impose on the audience our ideas of not to smoke in public, motivate and inspire them to protect our environment, to change their position, attitude, emotion and stance, we are speaking to persuade. If we speak to the audience to make them forget about their troubles, and tiredness or even get them to laugh, relax, or feel amused, then we are speaking to entertain.

Although we may find ourselves speaking with overlapping objectives, there is a primary purpose for our speech. For example: Arianna Huffington is the co-founder and editor-in-chief of *The Huffington Post*, a nationally syndicated columnist, and author of thirteen books. She informs her audience about the importance of sleeping.

(Arianna Huffington: Success Lies in Sleep)

"My big idea is a very, very small idea that can unlock(开启) billions of big ideas that are at the moment dormant(休眠) inside us. And my little idea that will do that is sleep. (laughter) (applause)

This is a room of type-A(A型血) women. This is a room of sleep-deprived(剥夺) women. And I learned the hard way(付出了沉重的代价) the value of sleep. Two and half years ago, I fainted from exhaustion. I hit my head on my desk, I broke my cheek bone. I got five stitches on my right eye. And I began the journey of rediscovering the value of sleep. And in the course of that, I studied, I met with medical doctors, scientists, and I'm here to tell you that the way to a more productive, more inspired, more joyful life is getting enough sleep. (applause)

And we women are going to lead the way in this new revolution, this new feminist(女权主义) issue. We are literally(实际上) going to sleep our way to the top, literally. (Laughter) (applause)

Because unfortunately, for men sleep deprivation(缺失) has become a virility(雄性,男子气概) symbol. I was recently having dinner with a guy who bragged that he had only gotten four hours' sleep the night before. And I felt like saying to him—but I didn't say it—I felt like saying, 'You know what? If you had gotten five, this dinner would have been a lot more interesting.' (laughter)

There is now a kind of sleep deprivation one-upmanship(胜人一筹的办法). Especially here in Washington, if you try to make a breakfast date, and you say, 'How about eight o'clock?' they're likely to tell you, 'Eight o'clock is too late for me, but that's okay, I can get a game of tennis in and do a few conference calls and meet you at eight.' And they think that means that they are so incredibly busy and productive, but the truth is they're not, because we at the moment, have had brilliant leaders in business, in finance, in politics, making terrible decisions. So a high I.Q. does not mean that you're a good leader, because the essence of leadership is being able to see the iceberg before it hits the Titanic. And we've had far too many icebergs hitting our Titanics.

In fact, I have a feeling that if Lehman Brothers(雷曼兄弟银行,2008年倒闭,引发

了导致美国并波及全球的金融危机) *was Lehman Brothers and Sisters, they might still be around. (applause) While all the brothers were busy just being hyper-connected*(高强度工作)*24/7, maybe a sister would have noticed the iceberg, because she would have woken up from a seven and a half-or eight-hour sleep and have been able to see the big picture*(大局).

So as we are facing all the multiple crises in our world at the moment, what is good for us on a personal level, what's going to bring more joy, gratitude, effectiveness in our lives and be the best for our own careers, is also what is best for the world. So I urge you to shut your eyes and discover the great ideas that lie inside us, to shut your engines and discover the power of sleep. Thank you. (applause)"

In this short talk, Arianna Huffington speaks both informatively, persuasively and in an entertaining way. The purpose of her speech is to share a small idea that can awaken much bigger ones: the power of a good night's sleep. She urges us to shut our eyes and see the big picture: We can sleep our way to increased productivity and happiness—and smarter decision-making. The main goal of her speech is to inform, but she does it in a very entertaining as well as convincing way at the same time.

Now we come to the step of asking ourselves these questions: what is my purpose? What is the goal of my speech? What do I want to accomplish? Then the purpose of our speech can be decided as the following:

- My purpose is to inform my audience about _____.
- My purpose is to persuade my audience to _____.
- My purpose is to entertain the audience with _____.

2.1.3 Deciding our theme and title

1) Guidelines on choosing a topic

There are two possibilities when we face a topic choice: an assigned topic and a selected topic. For the former, we don't have much freedom to handle, being confined to the limited area of topic. But for the latter, there is some room for us to maneuver when preparing for it, for besides our own personal inventory of information and knowledge, we can turn to the Internet or library, newspapers or magazines, or simply get ideas from listening and talking to people. One good way could be finding out and borrowing the similar topics that may be interesting to us and may have been talked about by other speakers in various public situations, including the speaking competitions.

Choosing the right topic comes along with determination of our purpose in the speech, which wins us the audiences' attention and favor from the beginning; the wrong topic, otherwise, spells disaster. The following guidelines may help us when choosing a topic.

a. Interesting to us

We must interest ourselves first, and then we can interest the audience. At least, we must be a concerned speaker.

b. Interesting to the audience

Try to make it interesting to our audience, on the condition that we know about our audience well, the relation between the audience and us, and their potential attitude and position towards our speech.

c. Appropriate to the situation

When Mao Zedong says what song we choose to sing depends on what hilltop we climb up to, it means exactly the appropriateness and fitness of our speaking environment, which includes not only the audience but the occasion, be it ever solemn, formal, festive, or joyous.

d. Appropriate to the time limit

There is usually a time limit for our speech, even if there isn't, we mustn't waste others' time, so we must consider the time amount available for us to give the speech when we do the research and preparation work.

e. Manageable

The topic must be familiar to us, within our grasp and access of resources.

2) Developing a thesis statement

A thesis statement is a complete declarative sentence which clarifies our central idea in the speech. It helps us stay focused on the topic once we have chosen a specific topic and decided our purpose in speaking. A thesis statement is different from a purpose in that a purpose is the general intent of our speech, while a thesis statement will be more specific and specifies the central idea of our speech. The function of a thesis statement is as follows:

- Letting the audience know what we want to say;
- Previewing the content of our speech;
- Including both the topic and the purpose of our speech;
- Maintaining the focus of our topic;
- Guiding us in determining what ideas we want and do not want to include in the speech.

When we plan our thesis statement, the following tips are worth considering.

a. Make sure our central idea is specific

Too vague or general an idea will not serve us well, nor will empty slogan shouting. We need to have a particular perspective, a specific point, and detailed supporting materials. For instance, in a speaking competition, the assigned topic for the contestants is about life long education. The topic is too general, and instead of generally talking about the importance of life-long education in a globalization context and an information age, one speaker starts her speech with a story about her aunt who goes to a university at the age of

40 and is enjoying her opportunity studying at a late age, and still she is planning to go to an American university for her MBA program. And then she refers to herself in the case, for one thing, about her taking extra classes like history even though she is an English major. Thus, her topic New Opened Doors is much more specific in both topic and perspective.

b. Write the statement in a full initiative phrase, not in a fragment

E. g. Spring Festival (less effective)

To inform my audience about Chinese Spring Festival (more effective)

c. The thesis is a statement, not a question

E. g. Should college students be allowed to choose their own teachers? (less effective)

To persuade my audience that college students should be allowed to choose their own teachers. (more effective)

d. Limit our statement to one distinct idea

E. g. To persuade my audience that the government should ban all cigarette advertising and that smoking should be prohibited in all public buildings. (less effective)

To persuade my audience that the government should ban all cigarette advertising. (more effective)

Or:

To persuade my audience that smoking should be prohibited in all public buildings. (more effective)

Keeping these guidelines in mind, and if we decide on our topic, know our purpose in speaking and have prepared a thesis statement, then we have completed the most difficult and frustrating step of speech making, and we are ready to go for the next step: to support our point.

Supporting What We Have to Say

A most probable contributing factor to a speech's failure can be the lack of lively, relevant and interesting supporting details, such as examples, quotations, stories, and so on. Once we have determined our subject and purpose, we then must decide how to achieve our purpose as effectively as possible. To avoid the pitfalls of confusing the listeners, the speaker should learn to first state his/her controlling ideas simply, then develop those ideas with good reasoning and evidence.

2.2.1 Presenting our idea first and straightforward

Unlike native speakers, Chinese tend to beat around the bush at the beginning of a speech, without giving an opening statement of assertion first. For instance, about the topic whether parents should buy their children going to college cars as presents, some speakers will not give their opening statement first, but elaborate a very detailed explanation of the news, or description of the background information, such as the development of economy, rising living standard etc., then the speaker will finally veer to his/her statement. This way of thinking and organizing a speech is confusing, therefore, unadvisable, for the audiences expect a controlling idea to be provided in a declarative sentence first, showing the speaker's position, stance and view.

Tips for presenting ideas:

1) A controlling idea is best expressed at the beginning. A straightforward opening is always appreciated.

2) A controlling idea must be produced in a simple declarative sentence. If it's too long, two confusions might occur: distracting and misleading. In this way, the opening statement may not be deemed as a thesis statement (a complete sentence of the purpose of a speech), but an entire speech itself.

3) A controlling idea should have a single purpose. It should be handled as a single case in a speech, as required by the principle of unity in a piece of writing. As we have discussed before, a multi-purposed speech is not only undesirable but also inoperable.

(*Lean on Me*, 1989)

"*They say, 'One bad apple spoils the bunch.' Well, what about 300? Rotten to the core*(腐烂透顶)! *Now, you're right, Mrs. Barrett: This is a war. It's a war to save 2 700 other students, most of whom don't have the basic skills to pass a state exam. Now, if you want to help us, fine. Sit down with your kids and make 'em study at night. Go get your families off welfare.*

Give our children some pride. Let 'em get their priorities straight. When Dr. Napier came to me offering this job, I saw the lightening flash. I heard the thunder roll. I felt breakers(大浪), *crashing, swamping*(淹没) *my soul.*

I fell down on my knees. And I cried, 'My God, why has thou forsaken(抛弃)*me?' And the Lord said, 'Joe, you're no damn good.' No, now I mean this more than you realize. 'You're no earthly good at all, unless you take this opportunity and do whatever you have to.' And he didn't say, 'Joe, be polite.' 'Do whatever you have to to*

> *transform and transmogrify（改变）this school into a special place* —*where the hearts and souls and minds of the young can rise, where they can grow tall and blossom out from under the shadows of the past, where the minds of the young are set free.'*
>
> And I gave my word to God! And that's why I threw those bastards out! And that's all I'm gonna say."

The principal of East Side High School is giving an inaugural speech on his first day at the school, which is now in disastrous chaos because of a number of bad students: hoodlums, drug dealers, and miscreants who have torn the place apart. The speaker focuses on his single purpose: to transform and transmogrify this school into a special place, and to achieve that purpose, he has to do three things: to give the children their pride, to let them get their priorities right, and to expel those bad apples of the bunch. In order to strengthen his persuasion, he appeals to God, making his speech strongly religious and effective. He clarifies his purpose straightforward and other details serve his purpose well in the speech.

2.2.2 Developing our ideas

As an essential step in speech preparation, we must first gather supporting material which refers to the information a speaker provides to develop and/or justify an idea or to persuade the audience. Before looking at the ways to support, we have to know the following principles of organizing supporting material in a speech.

1) Relevance

Each supporting detail should be clearly relevant to the point it is used to support.

2) Adequacy

Instead of one detail or example, sufficient amount of support is necessary to make the idea both clear and compelling to the audience.

3) Variety

A number of different forms of details are preferred instead of one type of support. A story, a statistic figure, a quote etc. may appear at the same time to support one idea.

4) Appropriateness

The type of support will have to meet the demands of the audience, and be fit for the occasion in the aspects of content, formality and style.

2.2.3 Ways to support our ideas

1) Specific detail

To develop an idea by specific detail is to list the details or break it down to its smaller parts. President Lyndon Johnson in his first address to Congress stated that, despite the recent assassination of John F. Kennedy, the country was still "capable of decisive action".

Then he continued by listing the specific details, expressed here as the new government's goals:

"From this chamber(房间,指白宫) of representative government, let all the world know and none misunderstand that I re-dedicate this Government <u>to the unswerving(始终如一的)support of the United Nations, to the honorable and determined execution of our commitments to our allies(盟友), to the maintenance of military strength second to none, to the defense of the strength and the stability of the dollar, to the expansion of our foreign trade, to the reinforcement of our programs of mutual assistance and cooperation in Asia and Africa, and to our Alliance for Progress in this hemisphere(半球).</u>"

(*All the King's Men*, 1949)

Announcer: Ladies and gentlemen, it gives me a great deal of pleasure to introduce to you that true man of the people, the next Governor of the state, Willie Stark!

Stark: My friends, my friends, I have a speech here. It's a speech about what this state needs. There's no need in my telling you what this state needs. You are the state and you know what you need. You over there, <u>look at your pants</u>. Have they got holes in the knees? <u>Listen to your stomach.</u> Did you ever hear it rumble(咕噜咕噜响) for hunger? And you, <u>what about your crops?</u> Did they ever rot in the field because the road was so bad you couldn't get them to market? And you, <u>what about your kids?</u> Are they growing up ignorant as dirt, ignorant as you 'cause there's no school for them? Now, I'm not gonna read you any speech [tosses speech]. But I am gonna tell you a story."

The speaker gives four details to support his purpose to make the people's life better: clothes, food, crops, education. From here, we can see the main function of providing such details is not to prove but to clarify, and to catch and hold the attention of the audience.

2) Description & explanation

A description tells us what something is like. An explanation is a statement that makes clear how something is done or why it exists or existed. It is like painting a verbal picture, which requires us to focus upon specific, concrete details.

For example, when telling her idea about the image of Beijing for hosting the Olympic Games, a student speaker gives a detailed description of three colors.

"What image does Beijing intend to create for itself once it has the opportunity to host the 2008 Olympics? It is known to all that Beijing Municipal(市政的)Government has already set the theme for the future games in New Beijing, Great Olympics. For me, the 2008 Olympics will be <u>a great green Olympics</u>, illuminated(点亮) with two more special colors, yellow and red. <u>First, yellow is a meaningful color.</u> The Yellow River is China's Mother River, and the cradle of Chinese civilization, we are of the yellow race, and descendants(后裔)of the Yellow Emperor. The color has a special origin and great significance for the Chinese people. Beijing is the capital of New China, and previously the capital of nine dynasties in Chinese history, so yellow will naturally add splendor to the 2008 Games. <u>Secondly, the 2008 Olympics will be a red pageant(盛会).</u> Red is another traditionally cherished color for the whole country; we adore red. On big occasions, we like to decorate our homes in red. It is the color of double happiness, representing joyous moments, auspiciousness(吉祥), enthusiasm and prosperity. Red is one of the most suitable colors to describe the future of Beijing. Beijing, together with the whole country, is becoming more and more prosperous(繁荣的)in the process of modernization. Should the 2008 Olympics be held in Beijing, the whole city will be a sea of red: the red torch, red flags, red flowers and the radiant(光芒四射的) faces of millions of joyful people. Above all, the 2008 Olympics will be a green Olympics, adding the green ingredient is essential in creating an appealing image, as we can't deny the fact that Beijing, at the moment, is not as green a city as what we like it to be. Striving for an environment appealing city has become a central task for all the citizens of Beijing. Big efforts have been made in pollution control, replanting and beautification of the city. According to a project entitled 'The Green Olympic Action Plan', between 1998 and 2007, Beijing, we have invested 100 million RMB in preserving and protecting the environment. Some 12.5 million trees and over 1 million acres of grass will be planted along the Fourth Ring Road (四环路). By then, the city's green area will make up 40% of its total. The city will also dredge(疏浚) its reservoirs, used as a water supply to Beijing residents, controlling industrial pollution, and moving out the 200 factories, presently located within the city proper(城区). Certainly, all of this is no easy task, but I'm sure all of us have confidence that we will realize these 'green' goals, for now, we have the full support and participation of the environmentally conscious citizens. Each citizen is showing great concern for every one of the steps the city government takes. As the saying goes, 'United, we stand', and a green Beijing will be achieved. When our aspiration(向往,渴望)

becomes a reality, it will be a unique Olympics. New Beijing, Great Olympics will be weaved of these three superb colors: yellow, red and green. Let us welcome it and look forward to it. Thank you!"

The vivid illustration of the three colors is interesting, surprising and appealing. A description of a person can also be necessary as shown in the following example.

(*Brian's Song*, 1971)

I'd like to say a few words about a guy I know, a friend of mine. His name is Brian Piccolo, and he has the heart of a giant and that rare form of courage which allows him to kid himself and his opponent — cancer. He has a mental attitude which makes me proud to have a friend who spells out 'courage' 24 hours a day, every day of his life.

Now you flatter me by giving me this award. But I say to you here and now, Brian Piccolo is the man of courage who should receive the George S. Halas award. It's mine tonight and Brian Piccolo's tomorrow. I love Brian Piccolo. And I'd like all of you to love him too. And tonight, you hit your knees(跪下): Please ask God to love him."

Here, a description of Brian Piccolo's personality is impressive: He has the heart of a giant and that rare form of courage which allows him to kid himself and his opponent—cancer. He has a mental attitude which makes us proud to have a friend who spells out "courage" 24 hours a day, every day of his life.

When using descriptions, we have some guidelines to keep in mind.

a. Use analogies if possible

Analogies show the similarities of two things, taking the advantage of the listener's prior knowledge, and helping them understand unfamiliar ideas, things and situations, so they have a clearer mental picture about what they hear.

b. Be organized

Get our descriptions organized in a reasonable progression. This forward sense of motion in our speech will add a living quality.

Description and explanation always go hand in hand. By using an explanation, a speaker may describe what category a thing belongs to, or explain the meaning of an idea, a concept or a definition.

(*Avatar*, 2009)

"You're not in Kansas(堪萨斯州)anymore. You're on Pandora(潘多拉星球). Ladies and gentlemen, respect that fact every second of every day. If there is a Hell, you might want to go there for some R & R(休息娱乐)after a tour on Pandora. Out there beyond that fence every living thing that crawls, flies, or squats(蹲)in the mud wants to kill you and eat your eyes for jujubes(果胶软糖). We have an indigenous(土著)population of humanoids(类人类)called the Na'vi. They're fond of arrows dipped in a neurotoxin(沾有神经毒素) that will stop your heart in one minute — and they have bones reinforced with naturally occurring carbon fiber(碳纤维). They are very hard to kill.

As head of security, it is my job to keep you alive. I will not succeed. Not with all of you. If you wish to survive, you need to cultivate a strong, mental attitude. You got to obey the rules: Pandora rules!"

Here the colonel explains to his soldiers the definition of Pandora Rules: in order to survive in a hell full of life-threatening elements, we must have a strong, mental attitude and obey the rules. Anyone who violates the rules is dead without zero warning.

3) Statistics

Providing numbers to explain or summarize facts and examples is an especially convincing way to make our point. Well-accredited and managed statistics makes our ideas carry more weight and exert more impact because they emphasize the magnitude of something. They are mainly used in the following ways: to express the magnitude or seriousness, to make quantitative comparisons, to suggest relationships between two or more factors involved and at last to summarize. When using this way, we must follow the tips below.

a. Identify our resources

Make sure our resources are reliable and identify them. This will make our speech credible.

b. Interpret the meaning of the statistics

The numbers won't speak for themselves thoroughly, so the audience needs our further explanation to understand better.

c. Round off the complicated numbers

When numbers are too long and complicated, and usually unnecessary, we need to round them off for the sake of the audience.

Here is one example where former General Motors executive, James M. Roche, used statistical information to make his point:

"Today, you can predict fairly accurately just how many alcoholics（酗酒者）there are in a company. If there are 100 employees, there are five to ten alcoholics. If there are 100,000 employees, you will find 5,000 to 10,000 alcoholics. At General Motors, we have more than 500,000 employees, so you will find 25,000 to 50,000 who are involved in an alcoholic problem."

(*The Great Debaters*, 2007)

"From 1914 to 1918, for every single minute the world was at war, four men laid down their lives. Just think of it: Two hundred and forty brave young men were hurled（抛入）into eternity every hour, of every day, of every night, for four long years. Thirty-five thousand hours; eight million, two hundred and eighty-one thousand casualties. Two hundred and forty. Two hundred and forty. Two hundred and forty. Here was a slaughter immeasurably（无法估量的）greater than what happened at Amritsar. Can there be anything moral about it? Nothing—except that it stopped Germany from enslaving all of Europe. Civil disobedience isn't moral because it's nonviolent. Fighting for your country with violence can be deeply moral, demanding the

greatest sacrifice of all: life itself. Nonviolence is the mask civil disobedience wears to conceal(掩盖)*its true face: anarchy*(无政府主义).*"*

In this speech, the speaker uses statistics to express the magnitude of casualties, thus illustrating the seriousness of the War. And also there is repetition of the figures to strengthen his point.

(Jay Walker speaking on English manias)

"Let's talk about manias(疯狂). *Let's start with Beatlemania*(披头士狂)*: hysterical*(歇斯底里) *teenagers, crying, screaming, pandemonium*(混乱). *Sports mania: deafening crowds, all for one idea—get the ball in the net.*

OK, religious mania. There is rupture(狂喜)*, there is weeping, there is visions. Manias can be good, manias can be alarming, or manias can be deadly.*

The world has a new mania, a mania for learning English. Listen as Chinese students practice their English by screaming it. (Students shouting: I want to change my life. I don't want to let my parents down. I don't ever want to let my country down. Most importantly, I don't want to let myself down.)

How many people are trying to learn English worldwide? <u>*Two billion of them*</u>*. In Latin America, in India, in South East Asia, and most of all, in China. If you're a Chinese student, you start learning English in the third grade by law. That's why this year China will become the world's largest English speaking country. Why English? In a single word: opportunity. Opportunity for a better life, a job, to be able to pay for school, put better food on the table. Imagine a student taking a giant test, for three full days. Her score on this one test, literally*(几乎)*determines her future.* <u>*She studies 12 hours a day for three years to prepare. 25% of her grade is based on English*</u>*. It's called Gao Kao.* <u>*And 80 million high school Chinese students*</u> *have already taken this grueling*(心力交瘁的)*test. The intensity to learn English is almost unimaginable unless you witness it. (Students shouting: Perfect, perfect. I want to speak perfect English. I want to speak perfect English. I want to change my life.)*

So is English mania good or bad? Is English a tsunami(海啸)*washing away other* languages? Not likely. English is the world's second language. Your native language is your life. But with English, you can become part of a wider conversation, a global conversation about global problems, like climate change, or poverty, or hunger, or disease.

The world has other universal languages. Mathematics is the language of science. Music is the language of emotion. And now English is the language of problem solving, not because America is pushing it, but because the world is pulling it. So English mania is a turning point, like the harnessing（控制）of electricity in our cities, or the fall of the Berlin Wall（柏林墙）. English represents hope, for a better future, a future where the world has a common language, to solve its common problems. Thank you."

This is both an informative and persuasive speech. The speaker uses a series of numbers showing the number of English learners and the intensity of English learning mania in China and the world.

4) Examples

When we want to make a general statement, we are searching for specific cases to support our point. So the format is in this way: first the general statement, then the supporting details. And the details can be representative cases. This is the way of using examples.

There are three types of examples: brief examples, extended examples and hypothetical examples.

a. Brief examples

Brief examples are short illustrations. The speaker can use just one or two, or many in succession. The following is a TED speech on "regretting".

(Kathryn Schulz talking on regretting)

"So, that's Johnny Depp（约翰尼•德普，好莱坞演员）, of course. And that's Johnny Depp's shoulder. And that's Johnny Depp's famous shoulder tattoo. Some of you might know that, in 1990, Depp got engaged to Winona Ryder（薇诺拉•赖德，好莱坞演员）, and he had tattooed on his right shoulder 'Winona forever'. And then three years later—which in fairness（公平地说）, kind of is forever by Hollywood standards—they broke up. And Johnny went and got a little bit of repair work done. And now his shoulder says, 'Wino forever'(幽默,wino 暗指酒,wine). (laughter) So like Johnny Depp, and like 23% of Americans between the ages of 16 and 50, I have a tattoo. I first started thinking about getting it in my mid-20s, but I deliberately(故意地)waited a really long time, because we all know people who have gotten tattoos when they were 17 or 19 or 23 and regretted it by the time they were 30. That didn't happen to me. I got my tattoo when I was 29, and I regretted it instantly. And by "regretted it", I mean that I stepped outside of the tattoo place—this is just a couple miles from here, down on the Lower East Side—and I had a massive emotional meltdown(情绪失控)in broad daylight on the corner of East Broadway and Canal Street, (laughter), which is a great place to do it because nobody cares. (Laughter). And then I went home that night, and I had an even larger emotional meltdown, which I'll say more about in a minute. And this was all actually quite shocking to me, because prior to this moment, I had prided myself on having absolutely no regrets. I made a lot of mistakes and dumb decisions, of course. I do that hourly. But I had always felt like, look, you know, I made the best choice I could make, given who I was then, given the information I had on hand. I learned a lesson from it. It somehow got me to where I am in life right now. And okay, I wouldn't change it. In other words, I had drunk our great cultural Kool-Aid(酷爱牌饮料)about regret, which is that lamenting(哀伤)things that occurred in the past is an absolute waste of time, that we should always look forward and not backward, and one of the noblest and best things we can do is strive to live a life free of regrets. This idea is nicely captured by this quote: things without all remedy(补救)should be without regard; what's done is done. It seems like kind of an admirable philosophy at first—something we might all agree to sign onto, until I tell you who said it.—Lady Macbeth, basically telling her husband to stop being such a wuss(懦夫)for feeling bad about murdering people. And as it happens, Shakespeare was onto something here, as he generally was. Because the inability to experience regret is actually one of the diagnostic(病理性)characteristics of sociopaths(病态者). It's so by the way, a characteristic of certain kinds of brain damage. So people have damage to their orbital frontal cortex(眶额前脑皮层)seem to be unable to feel regret in the face of even obviously very poor decisions. So if, in fact, you want to live a life free of regret, there is an option open to you. It's called a lobotomy(前脑叶白质切除术). But if you want to be fully functional and full human and fully humane, I think you need to learn to live, not without regret, but with it. So let's start off by defining some terms."

Here, the speaker begins with two examples, Johnny Depp's tattoo change on his shoulder and the speaker herself having had a tattoo and then regretted having it. By citing the two examples, she introduces the phenomenon in our life: regretting happens to us.

But note that the two examples in the speech are different: the first one is a brief example, and the second one is an extended one as discussed below.

b. Extended examples

When a speaker narrates, describes or illustrates one case in an elaborate way, he/she is using an extended example. The audience will be impressed with such a dramatic, emotionally compelling story or detailed description and analysis.

c. Hypothetical examples

A hypothetical example might be either brief or extended, but the difference lies in its unreal nature. The sentence usually begins with "Suppose/Imagine..., what would you do?" The purpose is obviously not to trick the audience, but to get them to identify themselves with someone in a particular situation or provoke their thoughts. In a speaking competition, the contestant might be asked by one of the judges to talk about how he/she would manage the city's traffic problems if he/she were the mayor of the city. Then the speaker will present his/her ideas as in a supposedly status of mayor.

(Professor Michael Sandel speaking on the moral side of murder)

"This is a course about 'Justice' and we begin with a story. <u>Suppose</u> you are the driver of a trolley car(有轨电车), and your trolley car is hurling(冲)down the track at 60 miles an hour. And at the end of the track you notice five workers working on the track. You try to stop but you can't, because your brakes don't work. You feel desperate because you know that if you crash into these five workers, they will all die. <u>Let's assume</u>(假设)you know that for sure. And so you feel helpless until you notice that there is, off to the right, a side track and at the end of the track, there is one worker working on the track. Your steering(转向)wheel works, so you can turn the trolley car, if you want to, onto the side track, killing the one but sparing the five. Here is our first question: <u>what's the right thing to do? What would you do? Let's take a poll</u>(举手示意)."

The professor is using an analogy to illustrate the dilemma of justice and a moral scenario. And the audience is really interested in discussing abstract philosophical concept in a hypothetical case study.

5) Anecdotes

Anecdotes are stories coming from our own real or imagined experience or from experiences of people we know. There are usually portraits of characters in an action, narrated in the first person, third person, or it's just a fictional story or historical event. The purpose is to make our details more memorable, interesting, personal and more impressive.

a. First Person Anecdote

The narrator is the speaker himself/herself about himself/herself as the central character. It's the easiest and most engaging type of anecdotes.

b. Third Person Anecdote

The central character is someone else rather than the speaker. It could be our friend, a stranger or just someone we heard from somewhere.

c. Fictional Story

A fictional story is a made-up one, or an imagined one, for the purpose of our speech.

d. Historical Event

Retelling a historical event can set up a reference context for our contemporary topic.

(*Norma Rae*, 1979)

"*On October 8th, 1970, my grandfather, Isaac Abraham Warshovsky, age 87, died in his sleep in New York City. On the following Friday morning, his funeral was held. My mother and father attended. My two uncles from Brooklyn attended. And my aunt Minnie came up from Florida. Also present were 862 members of The Amalgamated Clothing Workers and the Cloth, Hat and Cap Makers Union of America—also members of his family.*

In death, as in life, they stood at his side. They had fought battles with him, had bound the wounds of battle with him, had earned bread together and had broken it together. And when they spoke, they spoke in one voice and they were heard. And they were black and they were white and they were Irish and they were Polish and they were

Catholic(天主教徒) *and they were Jews—and they were one. That's what a union is— one.*

Ladies and gentlemen, the textile industry in which you are spending your lives and your substance, and in which your children and their children will spend their lives and their substance, is the only industry in the whole length and breadth(范围) of these United States of America that is not unionized(组成工会). Therefore, they are free to exploit you, to lie to you, to cheat you and to take away from you what is rightfully yours— your health, a decent wage, a fit place to work.

I would urge you to stop them by coming over to Room 31 at the Golden Cherry Motel and pick up a union card and sign it. Yes, it comes from the Bible, according to the tribes of your fathers: Ye shall inherit. But it comes from Reuben Warshovsky: Not unless you make it happen. Thank you."

Here the speaker urges the workers in the textile industry to organize a union so that their rights will be protected. The speaker begins by telling her grandfather's funeral and his earlier life to suggest one point: "When they spoke, they spoke in one voice and they were heard. And they were black and they were white and they were Irish and they were Polish and they were Catholic and they were Jews—and they were one. That's what a union is—one." By narrating her grandfather's life, the speaker has laid the ground for her point.

(*The Door in the Floor*, 2004)

"*There was a little boy who didn't know if he wanted to be born. His mommy didn't know if she wanted him to be born either. They lived in a cabin, in the woods, on an island, in a lake, and there was no one else around. And in the cabin — there was a door in the floor.*

The little boy was afraid of what was under the door in the floor, and the mommy was afraid, too. Once, long ago, other children had come to visit the cabin for Christmas. But the children had opened the door in the floor and had disappeared down the hole. The mommy had tried to look for the children, but when she opened the door in the floor, she heard such an awful sound that her hair turned completely white, like the hair of a ghost. And, the mommy had also seen some things, things so horrible, you can't imagine them.

And so the mommy wondered if she wanted to have a little boy, especially because of everything that might be under the door in the floor. And then she thought, 'Why not? I'll just tell him not to open the door in the floor.'

Yet, the little boy still didn't know if he wanted to be born into a world where there was a door in the floor. But, there were some beautiful things in the woods, on the island, and in the lake. 'Why not take a chance?' he thought.

And so, the little boy was born, and he was happy, and his mommy was happy again, too. Although she told the boy, at least once every day, 'Don't ever, not ever, never, never, never — open the door in the floor.' But, of course, he was only a little boy. If you were that little boy, wouldn't you want to open that door in the floor?"

Here the speaker uses an anecdote to inspire the listener, the little boy.

Organizing the Body of Our Speech

A general strategy of a speech is said to be about the following three parts:
Tell us what you are going to tell us.
Tell us.
Tell us what you told us.

One reason why the audience has trouble following the speaker is disorder and disorganization of the speech. Disorder is discomforting. Well-organized speeches are easier to remember and can make our speech more credible. This part deals with how to prepare the main points, how to select and arrange the main points, and at last how to make our transitions smooth and effective.

2.3.1 Presenting the main points

As the central features of our speech, main points are the major divisions of the speech. We must select them carefully and phrase them precisely. There are some overall principles for a good arrangement of main points.

1) The main points must be limited

The range from two to five points is recommended. And the audience will find that the 3-point structure works best. Too many points will confuse and exhaust the audience, and inconvenience the speaker himself/herself.

2) Make sure each point works for the topic

Irrelevant and defocused points must be discarded.

3) Use a parallel structure

Using parallel structure facilitates our memorizing the speech and guiding ourselves in the speech.

For example: in a school opening speech to the freshmen in a college, the teacher speaks about how to be a good college student. He lists his main points in this way:

> Specific Purpose: To inform the audience of how to be a good college student
> Main points:
> Ⅰ. You must be a student of good habits
> Ⅱ. You must be a student of critical thoughts
> Ⅲ. You must be a student of concentration and devotion
> Ⅳ. You must be a student of adventurous spirit
> Ⅴ. You must be a student of social skills

Using parallel structures can make our points clear and easy to remember when we prepare our speech.

4) Use concise and simple words or phrases

Too complicated sentence structures will not help either the speaker or the audience.

5) Use good cohesion devices

Good cohesion devices make the sentences run into and connect each other in a smooth and continuous way. Please see "2.3.3 Transition".

2.3.2 Ways to organize the main points

Dividing the topic into a number of smaller units helps the audience follow our ideas better. Which pattern of organization to use depends on what principle of division we choose to adopt. Here are some ways to arrange our main topics.

1) Topic order

It is the most common way of organizing main points.

(*Ladder 49*, 2004)

"It's never an easy thing saying goodbye to a brother firefighter. It's not. And this time, particularly, it is difficult for me because I watched Jack grow into a, well, into one of the finest firefighters I've ever known. He joined this department because he wanted to help people. Who knows how many homes are still standing because Jack was there; how many lives were spared? He gave his life for that cause.

We'll never forget you, Jack, and we are better for having known you. But I make you this one promise: Tomorrow, when that bell rings, we will be back on the truck, because you were the bravest of the brave.

People are always asking me: How is it that firefighters run into a burning building when everyone else is running out? Well, Jack, you answered that question by saving another man's life. Your courage is the answer.

And today, we will be as brave as you by not mourning(哀悼) you, but by celebrating your life. So, I'd like everyone to stand up and celebrate the life of Jack Morrison."

In this eulogy, the speaker gives a speech in the following points:
- Jack Morrison is one of the finest firefighters.
- We will be as brave as you.
- We celebrate his life.

2) Time or chronological order

The order follows the sequence where events occur in time order or processes are discussed step by step. e.g.

Specific Purpose: To inform the audience of the steps to a successful job interview.
Main Points:
 Ⅰ. Prepare thoroughly
 Ⅱ. Arrive promptly
 Ⅲ. Enter confidently
 Ⅳ. Communicate effectively
 Ⅴ. Follow up immediately

(Ang Lee speaking after winning BAFTA)

"Thank you. I love this thing. It's the greatest statue of all awards, I think. Thank you BAFTA(英国电影和电视艺术学院) for giving me this great honor, again. You've been always very nice to me since my little film, *The Wedding Banquet*(《喜宴》), 13 years ago. One good example would be one of my movie(s) like *The Ice Storm*(《冰风暴》) again (got) no critical acclaim(好评) except (that) it was mentioned here in the BAFTA and it has no commercial success except it's a big success in England. I don't know what makes me so connect to you. I'm pretty sure it's not the food (laughter from audience). Anyway, (a lot of people) it's always great to be here. Most of all I'd like to grab this chance to give a sincere thank you to you, that for your education, for your support, and drill me to the ground(彻底磨炼) to help me overcome the fear. And many Asian directors' mental obstacles(心理障碍) directing an English language film. It is still scary, but not as bad as making *Sense and Sensibility*(《理智与情感》). So here I am. I feel very privileged to have the chance to participate in the making of *Brokeback Mountain*. It's a very special project."

In his speech, Ang Lee expresses his gratitude to BAFTA for their special favor to him by reviewing, in time order, his four films (*The Wedding Banquet*, *The Ice Storm*, *Sense and Sensibility*, *Brokeback Mountain*) which were well received in England.

3) Space order

If we arrange the ideas according to geographical location, give directions, describe a scene, place, person, or an object, we need to arrange our points in a way that gives the speech a sense of progression. E. g. we give an introduction of the location of our school probably in different directions and parts: the east, the central part, the west, etc. and usually there is a controlling point which governs the whole area and starts our description.

4) Causal order

When we try to explain a reason, we are using causal order. There are two different varieties: cause-effect order, and effect-cause order. The first one emphasizes the effects, and the second one examines the causes. E. g. when we intend to explain why we propose banning smoking in public places, we would try to give reasons to support this point in an effect-cause way:

Specific Purpose: Smoking in public places should be banned

Main Points:

  I. Smoking causes several deadly health problems

  II. Smoking in public is a fire hazard

  III. Smoking pollutes the air and environment

  IV. Smoking is rude in formal social settings

（300，2007）

  Spartan Council Loyalist：*May I give the floor now to the wife of Leonidas and Queen of Sparta.*

  Queen Gorgo：*Councilmen*（议员们），*I stand before you not only as your Queen*：*I come to you as a mother*；*I come to you as a wife*；*I come to you as a Spartan*（斯巴达）*woman*；*I come to you with great humility*（谦逊）.

  I am not here to represent Leonidas；*his actions speak louder than my words ever could. I am here for all those voices which cannot be heard*：*mothers*，*daughters*，*fathers*，*sons*—*300 families that bleed for our rights*，*and for the very principles this room was built upon.*

  We are at war，*gentlemen.* <u>*We must send the entire Spartan army to aid our King in the preservation*（保护）*of not just ourselves*，*but of our children.*</u>

  <u>*Send the army for the preservation of liberty. Send it for justice. Send it for law and order.*</u>

  <u>*Send it for reason.*</u> *But most importantly*，*send our army for hope*—*hope that a king and his men have not been wasted to the pages of history*—*that their courage bonds*（团结）*us together*，*that we are made stronger by their actions*，*and that your choices today reflect their bravery.*"

  In this speech, The queen calls on sending the army, and then she gives the reasons why they should do so by such sentences as "send the army for..."

  In the movie *Invictus*（2011，Morgan Freeman），President Mandela urges the National Sports Committee of South Africa to retain the white man's rugby team Springbok which was made up of all white men players and was hated by the black people in South Africa.

(*Invictus*, 2009)

"I thank you. Please. Brothers. Sisters. Comrades. I am here because I believe you have made a decision with insufficient information and foresight. I am aware of your earlier vote. I am aware that it was unanimous(全票通过). Nonetheless, I believe we should restore(恢复) the Springboks. Restore their name, their emblem(标志) and their colors immediately.

Let me tell you why. On Robben Island, in Pollsmoor Prison(曼德拉曾被囚禁的地方), all of my jailers were Afrikaners(非洲白人). For 27 years, I studied them. I learned their language, read their books, their poetry. I had to know my enemy before I could prevail against him. And we did prevail, did we not? All of us here, we prevailed. Our enemy is no longer the Afrikaner. They are our fellow South Africans, our partners in democracy. And they treasure Springbok rugby. If we take that away, we lose them. We prove that we are what they feared we would be. We have to be better than that. We have to surprise them with the compassion(同情), with restraint(克制) and generosity. I know all of the things they denied us, but this is no time to celebrate petty revenge. This is the time to build our nation, using every single brick available to us, even if that brick comes wrapped in green and gold(南非橄榄球队的颜色标志为绿色和金色). You elected me your leader. Let me lead you now."

President Mandela gives three reasons to explain why people should support and retain the rugby team: ① We had to know our enemies before we could prevail them; ② They are our fellow South Africans, our partners in democracy, not our enemy; ③ This is the time to build our nation, using every single brick available to us.

5) Comparison and contrast

When we explore the similarities and differences between two or more things, we call this compare and contrast. Compare explains how things are similar, and contrast, how they are different. We use compare and contrast in our daily lives though we may not be aware of it, e. g. a teacher explaining the US Congress by comparing it with China's People's Congress to find out the differences or similarities. A student compares two universities to find out their differences when choosing between them to go to. There are two outline orders: subject by subject, and topic by topic, as follows.

a. Subject by subject

The speaker discusses the various aspects of one item before going to the other.

Thesis statement: university X is better than university Y

Ⅰ. University X

    A. Campus environment

    B. Teaching staff

    C. Student body

    D. Facilities

Ⅱ. University Y

    A. Campus environment

    B. Teaching staff

    C. Student body

    D. Facilities

b. Topic by topic

The speaker discusses both items under each of the various aspects compared/contrasted.

Thesis statement: university X is better than university Y

Ⅰ. Topic 1: Campus environment

    A. University X

    B. University Y

Ⅱ. Topic 2: Teaching staff

    A. University X

    B. University Y

Ⅲ. Topic 3: Student body

    A. University X

    B. University Y

Here is one example:

When a senator argues for defending the American aid to South Vietnam, he compared the Vietnamese to South Koreans, "We should reiterate our determination to try to find a viable, freely elected government for South Vietnam, pursuing very much the same policy that we pursued... in South Korea, and for the very same reason."

But another senator was quick to object to the comparison,

"Has the Senator noted the marked difference in the attitude of the South Koreans from that of the South Vietnamese? The South Koreans were opposed to the Communists. They fought bravely and incurred(导致) many losses. The United States went in there to help those who wanted to help themselves. There seems to be a lack of will on the part of the South Vietnamese to wage a fight against the Communists. It contrasts with the will to fight of the Koreans. That is the basis of our difficulty in Vietnam."

This is a contrast arrangement of subject-by-subject in the short form.

Another example:

(*The Fountainhead*, 1949)

"*The creator stands on his own judgment; the parasite*(寄生虫) *follows the opinions of others. The creator thinks; the parasite copies. The creator produces; the parasite loots*（打劫）. *The creator's concern is the conquest of nature; the parasite's concern is the conquest of men.*

The creator requires independence. He neither serves nor rules. He deals with men by free exchange and voluntary choice. The parasite seeks power. He wants to bind all men together in common action and common slavery. He claims that man is only a tool for the use of others—that he must think as they think, act as they act, and live in selfless, joyless servitude（劳役）*to any need but his own.*"

In this speech of contrast, the first paragraph follows the topic by topic order, while the second paragraph is subject-by-subject order.

c. Combined patterns

The speaker's first responsibility, in order to speak effectively, is to discover what he has to say and why he is saying it. Then, he must find the specific patterns especially suited to his subject and purpose. Particular patterns are suited to particular speech units. In the first unit, time order might be used, then in the second, causal order. The speaker who takes the first steps of careful analysis and the subsequent steps of skillful organization is more likely to achieve his purpose.

2.3.3 Transition

Transitions keep all the elements of the speech flowing together. On the one hand, the listeners need help, i.e. guidance and direction, to follow the speaker moving from one point to the other. And on the other hand, transitions allow the speaker to show the connections between all the elements of the speech, relate all the different parts of the speech to the main purpose, and help the audience see how everything fits together into a complete and coherent speech, and the relationship between the introduction and the first main point of our speech, and between each of the main points of our speech.

Transitions are not just verbal. Effective speakers use body movement as a transition device. Speakers plan purposeful movement to show the audience, literally, that the speech is "moving" to a new point. In most instances, speakers will start in the center of the room for the introduction, move slightly to one side for the first point, move slightly to the other side for the next point (and so on as needed), and then move back to the center for the conclusion. This movement, tied to verbal transition devices, makes it much simpler for the audience to follow the structure of the speech.

(*Mrs. Miniver*, 1942)

"We, in this quiet corner of England, have suffered the loss of friends very dear to us. Some close to this church: George West, choir（合唱）boy; James Bellard, station master and bell ringer and a proud winner, only one hour before his death, of the Belding Cup for his beautiful Miniver rose; and our hearts go out in sympathy to the two families who share the cruel loss of a young girl who was married at this altar（祭坛）only two weeks ago.

The homes of many of us have been destroyed, and the lives of young and old have been taken. There is scarcely a household that hasn't been struck to the heart. And why? Surely you must have asked yourself this question. Why in all conscience should these be the ones to suffer? Children, old people, a young girl at the height of her loveliness. Why these? Are these our soldiers? Are these our fighters? Why should they be sacrificed?

I shall tell you why.

Because this is not only a war of soldiers in uniform. It is a war of the people, of all the people, and it must be fought not only on the battlefield, but in the cities and in the villages, in the factories and on the farms, in the home, and in the heart of every *man, woman, and child who loves freedom!*

Well, we have buried our dead, but we shall not forget them. Instead they will inspire us with an unbreakable determination to free ourselves and those who come after us from the tyranny and terror that threaten to strike us down.

This is the people's war! It is our war! We are the fighters! Fight it then! Fight it with all that is in us. And may God defend the right."

Here, the speaker uses "And why?" as a preparatory transition to the next point. And "I shall tell you why." serves as the boundary of the speech bridging one part and the next. Hence, the functions of good transitions are the following:

- It prepares for a point we are going to make.
- It directs the audience about where we are in our speech.
- Emphatic transitions will add emphasis.

Tips on using transitions:

1) Transitions are better used in varied ways

Repetition of the same transitional phrase will sound boring, so we can use an affirmative statement to begin the first point, and a rhetorical question for the second point. Chinese speakers tend to list their main supporting points by proceeding "firstly, secondly, thirdly, fourthly...lastly", which look neat but sounds monotonous and boring.

2) Don't overuse transitions

Overused transitions may make the speech sound like a shopping list, disorganized, confusing and random. A good speaker will know how to control the flow of his speech in natural ways. And we don't see many transitions in great speeches. In Steve Jobs' speech, when he begins his speech by telling three stories, he states that he will tell just three stories of his life. Then he connects his parts by such simple transitional expressions like: *The first story is about connecting the dots*; *my second story is about love and loss...*; *my third story is about death....* The three stories are only connected by three transitions.

3) Useful connections and signposts in transition

Such short statements as "first", "second", and "next" are called signposts because they quickly point out to the audience where we are now and where we are going in the speech. Signposts are generally a specific and shortened form of a transition or connection, either a word or a phrase, either an idiom or a clause (sentence), giving the listener a direction in time, space, sequence, or logical reasoning context. Signposts provide quick cues to the audience so that they know how a speech moves from one point to another.

Spatial development

across from...   opposite to...
adjacent to...   close to...
in the distance,   beyond that point,

on the left (right),
to your (left) right,
on top of...
at the bottom of...
as far as...
look beyond...
at the back,
looking from outside,
from this point on,
from this point of view,
from this perspective,
standing here/between/in the middle of...
stepping off...
stepping into...
between... and...
all the way through...
just as...
beneath my feet,
then my eyes travel to...
as I look up,
under... lies a...
down there is a...
as you go along,
this will take you to...

Sequence

first of all,
to begin with
the first step is...
by the time...
lets' start with...
first things first,
let me start by saying,
let's move on to...
now we come to...
that brings us to...
that covers...
let's get back to...
the former... the latter...
following the...
after this,
by following this,
in summary,
in conclusion,
on the first day...
on the morning/in the evening...
starting from...
let us see how...
in this way,
that is to say,
now you are ready to...
one important part of it is...
in the next hour or so,
here comes the crucial step (critical point)...

Dividing and classifying

one way of doing this is...
another type of... is...
unlike.../like...
in comparison,
... falls into... categories,
... can be divided into... classes/groups
the former... the latter...
among the former (latter)...
one of the features is...
in other words,

Cause and effect

the first reason is...
one of the main reasons is...
one reason is...
another good point is...
Why do I...? Why don't I...?
Let me tell you why.
not because... but because...
the fact that... is the main reason for...

to justify my...
in suggesting...my point is...
one more reason...is that...
I do it for the reason that...
because of this,
therefore,
as a result,
consequently,
a multitude of factors could account for...
another contributing factor is...
Why are...? For one thing...for another...
perhaps the primary reason is...
...is solely responsible for...
among the most convincing reasons given, one should be emphasized...

by...I mean...
that matters because...
What I find is that...
I support this decision because...
with this in mind,
accordingly/consequently/as a result...
for this reason,
seeing that,

Comparing and contrasting

similarly/in the same way,
on the contrary,
meanwhile,
from a similar perspective...
a comparison of...reveals that...
my preference is...
instead of...
another similarity is...
this is connected to...
the first difference is...
unfortunately,
the analogy between...and...is...
equally important,
on the one hand...on the other...
although...and...differ greatly, they share some common ground.

whereas
on the other hand,
in (by) contrast,
equally important
it is better to...than to...
I prefer to...
...as opposed to...
something else similar is...
between the two...
one difference between...and...is...
not surprisingly,
in this same regard,
accordingly
in the same way,

Concession

even though...
admittedly,
although it is true that,
it may sound true, but...
call me a pessimist, but...
hard as I've tried,...
while I understand why...I can't agree...

regardless of...
there is no doubt
it is true that...but...
in spite of the fact that...
much as...

Exemplifying

for instance,
as a case in point,
namely,
for one thing,
to illustrate,
according to statistics,
on the whole,
it is often the case that...
a classic instance is...
to support my argument,...

for example,
take... as an example,
that is,
as an illustration,
let me illustrate,
consider... for example,
let me cite as proof,
if we look at this...
in both cases,
suppose...

Summarizing and concluding

to sum up,
therefore,
finally,
in conclusion,
all in all,
to put it in a nutshell,
to bring my speech to a conclusion,
from what I've explained,
as we can see,
so, ladies and gentlemen,...
my dear friends, my fellow classmates,...
I'd like to conclude my speech by saying that...
with my speech come to a close, I'd like to...
Let's recap/review what we have discussed today.

in summary,
in brief,
in short,
to conclude,
in a word,

Highlighting

on a personal/serious/optimistic note, regrettably,
it is well-known that...
with... in mind,
in particular,
it goes without saying that...
as a saying goes in China,...
as long as...
in other words,
generally speaking,
please bear with me,
one good point is...

as for...
please bear in mind that...
especially,
to put it in another way,
for the record,
I'd like to bring your attention to...
let me rephrase that,
according to statistics,
let us take a look at...
we cannot ignore the fact that...

Stating personal views

personally, honestly, frankly, seriously,

in my defense/to justify myself,

please let me explain,

as for me/if you ask me,

it would seem to me (that)...

as far as I am able to judge.../as far as I am concerned...

as far as my memory serves me right,

I'd like to point out (that)...

from my point of view,

if you want my opinion, I'd say...

well, the point I'm trying to make is (that)...

That's not quite what I meant. What I really meant was...

all I am trying to say is...

well, let me put it in another way...

What I am trying to say (get at) is...

Referring to the audience

Ladies and gentlemen,

May I please have your attention?

My dear fellow citizens (classmates, teachers...)

As I'm sure we'd all agree...

We have all experienced...

You may still remember...

I'd like to direct your attention to...

How many of you have... please raise your hand?

As you (we) all know...

We still remember...

Have you ever...?

Some people among the audience may wonder...

I'd like to ask one of you to...

So my dear friends, would you please...?

Who among you has...?

I'd like to take a poll...

Let me share with you a story...

Believe men when I tell you...

You might find it hard to believe...

With your permission, I'd like to...

Let me remind you that...

I'd like to refresh your memory that...

2.4 Beginning of Our Speech

When we stand in front of an audience, we have very little time to set the stage for a successful speech, for audience members begin evaluating us immediately. What we sometimes forget since we are so focused on the words we have to say is that we are being evaluated even before we open our mouths.

2.4.1 The functions of a good beginning

Speech introductions are an essential element of an effective public speech. Some of us begin with unimaginative phrases like, "My speech is about...", "Today I am going to talk about...", "My topic is..." or other similar repetitions. Some Chinese speakers even start their speech with "Today, I'm going to give you a lecture about..." A good beginning of our speech is crucial in the following senses.

1) Grabbing the audience's attention

Our first goal is to create an opening that captivates the listener's undivided attention. When an audience has decided to listen to us—when we have gained their attention and interest—we still need them to think favorably of us. The most effective way of doing this is by establishing our credibility to speak.

- Be appropriately attired for a public presentation
- Make eye contact with the audience BEFORE we speak
- Speak clearly, fluently and confidently

2) Helping the audience form their initial judgment of the speaker at the very beginning

A poor introduction will lose the chance from the audience of a fair and just judgment of the content of the speech and even of the speaker's character, so we cannot afford to communicate a bad impression at the beginning if the value of our speech is wrongly presumed.

3) Introducing the content

In all speeches, there should be this one sentence, this one statement that succinctly and accurately lets the audience know what the speech will be about and what the speaker plans to accomplish in the speech. Speakers, especially novice speakers but also experienced ones, are so concerned with the content of the speech that they forget to let us know about the purpose. A good thesis statement clearly announces the topic and purpose of the speech. The thesis statement lets the audience know what the speech is about and what we as a speaker want to accomplish. The preview statement lets the audience know HOW we will develop the speech as a roadmap — a direction for the speech that leads to a successful conclusion. A preview lets the audience know what will come first, what will come next, and so on, to the end of the speech. Meanwhile, a clearly and precisely highlighted framework of our speech in the beginning will exert a good command of the whole speech.

4) Setting the tone and establishing a mood

Whether our speech will be about a serious topic or a lighthearted one is indicated by the tone of our speech in the beginning: to open in a humorous way or a serious way. A serious opening will heighten the audience's concern and evoke a deep thought, while a humorous one will ease and calm the audience.

5) The last but not the least, creating a favorable bond with the audience

It's about how the audience will think of us as a person as well as a speaker: how enthusiastic, warm and friendly we sound and how we signal to them that our topic is of their interest. By knowing that, we will win their hearts with better odds from the start.

2.4.2 Ways to introduce our speech

Let's look at the following potential introduction techniques. This is not an exhaustive list, and many of these introduction techniques can be combined or adapted to fit the needs of the speaker, the occasion and the audience. Regardless of the specific technique used in the introduction, all introductions still need to meet the five basic functions of an introduction listed above.

1) Taking a poll in the audience

Taking a poll in the audience is to ask them a question and investigate the status quo, stance and viewpoint about an issue. Remember to give feedback to the result of your investigation. The question usually begins with "How many of you... please show me your hands." E.g. A speaker wants to tell how important pigs are to us in our everyday life. She begins her speech this way,

"Hello, I would like to start my talk with actually two questions. And the first one is 'How many people here actually eat pig meat?' Please raise your hand. Oh, that's a lot. Um...And 'How many people have actually seen a live pig producing this meat? In the last year.' In the Netherlands where I come from, you actually never see a pig, which is

really strange, because on a population of 16 million people, we have 12 million pigs. And well, of course, the Dutch（荷兰人）can't eat all these pigs. They eat about 1/3, and the rest is exported to all kinds of countries in Europe, and the rest of the world. A lot goes to the UK, Germany. And what I was curious about... 'cause historically the whole pig would be used up until the last bit, so nothing would be wasted. And I was curious to find out if this was actually still the case. And I spent about three years researching. And I followed this one pig with number 05049, all the way up until the end and to what products it's made of. And in these years, I met all kinds of people, like, for instance, farmers and butchers, which seems logical. But I also met aluminum mold（铝合金模具）makers, ammunition（弹药）producers, and... well... all kinds of people."

  2) Asking a rhetorical question

  As a good technique to get audience involvement and interest, a question can be asked to start our speech. There are two types of questions: actual and rhetorical. An actual question needs the answer of the audience at the moment and on the spot. A rhetorical question is one that the questioner answers it himself/herself, or the questioner has hinted the answer already to the listener. We need to be careful when we ask questions.

  • We must carefully deliver the question. Even if we think the question is rhetorical, our audience may not know this and may answer the question.

  • Learn to use timing and pause. Too often, speakers will use a question, or a series of questions, as an introduction — but then give the audience no time to either think about the answer or answer the question.

  • We also need to be careful to use eye contact in asking questions, since we are above all asking for audience involvement and our eye contact requests that involvement.

(*A Beautiful Mind*, 2001)

"Thank you. I've always believed in numbers and the equations（等式）and logics that lead to reason. But after a lifetime of such pursuits, I ask, 'What truly is logic?' 'Who decides reason?'

> *My quest* (追寻) *has taken me through the physical, the metaphysical* (玄学), *the delusional* (妄想)—*and back. And I have made the most important discovery of my career, the most important discovery of my life: It is only in the mysterious equations of love that any logic or reasons can be found.*
>
> *I'm only here tonight because of you* [*wife, Alicia*]. <u>*You are the reason I am. You are all my reasons. Thank you.*</u>"

The speaker answers the questions asked by himself.

3) Using a quotation

It is a common introductory technique to use a quotation which can be borrowed from a person of fame, authority or special expertise, or it comes simply from a passage of a book. When we quote that well-known figure, we are, in a sense, borrowing some of that person's credibility for our speech, enhancing our credibility with the audience. Even when we use a less than well-known figure, the quotation can be effective if it nicely sets up our speech topic and is something to which our audience can relate. A word of advice when using a quotation: the quotation must be relevant. In the following example, the speaker quotes directly from the Bible.

(*The Help*, 2011)

> "*Please open our Bibles to Exodus*(《出埃及记》). *Chapter four, verse ten. God having asked Moses*(摩西)*to free the Israelites, Moses answered,* "*Oh, my Lord. I am not eloquent*(雄辩的). *I am slow of speech and slow of tongue.*" *See, courage isn't just about being brave.* (*Audience: Amen*) *Courage is daring to do what is right, in spite of the weakness of our flesh*(力不从心). *And God tells us, commands us, compels*(迫使)*us to love. Amen?* (*Audience: Amen*)
>
> *See, love as exemplified*(代表)*by our Lord Jesus Christ, is to be prepared to put yourself in harm's way*(临危不惧)*for your fellow men. And by your fellow man, I mean your brother, your sister, your neighbor, your friend and your enemy. If you can love your enemy, you already have the victory. Let's stand. All right!* (*Audience singing*)"

The priest is quoting a chapter from the Bible calling on people to have the courage to be brave and to love.

(*The Contender*, 2000)

"Thank you. Napoleon once said, when asked to explain the lack of great statesmen in the world, that 'to get power you need to display absolute pettiness（渺小）; to exercise power you need to show true greatness.（伟大）' Such pettiness and such greatness are rarely found in one person. I look upon the events of the past weeks and I've never come so to grips（理解）with that quotation.

For ladies and gentlemen of this Congress, it pains my soul to tell you that you have brought blood and shame under this great dome（国会大厦）. Your leadership has raised the stakes（危险）of hate to a level where we can no longer separate the demagogue（煽动者）from the truly inspired."

In the movie, the President proposes to the Senate the nomination of Senate Laine Hanson, a woman to be vice president, but hatred and prejudice run rampant against the proposal. The speaker uses Napoleon's words to criticize the dark side of power fight in the White House.

4) Telling stories

To tell a story or an anecdote is an effective way to attract the audience in the beginning. Human beings love stories. In all cultures, stories are used to communicate and share values, traditions and knowledge. Stories have a built-in structure that everyone recognizes and expects. Stories have a beginning, middle and end, and this built-in structure allows the audience and the speaker to immediately share this experience of starting, climax and ending of the story.

The speaker may tell a story in the first or third person. Both can attract the audience's attention.

The following is the beginning part of a speech given by President Obama in 2009 on school opening day by telling a story in the first person.

(President Obama speaking on the school opening day)

"Thanks, everybody go ahead and have a seat. How is everybody doing today? How about Tim Spicer? I am here with students at Wakefield High School of Arlington Virginia, and we've got students tuning in (收看) from all across America, from Kindergarten to 12th grade. I am just so glad that you could all join us today, and I wanna thank Wakefield for being such an outstanding host. Give yourselves a big round of applause for that. I know that for many of you, today is the first day at school, and for those of you in Kindergarten, or starting middle or high school, it's your first day in the new school, so it's understandable if you are a little nervous. I imagine that some seniors are feeling pretty good right now, with just one more year to go. And no matter what grade you're in, some of you are probably wishing it was still summer and you could stay in bed just a little bit longer this morning. I know that feeling. When I was young, my family lived overseas. I lived in Indonesia for a few years, and my mother, she didn't have the money to send me where all other American kids went to school, but she thought it was important for me to keep up with American education, so she decided to teach me extra lessons herself, Monday to Friday. But because she had to go to work, the only time she could do it was 4:30 in the morning. Now as you might imagine, I wasn't too happy about getting up that early. And a lot of times, I fall asleep right there at the kitchen table, but whenever I complained, my mother would just give me one of those looks, and she would say, 'This is no picnic (容易的事情) for me either, buster (小鬼).' So I know that some of you are still adjusting to being back at school. But I am here today, because I have something important to discuss with you."

Here is another story told by Yang Lan in third person in her speech at TED.

(Yang Lan speaking at TED on young people in China)

"The night I was heading for Scotland, I was invited to host the final of China's Got Talent show in Shanghai, with 80,000 live audiences in the stadium. Guess who was the performing guest? Susan Boyle. And I told her, 'I'm going to Scotland the next day.' She sang beautifully, and she even managed to say a few words in Chinese, 'Song ni cong', so it's not like 'hello' or 'thank you' those ordinary stuff. It means 'green onion for free'. Why did she say that? Because it was a line from our Chinese parallel (对等人物) Susan Boyle, a 50 some-year-old woman, a vegetable vendor (小贩) in Shanghai who loves singing western opera, but she didn't understand any English or French or Italian, so she managed to fill in the lyrics with vegetable names in Chinese. And the last sentence of Nessun Dorma (今夜无人入睡) that she was singing in the stadium was 'green onion for free'. So Susan Boyle was saying that, and 80 000 live audiences sang together. That was hilarious (捧腹)."

5) Using humors

The use of humor in an introduction can be one of the most effective types of introductions—if done well. Humor can create a connection between the speaker and audience, can get an audience relaxed and in a receptive frame of mind, and can allow an audience to perceive the speaker (and the topic) in a positive light. Here is one example from a movie, where the speaker is addressing his potential business partners.

(R.V., 2006)

"Hi, everybody, sorry I'm late. I just came down that mountain, and next time I'll use a road. I guess you guys didn't get the memo(备忘录)about extreme casual. I love your wilderness(野外)so much, I decided to wear it. It's kind of wild journey getting here. If you ever wanna really find out about yourself, put your family in an RV(娱乐旅行车)and drive, I've seen some amazing stuff. I've fought wild raccoons(浣熊)and won; I've been in the desert to a place where it's not the end of the world, but you can see it from there."

The speaker makes it to a business presentation through a great deal of ordeal, looking dirty and messy all over, but the lighthearted humor lessens the embarrassment. Using humors can be tricky sometimes, however, when a speaker normally is not a funny person but forces him to be so in his speech, or an ill-timed or misplaced joke will be a deadly pitfall.

6) Personal reference

A personal reference may be a narration, a description or an explanation referring to the speaker himself/herself. The purpose is to prepare for the introduction of the topic in the speech. By noting our personal interest, we will demonstrate our credibility by showing our knowledge and experience with this topic.

(Tucker: The Man and His Dream, 1988)

"When I was a boy, I used to read all about Edison and the Wright brothers, Mr. Ford. They were my heroes. Rags to Riches(《从贫穷到富有》)—that's not just the name of a book, that's what this country was all about. We invented the 'free enterprise' system, where anybody, no matter who he was, where he came from, what class he belonged to—if he came up with a better idea about anything, there's no limit to how far he could go.

I grew up a generation too late, I guess, because now the way the system works, the loner, the dreamer, the crackpot(狂想家)who comes up with some crazy idea that everybody laughs at, that later turns out to revolutionize the world—he's squashed(压制) from above before he even gets his head out of the water because the bureaucrats(官员),

they'd rather kill a new idea than let it rock the boat(捣乱)！！ *If Benjamin Franklin were alive today, he'd be thrown in jail for sailing a kite without a license!*"

The speaker refers to himself by telling us the heroes he admired in his childhood, but the system where free enterprise was encouraged is now different, because the bureaucrats kill new ideas.

(*Malcolm X*, 1992)

"*My high school was a black ghetto*(贫民窟)*in Roxbury, right here in Boston. I got my college education on the streets of Harlem in New York City. I took my Masters degree in prison over the course of six and a half years. In fact, my old burglary hangout*(偷盗点)*is just outside this campus. I lived like an animal. I stole. I used drugs. I smoked reefers*(大麻), *cocaine. I committed adultery*(通奸).

Had it not been for the Honorable Elijah Muhammad, I'd have surely been in an insane asylum(疯人院), *or dead, or possibly even the murderer of one of you.*

So what is Mr. Muhammad trying to do? He's trying to get us on God's side, so that God will be on our side and help us fight our battles.

When the negro, the so-called negro in America gets on God's side and listens to the teachings of the Honorable Elijah Muhammad, he'll wanna get off drugs. He'll wanna get away from a life of crime. He'll wanna get away from committing adultery and fornication(私通). *Then he would wanna get off the welfare. He would wanna get a job. He would wanna earn a living and take care of his family, and his family would respect him. His son will say, 'I'm proud that that's my father.' His wife will say, 'I'm proud that that's my husband.'*

'Father' only means that you're taking care of your children—that's what it is to be a father. 'Father' doesn't mean that you're havin' some babies. Anybody can have a baby. Havin' a baby does not make you father. Anybody can go out and get a woman. But not anybody can take care of that woman. There's another word for it: It's called 'responsibility'."

In this speech, the speaker relates his own childhood experience as a transformed young man from a villain and a degenerate because of the influence of Father Muhammad. Then he continues to preach on the importance of believing God, of believing the teachings of Mr. Muhammad. At last he defines the meaning of being a real father—a man of responsibility.

7) A startling statement

A startling statement is aimed to shock the audience, so that an effect of suspense is achieved to quickly grab the audience's attention, and also the audiences are encouraged to listen further as we present the context of the startling statement. When we startle the audience, we set them up to want to hear the rest of the story.

(*Wall Street 2*, 2010)

"You're all pretty much fucked(被害惨了). You don't know it yet, but you're the Ninja(忍者)generation: no income, no job, no assets. You got a lot to look forward to. Someone reminded me the other evening, that I once said, 'Greed is good.' Now it seems it's legal. But folks, it's greed that makes my bartender buy three houses that he can't afford, with no money down(首付款). And it's greed that makes your parents refinance (贷款购买)their $200,000 house for 250. And then they take the extra 50 and they go down to the mall. And they buy a plasma(等离子)TV, cell phones, computers, an SUV, and hey, why not a second home while we are at it? Because, gee whiz(天啊), we all know that prices of houses in America always go up, right? It's greed that makes the government in this country cut the interest rate to 1% after 9/11, so we could all go shopping again. They got all these fancy names for trillions of dollars of credit, CMOs, CDOs, SIVs, ABSs(都是在美国发行的信用卡的名字). I honestly think there's maybe only 75% people in the world who know what they are. But I'll tell you what they are. They're WMDs. Weapons of Mass Destruction(大规模破坏性武器). That's what they are."

In this speech, the speaker stuns the audience by warning them of their bleak prospects because of the worsening financial environment. Then he breaks down the situations in detail. The examples listed are both humorous and pungent.

8) Previewing the main points

This is a very simple and down-to-earth way of opening a speech. The audience will get the gist of our speech, the points we want to make, and even the duration of our speech from this way of opening. The preview is essentially an outline—an oral outline—of the basic organizational pattern of the speech. Previews allow the audience to pay attention to the content because they already know the structure. Remember, though, that the basic structure of a speech is not linear, it is circular. Organizational patterns have the conclusion, as we will see later in this section, bringing us back to the beginning.

E. g. The speech made by Steve Jobs at Stanford University. He begins his speech like this:

Today I want to tell you three stories from my life. That's it. No big deal. Just three stories.

9) Expressing gratitude

Usually this comes at the end, but the difference lies in the fact that ending acknowledgment is devoted to the audience, while the beginning is to the organizer, the sponsor or the presenter of the activity. The following is a part from US President Obama's speech when he visited Shanghai in 2009. This is a beginning combining both expressing gratitude and previewing the main points.

(Obama speaking to the Shanghai youth)

"It's a great honor for me to be here in Shanghai, and to have this opportunity to speak with all of you. I'd like to thank Fudan University's President Yang for his hospitality and his gracious welcome. I'd like to thank our outstanding Ambassador, Jon Huntsman, who exemplifies(代表)the deep ties and respect between our nations. I don't know what he said, but I hope it was good. What I'd like to do is to make some opening remarks, and then what I am really looking forward to doing is taking questions, not only from students who are in the audience, but also we've received questions online, which will be asked by some of the students who are here in the audience as well as by Ambassador Huntsman. And I am really sorry that my Chinese is not as good as your English, but I'm looking forward to this chance to have a dialogue. This is my first time travelling to China, and I'm excited to see this majestic(伟大的)country."

President Obama gives thanks to the two persons involved in his visit, and then previews the content in the speech.

10) Performing

It's an unusual way to open a speech by giving a performance, such as singing a song, playing a trick, mimicking some acts like dancing and so on. It may be a pitfall to open in this way, for the audience may find it overacting or pretentious, but on the other hand could be unexpectedly effective. Mostly performance is only an aid to the speech.

(*Other People's Money*, 1991)

"*Amen. And amen. And amen. You have to forgive me. I'm not familiar with the local custom. Where I come from, you always say 'Amen' after you hear a prayer. Because that's what you just heard—a prayer. Where I come from, that particular prayer is called 'The Prayer for the Dead'. You just heard The Prayer for the Dead, my fellow stockholders, and you didn't say, 'Amen'.*"

The speaker performs the act of a priest in the church, and the effect can be unexpected and stunning.

2.4.3 Some common faults in opening a speech

1) Do not use clichés

Such common but ineffective statements as "I'm really nervous." "My speech is about...", "Today I'm going to talk about..." "I'm going to give you a speech about..." are better avoided, because they are repetitious, unimaginative, unattractive and thus boring.

2) Do not apologize

It's a habitual act or mostly a way of showing modesty for Chinese speakers to apologize at the beginning, either for personal physical ailment, for ill preparation or for a lack of certain equipment or material, and even for his/her own poor English level. Such beginning statements like "Please forgive me. I'm nervous." "I'm sorry about this cough I am having today." "I'm sorry my English is poor." etc. The worst apology would be saying that we are little prepared or unprepared. Why on earth are we standing here? Even if we are not well prepared, there is nothing for us to apologize about, but to continue by saying something like, "I haven't prepared for the occasion, but I would just say a few words from my heart."

3) Do not overdo our introduction

Usually, the speaker is on a time limit, and even if there is no time limit, most people will simply not pay attention to a speech that goes on and on and on.

What's more, the body of the speech is the heart of our speech, the introduction of our speech needs to be concise and succinct. There is no magic formula for the length of an introduction, and we do need to meet all five functions in our introduction. However, if we are unable to complete our introduction in the first 60-90 seconds of most speeches, we have probably gone too long.

Overdoing an introduction is a common problem for Chinese speakers, for they tend to beat around the bush a lot before turning to the point. For example, when a speaker talks about an overwhelming and controversial phenomenon in China—Naked Marriage, he/she will spend a long time elaborating the background before presenting his/her own opinion, which is quite unnecessary if our audience is already familiar with this background. If we spend more time opening an introduction than presenting our point, we are putting the cart before the horse. It is probably better to be briefer than more lengthy. Get to our point, present it specifically, directly and briefly.

4) Avoid irrelevant subject in the opening unless for humor purpose

It's misleading and confusing to provide irrelevant information in the beginning. E. g. In our speech on campus love, if we begin verbosely on student's campus life, the audience would lose themselves in confusion: what is your point?

5) Nervousness kills the beginning

Try to calm ourselves and take a deep breath before starting our speech. Nervousness causes two bad things: lack of eye contact with the audience, and projecting a poor image, thus poor credibility in front of the audience.

Ending of Our Speech

2.5.1　Effects of a good ending

Before we start looking at the functions, we have to know that the basic structure of a speech is not linear but circular. Speeches should not take us on a straight line from A to Z. Speeches should take us in a circle from A to Z. that means we start at the top of the circle with the introduction, work all the way around the circle, and end up back at the top with the conclusion. All the parts fit together and flow together in this circle, and the conclusion takes us right back to the introduction—with an enhanced understanding of that introduction.

In Chinese, there is a piece of good advice and a criterion for composing a fine article, "the crest of the phoenix, the belly of the pig and the tail of the leopard", which means a good article should begin charmingly, develop fully, and end powerfully, so should a good speech. Just as the advice metaphorically indicates, the ending should be forceful, deciding and sweeping, which can be achieved in the following ways and serve the following functions.

1) To create a sense of completeness to the speech

It is said that a good ending should require about 5%-10% of our total speaking time. So in a three minute speech, the ending should take up approximately 9-18 seconds. This time frame will leave the audience a sufficient impression of a complete ending.

2) To win the audience for the last time

Special efforts must be made to increase the ethos (bonding) so as to avoid negative reaction from the audience.

3) To reinforce our points

No matter what methods we employ, the purpose is to strengthen our purpose, consolidate our points, and ultimately to convince the audience.

2.5.2 Effective and common ways to end our speech

1) Appealing to the audience

Appealing to the audience is to call for actions among them. It can be a persuasive way to end our speech, passionately urging for an act to happen or a measure to take. In presenting our appeals to the audience in the ending of the speech, we can take advantage to increase the likelihood of our audience acting on our appeals.

(*Romero*, 1989)

> "I'd like to make an appeal in a special way to the men in the army. Brothers, each one of you is one of us. We are the same People. The farmers and peasants that you kill are your own brothers and sisters. When you hear the words of a man telling you to kill, think instead in the words of God, 'Thou shalt not kill!' No soldier is obliged to obey an order contrary to the Law of God. In His(上帝)Name and in the name of our tormented people who have suffered so much, and whose laments(悲伤)cry out to heaven: I implore(恳求)you! I beg you! I ORDER you!! STOP THE REPRESSION!!!"

The speaker ends his speech by appealing to the army men not to kill the farmers and peasants. The ending part of the speech is forceful: I implore you! I beg you! I order you! Stop the repression!

2) Restating our points in summary

A conclusion is structural in function. Just as the introduction must include a statement of the purpose of the speech, as well as a preview of the main ideas of the speech, the conclusion must include a restatement of the thesis and a review of the main ideas of the speech. The review and restatement are mirror images of the preview statement in the introduction. Structurally, the restatement and review bring the speech back to the top of the circle and remind the audience where we started. Functionally, they help cue the audience that the end of the speech is coming up.

Using pointers to signal that we have reached the ending part of our speech: "Now let's recap our three points." "And so, what have we said today? First...", "To bring my speech to a conclusion, I'd like to sum up the main points..." E. g. A speaker, after giving facts and evidences to the audience that when we have made big plans for ourselves, we shouldn't tell others, concludes his speech in this way: "So next time, when you're tempted to tell people your goal, what would you say? (Audiences respond) Exactly, well done." Concluding in this way is a good echo to the beginning of our speech and forms a good completion, too.

In the conclusion of this speech, one effective method to summarize and wrap-up is to simply restate the thesis and preview—but in the past tense, since we have now heard the speech.

By restating the thesis and reviewing the main ideas, we once again take advantage to create a complete and coherent structure to our speech.

3) Using a quotation

If someone has said something better and more authoritative than us, then quote it. Don't forget to refer to the origin we are quoting from before or after we use it.

(*The Great Debaters*, 2007)

"*In Texas, they lynch*(用私刑)*Negroes. My teammates and I saw a man strung up by his neck—and set on fire. We drove through a lynch mob*(暴徒)*, pressed our faces against the floorboard*(车底板)*. I looked at my teammates. I saw the fear in their eyes; and worse—the shame. What was this Negro's crime that he should be hung, without trial, in a dark forest filled with fog? Was he a thief? Was he a killer? Or just a negro? Was he a sharecropper*(佃户)*? A preacher? Were his children waiting up for him? And who were we to just lie there and do nothing? No matter what he did, the mob was the criminal. But the law did nothing—just left us wondering why. My opponent says, 'Nothing that erodes*(腐蚀)*the rule of law can be moral.' But there is no rule of law in the Jim Crow South, not when Negroes are denied housing, turned away from schools, hospitals—and not when we are lynched. Saint Augustine said, 'An unjust law is no law at all', which means I have a right, even a duty, to resist—with violence or civil disobedience*(非暴力抵抗)*. You should pray I choose the latter.*"

In the end, the speaker quotes Saint Augustine's famous remark, with a powerful and sweeping impact.

4) Telling a story

Stories also make excellent conclusions, and can be used as conclusions in at least two ways. First, we can complete the story that we started in the introduction. Alternatively, we can retell the story, and this time the story will reflect what we have learned from our speech. Either method provides coherence and closure to the story and the speech.

J. F. Kennedy told a story in his speech.

"... we must think and act not only for the moment but for our time. I am reminded of the story of the great French Marshal Lyautey, who walked one morning through his garden with his gardener. He stopped at a certain point and asked the gardener to plant a tree there the next morning. The gardener said, 'But the tree will not bloom for one hundred years.' The Marshal looked at the gardener and replied, 'In that case, you had better plant it this afternoon.'"

5) Inspiring and motivating

Issuing an inspirational appeal or challenging the audience with an emotional conclusion, we give a sense of climax in the end. The following ending part is a speech by Thomas Paine, a famous politician in the Independence War in America. He ends his speech in this way.

"Is life so dear, or peace so sweet, as to be purchased at the price of chains and slavery? Forbid it, Almighty God! I know not what course other may take, but as for me, give me liberty or give me death!"

(*City Hall*, 1996)

"*That's why I ask you now to join me. Join me, rise up with me; rise up on the wings of this slain(被杀害的)angel. We'll rebuild on the soul of this little warrior. We will pick up his standard and raise it high! Carry it forward until this city—your city—our city—his city—is a palace again! Is a palace again!*"

The speaker ends his speech with a strong urge and appeal.

The following speech made by incumbent(在位的) US President Barrack Obama calls for people to fight against domestic violence.

(President Obama speaking on fighting domestic violence)

"Tonight we celebrate artists whose music and message help shape our culture, and together we can change our culture for the better by ending violence against women and girls. Right now, nearly one in five women in America has been a victim of rape or attempted rape. And more than one in four women has experienced some form of domestic violence. It's not OK. And it has to stop. Artists have a unique power to change minds and attitudes, and get us thinking and talking about what matters. And all of us, in our own lives, have the power to set an example. Join our campaign to stop this violence. Go to ItsOnUs.org, and take the pledge(宣誓), and to the artists at the Grammies(格莱美音乐奖) tonight, I ask you to ask your fans to do it, too. It's on us, all of us to create a culture where violence isn't tolerated, or survivors are supported, and where all our young people, men and women, can go as far as their talents and their dreams will take them. Thanks!"

In this speech, President Obama first depicts the serious situation of domestic violence going on in America, and then urges people to join the campaign and set an example to stop it. At last, he issues a strong appeal to the artists to play their role in inspiring our young people to realize their dreams.

(A woman speaking on domestic violence)

"My name is Brooke Axtell, and I'm a survivor of domestic violence. After a year of passionate romance with a handsome, charismatic(有性格魅力的)man, I was stunned when he began to abuse me. I believed he was lashing out(猛打，攻击)because he was in pain and needed help. I believed my compassion(同情)could restore him and our relationship. My empathy(同情心)was used against me. I was terrified of him and ashamed I was in this position. What bound(相联系)me to him was my desire to heal him. My compassion was incomplete because it did not include me. When he threatened to kill me, I knew I had to escape. I revealed the truth to my mom and she encouraged me to seek help at a local domestic violence shelter(救助所). This conversation saved my life. Authentic love does not devalue another human being. Authentic love does not silence, shame, or abuse. If you're in a relationship with someone who does not honor and respect you, I want you to know that you're worthy of love. Please reach out for help. Your voice will save you. Let it extend into the light; let it part(分开)the darkness, let it set you free to know who you truly are: valuable, beautiful, loved."

The speaker combines description, narration and explanation in an effort to urge people to face up to domestic violence and to love and value themselves.

6) Making a promise

This way of ending is especially common for campaign candidates in their speech, so as to win their votes.

(*All the King's Men*, 1949)

"This much I swear to you—these things you shall have: I'm going to build a hospital, the biggest that money can buy, and it will belong to you. And any man, woman or child who is sick or in pain can go through those doors and know that everything will be done for them that man can do: to heal sickness, to ease pain. Free! Not as a charity, but as a right. And it is your right. Do you hear me? It is your right.

And it is your right that every child should have a complete education; that any man who produces anything can take it to market without paying toll(付费). And no poor man's land or farm can be taxed or taken away from him. And it is the right of the people that they shall not be deprived of(剥夺)hope."

The candidate running for the governor gives his people promises on the hospital, education, taxes, etc.

7) Expressing hope, good wish and resolution

(*Nixon*, 1995)

"I say to you tonight—I say to you tonight we must have a new feeling of responsibility, of self-discipline. We must look to renew state and local government. We must have a complete reform of the big, bloated (肿胀的) Federal Government. Those of us in public service know we can have full prosperity in peace time. Yes we can cut the defense budget. We can reduce our conventional forces (常规部队) in Europe. We can restore the natural environment. We can improve health care and make it more available to all people. And yes we can have a complete reform of this government. We can have a new American Revolution!"

The underlined sentences with model verbs "must" and "can" express vows with a sense of forceful progression.

Here is a speech made by the commander of a peacemaking corps stationed in Yugoslavia, encouraging the soldiers and instilling them with hope.

(*The Whistleblower*, 2010)

"You come here today as a beacon (灯塔) of hope. As representatives of our highest aspirations (向往), you have been hired by Democrat Security to represent the US as monitors (观察员) for the United Nations. In the next few months, you will protect the rule of law where lawlessness is run rampant (猖獗). The 1995 Dayton Peace Accords (协议) ended this war, dictating (规定) that an international police task force, you, would smooth the transition from war to peace. During your training you will see that peace is hard won than war, that every morning's hope is haunted (笼罩) by yesterday's nightmare. As representatives of the United Nations, we stake our highest values, even our lives on the belief that we can rebuild, we must renew and we will witness the rebirth of this country."

8) Ending with a startling statement

It can be a good way to open and end our speech with a startling statement. Startling statements now take on new meaning because of all that we have told the audience in our speech. Repetition of startling statements should provide audiences with a key reminder of the main point of our speech.

(*Network*, 1976)

> "*You're beginning to believe the illusions*(幻觉)*we're spinning*(创造) *here*! *You're beginning to think that the tube*(口语：电视机)*is reality and that your own lives are unreal. You do whatever the tube tells you...*
>
> *You dress like the tube. You eat like the tube. You raise your children like the tube. You even think like the tube. This is mass madness, you maniacs! In God's name, you people are the real thing. We are the illusion!*
>
> *So turn off your television sets. Turn them off now! Turn them off right now! Turn them off and leave them off. Turn them off right in the middle of this sentence I'm speaking to you now. Turn them off!!*"

In this speech, the speaker advocates that television gives us only the unreal world, and the illusions. He urges us to get rid of this illusion by turning off TVs and live a real life.

9) Expressing thankfulness

End our speech by showing gratitude to the person(s) who has/have assisted us in preparing the speech, and giving the speech, and also the audiences for their time and attention.

10) Challenging the audience

We can challenge the audience by urging them to do the right thing and do it in a prompt fashion in the end, but still it's also for the purpose of inspiring and actuating the audience.

Former President Lyndon Johnson, in a speech announcing a major policy initiative known as the Great Society, concluded this speech with a series of challenges to his audience. The challenges were significant in that the speech was delivered as a commencement address at the University of Michigan, at a time in American society when college and university students were protesting many government actions.

"For better or for worse, your generation has been appointed by history to deal with those problems and to lead America toward a new age. You have the chance never before afforded to any people in any age. You can help build a society where the demands of morality, and the needs of the spirit, can be realized in the life of the Nation.

So, will you join in the battle to give every citizen the full equality which God enjoins and the law requires, whatever his belief, or race, or the color of his skin?

Will you join in the battle to give every citizen an escape from the crushing weight of poverty?

Will you join in the battle to make it possible for all nations to live in enduring peace — as neighbors and not as mortal enemies?

Will you join in the battle to build the Great Society, to prove that our material progress is only the foundation on which we will build a richer life of mind and spirit?

There are those timid souls that say this battle cannot be won; that we are condemned to a soulless wealth. I do not agree. We have the power to shape the civilization that we want. But we need your will and your labor and your hearts, if we are to build that kind of society."

(*The Girl in the Café*, 2005)

"And tomorrow, eight of the men sitting around this table actually have the ability to sort this out by making a few great decisions. And if they don't, someday someone else will, and they'll look back on us lot and say, 'People were actually dying in their millions, unnecessarily, in front of you, on your TV screens. What were you thinking? You knew what to do to stop it happening and you didn't do those things. Shame on you.'

So that's what you have to do tomorrow: Be great, instead of being ashamed. It can't be impossible. It must be possible..."

With a rhetorical question and a strong urge, the speaker challenges the audience.

(Leonardo Dicaprio speaking after winning the Academy Award for Best Actor in 2016)

"Thank you all so very much. Thank you to the Academy, thank you to all of you in this room. I have to congratulate the other incredible nominees this year, for their unbelievable performances. The Revenant(《荒野猎人》)was a product of the tireless efforts of an unbelievable cast and crew(演职人员)I got to work alongside. First off, to my brother in this endeavor("努力,事业",这里指该影片), Mr. Tom Hardy(该片中演对手戏的英国演员). Tom, your fierce talent on screen can only be surpassed by your friendship off screen. To Mr. Alejandro Innaritu(该片导演), as the history of cinema unfolds(展开), you have forged(锻造)your way into history these past 2 years, what an unbelievable talent you are. Thank you to you and Chivo for creating a transcendent(超越的)cinematic experience for all of us. Thank you to everybody at Fox(福克斯影业公司)and New Regency(新摄政影业公司). A particular honor, Melching, you're the champion of this endeavor. My entire team. I have to thank everyone from the very onset(开端)of my career. Mr. Caton Jones, for casting me in my first film; Mr. Scorsese, for teaching me so much about the cinematic art form. To Mr. Rick Yorn, thank you for helping navigate(导航,引导)my way through this industry and to my parents, none of this would be possible without you. And to my friends, I love you dearly; you know who you are.

And lastly I just want to say this: Making The Revenant was about man's relationship to the natural world. A world that we collectively(集体)felt in 2015 as the hottest year in recorded history. Our production needed to move to the southern tip of this planet just to be able to find snow. Climate change is real; it is happening right now. <u>It is the most urgent threat</u> facing our entire species(物种), and <u>we need to</u> work collectively together and stop procrastinating(拖延). <u>We need to</u> support leaders around the world who do not speak for the big polluters, and the big corporations, but who speak for all of humanity, <u>for the indigenous</u>(本土)people of the world, <u>for the billions and billions of *underprivileged people out there who would be most affected by this. <u>For</u> our children's children, and <u>for</u> those people out there whose voices have been drowned out by the politics of greed. I thank you all for this amazing award tonight. <u>Let us not take this planet for granted. I do not take tonight for granted.</u> Thank you so very much."*

In this speech, after acknowledging all other colleagues, the speaker urges and appeals to the audience and people around the world to take action for the threat of climate change and for our future. Please note the underlined words: ...the most urgent threat, we need to, for... The sentence "Let us not take this planet for granted. I do not take tonight for granted" gives the audience a deep impression.

2.5.3 Tips on how to give a good conclusion

(1) Don't apologize in the end. An apology is seen as an excuse for a lack of confidence and competence. Such expression as "Sorry for taking up your time" may sound polite in Chinese culture, but it may offend the audience.

(2) Use signposts before ending our speech. An abrupt and unexpected ending will harm our speech, sacrificing all the deserved merits. Use signaling words such as "Now let's restate our three main points", "To bring my speech to an end, I'd like to sum up the three points"; "And so, what have we said? First...";"So, my dear friends..."; "So, Ladies and gentlemen..."; "I'd like to finish up by saying..."

(3) Be brief and crisp. Just think of the time!

(4) Thank the audience. And remember to look at them when saying that! Don't continue to speak when you're exiting the lectern. Say "thank you" with a nod or a bow, then leave.

(5) Don't deviate. Don't add new material or information in our conclusion. Digressing and deviating may harm our speech greatly with the impression that we are ill prepared, indecisive and unconvincing. If possible, leave those things in the question-answer session.

2.6 Outlining Our Speech

Outlines are for two purposes: to help us write the speech, and to help remember and deliver the speech. There are two kinds of outlines, preparation outline, and delivery outline. A preparation outline helps us prepare the written version, i.e. the manuscript of our speech, and a delivery one, the speaking version. A preparation outline precedes the delivery outline, serving as a written aid for our speech. While the delivery outline prepares for the presentation of the speech itself. In this section, we look at them respectively.

2.6.1 The preparation outline

As in writing, a good speech follows the same rules of unity and coherence: the wholeness and smoothness of our speech. There are the following major parts of our preparation speech: the specific purpose, the central idea (theme), introduction, the body and the conclusion. And each part is linked up with main ideas, sub-points and supporting materials, as well as transitional signposts. The finished preparation outline is a detailed map of our speech.

1) Preparing a preparation outline

A good outline is created in consideration of the following elements.

a. Putting down the specific purpose first

Put it down at the top of the preparation outline. A complete sentence is advised to write out the topic, specific purpose and thesis statement of our speech.

b. Using proper indenting

Indent to list our main points and sub-points. The structure will be clearer visually in this way.

c. Using standard numbering

Roman numerals, capital letters, Arabic numerals, and lower case letters are used in the sequence of main points, major divisions, minor divisions and further divisions.

d. Identify the sources

Attach with the outline a list of the sources we consulted in preparing the speech in the end, i.e. the magazines, newspapers, and internet sources, and so on.

The following is a formal preparation outline framework

Title

Topic:

Specific purpose:

Thesis Statement:

Introduction

Ⅰ. Attention-getting device
Ⅱ. The purpose or thesis statement
Ⅲ. The preview of the speech
Ⅳ. Transition into the body

续表

Body

Ⅰ. First main point
    A. First sub-point
        1. First further sub-point
        2. Second further sub-point
    B. Second sub-point
Ⅱ. Second main point
    A. First further sub-point
    B. Second further sub-point
        1. First division
            a. Fact one
            b. Fact two
        2. Second division
Ⅲ. Transition into conclusion

Conclusion

Summary statement：_____
Closure：_____

Bibliography

---

2) A sample preparation outline

Title

Topic：The college library in the internet age

Specific purpose：To inform the audience about the use of library in the modern age

Thesis Statement：The library still plays a very important role in our college in the internet age

Introduction

Ⅰ. (Attention-getting device) Asking a question, taking a poll (How many...; Purpose of going to...)
Ⅱ. (The purpose or thesis statement) To inform the audience about the importance of library in our college
Ⅲ. (The preview of the speech) The importance and use of our library
Ⅳ. (Transition into the body) In order to make good use of our library, what do we have to do?

续表

Body

Ⅰ. (First main point) The school library is a great help in our course study and exam preparations.
    A. (First sub-point) For course studies, we go there to find extra resources.
        1. (First further sub-point) To preview and review our lessons, we use the library for better understanding of the writer and the background of the text.
        2. (Second further sub-point) To complete the assigned projects, the library is a good help.
    B. (Second sub-point) To prepare for exams and term papers, we need the numerous resources of the library.
        1. (First further sub-point) For preparing exams, the library's quiet environment is a great place to go.
            a. (fact one) The reading rooms in the library are always packed with keen students.
            b. (fact two) There are even bags and books on the desks and chairs announcing the preoccupation of the seats.
        2. (Second further sub-point) For a term paper, the library is a tool you can't do without.

Ⅱ. (Second main point) The library is a great place for leisure time.
    A. (First sub-point) The library isn't just a place for studying, but also for fun reading and leisure time.
        1. (First further sub-point) We go there to read for fun.
            a. (fact one) The various magazines and newspapers are waiting for us to flip through.
            b. (fact two) The Internet-accessed computers are another great resource.
        2. (Second further sub-point) We go there to enjoy the quietness of the free time.
    B. (Second sub-point) To enlarge our scope of knowledge, we also go there to read major-related materials.

Ⅲ. Transition into conclusion: Modern document indexing and researching tools are a great help and the quiet atmosphere is an ideal place for study and fun reading.

Conclusion

Summary statement: The school library is an ideal place for us to go after school time.
    Closure: Why should we ignore and waste such a fine and fun place on our campus?

Bibliography

1) How to Use a Library, Lei Jun. Beijing: Beijing University Press, 1999.
2) Library Services Manual.
3) Personal Interview with Mr. Wang Haiqiang, Head Librarian of Jingchu University Library.

2.6.2 The Delivery outline

It is a briefer outline with key words, phrases to aid our memory in the process of giving the speech. We can use this in our speech—to look down at it from time to time (not to fix our eyes on it) and make sure we're covering all the right points and details in the right order.

1) How to make a delivery outline?

a. Write in single words or phrases

Avoid complete sentences, and make it as brief as possible. In this way, we are the only person who can make out our handwriting and understand the way of arrangement. For a delivery outline, it is the ideas that count, not the wording, so do not overwhelm us by racking our brains for sentence structures.

b. Use a parallel structure

Corresponding to the preparation outline, the two outlines should follow the same pattern.

c. A complete form

Include the following parts as short as possible: introduction, conclusion, transition and supporting materials.

d. Use a card

Transfer the outline to a note card, so it is handy to carry around and hold during the speech.

e. Prepare early

Prepare the delivery outline early enough so we have time for practice.

2) A sample delivery Outline

Here we have a delivery outline according the preparation outline above.

Introduction

Ⅰ. (Attention-getting device) How many...; What is the purpose of going to...?

(The purpose or thesis statement) To inform the audience about the importance of library in our college.

Ⅱ. (The preview of the speech) The importance and use of our library.

Ⅲ. (Transition into the body) In order to make good use of our library, what do we have to do?

Body

Ⅰ. A great help in course study and exam

   A. For course studies, extra resources

      1. Preview and review

      2. Assigned projects

   B. Exams and term papers

      1. For preparing exams

         a. Always packed with keen students

         b. Bags and books occupying the seats

      2. For a term paper

> 续表
>
> Ⅱ. Fun reading and leisure time
>   1. For fun
>   a. Magazines and newspapers
>   b. The internet-accessed computers
>   2. The quietness
> Ⅲ. Major-related materials
>   Transition into conclusion: Modern document indexing and researching tools are a great help and the quiet atmosphere is an ideal place for study and fun reading.
>   -
>   Conclusion
>   Summary statement: Reference to the audience
>   Closure: Why ignore and waste?

2.7 Rehearsing Our Speech

Being the last step before getting onto the stage to speak, practicing and rehearsing is crucial to a successful speech. We can never imagine a good speech to be delivered without a good thorough practice and rehearsal. Even those seasoned statesmen will go all out for repeated practices before getting onto the stage with the acquired advice from other people on the content, voice and facial expressions. When we rehearse and practice, here are some guidelines for us to follow:

1) Focus on the message

We are speaking not to show off our oratory, but to make sense of our points and get across the message.

2) Record our speech

Do not use a mirror, for it is distracting when we look at ourselves in the mirror and talk. Use a camcorder placed in front of us, and we can even imagine it as our audience.

3) Emulate a speaking condition

Imagine our real speaking conditions, the podium, the capacity of the room, the layout of the seats, the microphone, and so on. If possible, find a friend, an expert or a colleague as a real audience who listens and gives us feedback.

4) Practice our time control

Don't steal other speaker's or the audience's time, and confine our speech to the time limit. If it is too long, leave out some point or detail; if it is too short, add something else, an example, for instance. In a speaking competition, violating the time limit rule is not allowed.

Topics for One-Minute Speech Practice

1. How do you understand the statement "We all live under the same sky, but we don't all have the same horizon?"
2. Has the internet narrowed or increased the distance between people?
3. Do you think good health can be bought?
4. Are western holidays a sign of modern China or sacrificed traditions to commercial interests?
5. Spring festival, to eat outside in the restaurant or cook at home?
6. Postgraduate study to us, necessary or unnecessary?
7. What improper behaviors do Chinese people have when using a mobile phone?
8. Is it a waste of talent for a college student to work in the rural area?
9. How has the Internet changed your life?
10. Do you read classical Chinese literary works? Why or why not?

Varieties of Public Speaking
演讲的种类

There are always three speeches, for every one you actually gave. The one you practiced, the one you gave, and the one you wish you gave. —Dale Carnegie
你完成的每一次演讲实际上有三种版本:你练过的演讲,你给出的演讲,以及你希望给出的演讲。□ 戴尔·卡耐基

It usually takes me three weeks to prepare a good impromptu speech. —Mark Twain
做好一场即兴演讲,我通常要花三个星期时间来准备。□ 马克·吐温

本章要点

- 按照演讲功能和目的分类的演讲
- 按照演讲方式和方法分类的演讲
- 演讲中的问答环节特点和策略

3.1 Speaking Informatively

According to the purpose and function of a speech, there are three major varieties: speaking informatively, speaking persuasively and speaking to entertain. Informative and persuasive speeches are the most used and learned in American colleges, and therefore, the most important.

3.1.1 The definition of informative speaking

By speaking informatively, we mean providing interesting, useful, and unique information to our audience. In one survey, graduates from five US colleges were asked to rank the speech skills most important to their jobs. They rated informative speaking number one. In another survey, 62 percent of the respondents said they used informative speech "almost constantly". (Lucas, 2007) As a loose and general term, informative speech does not only confine its meaning to providing information or knowledge concerning a particular fact or circumstance, but also refers to explanatory and expository endeavors. The following occasions are not unfamiliar to us: a business manager explaining next year's budget; a marketing executive presenting his strategy to the board members at the board meeting; an architect reviewing plans for a new building; a military officer briefing subordinates; a teacher in the classroom explaining a concept; a student presenting in front of the classmates. There are endless situations where people need to inform others.

For students in this case, one of our first classroom activities probably will be to give a brief summary of a reading assignment or defend an argument, or to describe an object and show how something works, or report an event and explain a concept. The criteria for judging our speech will be accuracy of the information, clarity of narration, strong support of evidence and whether it's interesting enough to be accepted by the audience.

Speaking to inform is to share information with our audience, i.e. telling about objects, events, places, people, procedures, concepts or issues. The speaker acts as a teacher using definition, explanation, illustration, clarification and other skills to achieve that purpose, which is to enhance their understanding and knowledge of some information.

3.1.2 Types of informative speech

1) About objects

Anything tangible, visible and stable in form are included, such as toys, cameras, cars, volcanoes, chopsticks, and so on. The purpose is mostly focused on one aspect of the object, preferably not everything. The ways to develop it are usually topically, chronologically and spatially.

2) About places

A tour guide will give a speech about a particular historical site. The three ways of development, i.e., spatially, chronologically and topically can also be used to describe a place. A speech about the Yangzi River can be organized spatially according to the three parts—upper, middle and lower reaches; an introduction to the history of our university can be developed chronologically; and informing the audience about the architectural features of the school buildings will be organized in topical order.

3) About events

There are two kinds of events: one without the speaker's involvement, for instance, a speech to tell our audience about the activities of Spring Festival in China; and one with the speaker's involvement, when we describe to the audience the event or experience we've had. A vivid description is essential and the development is usually in chronological order.

4) About people

Be it about someone we know or someone famous, living or dead, listeners are interested in hearing about the real person stories. The focus is on the unique quality, career achievements or significant life features as well as the implications. The methods to develop may involve chronological order and topic order.

5) About processes

It is about how something is made, done or how it works. The process may involve a few steps, so it's usually time-ordered sequence. When giving a how-to topic speech, sometimes the speaker needs to demonstrate with specific aids, such as an object, a model, a slide show, a video clip, etc, to demonstrate.

6) About concepts

While objects, processes and events are concrete topics to talk about, concepts are abstract ones which deal with beliefs, ideas, theories, principles, and so on. Definitions are usually given to develop this speech. The first example is a presentation given by a manager of a company to a Japanese client on his visit.

(Don making a presentation to a Japanese client)

"*Welcome to Bibary Systems. We are very honored to have the opportunity of making this presentation to you, Mr. Sakai. In the next hour and half, we hope to show that one, Bibary Systems has the right product range*(产品类型)*for today's market place, and ambitious plans for the future. Two, that our market share*(市场占有率)*in Europe is growing at a steady rate. Three, that our marketing strategy in the US is very successful. And lastly, four, that we can be a major player in the Far Eastern markets, and we're sure that we can be a major player in these markets. If you have any questions, please feel free to interrupt at any time, but first of all, some background information on Bibary Systems.*"

In the business presentation above, a standard procedure is followed: welcoming introduction—the time limit—the purpose—the agenda—questions invited.

In the following example, the speaker talks on "metaphor".

(TED speaking: Metaphor)

"Metaphor lives a secret life all around us. We utter about six metaphors a minute. Metaphorical thinking is essential to how we understand ourselves, how we communicate, learn, discover, and invent. But metaphor is a way of thought before it is a way with words. Now to assist me in explaining this, I have listed the help of one of our greatest philosophers, the reigning(在位的,现任的) king of metaphorians(隐喻学家), the man whose contributions to the field are so great that he himself has become a metaphor. I am of course, referring to none other than Elvis Presley(猫王). Now All Shook Up is a great love song. It's also a great example of how whenever we deal with anything abstract, ideas, emotions, feelings, concepts, thoughts, we inevitably resort to(求助于) metaphor. In All Shook Up, a touch is not a touch, but a chill; lips are not lips, but volcanoes; she is not she, but a buttercup(毛茛花); a love is not love, but all being shook up(神魂颠倒). In this, Elvis is following Aristotle's classic definition of metaphor as the process of giving a thing a name that belongs to something else. This is the mathematics of metaphor. Unfortunately it's very simple, $X=Y$. This formula works wherever metaphor is present. Elvis uses it, so does Shakespeare, his famous line from Romeo and Juliet, Juliet is the sun. Now, here Shakespeare gives the thing, Juliet, a name that belongs to something else, the sun. But whenever we give a thing a name that belongs to something else, we give it a whole network of analogies(类比), too. We mix the match where we know about the metaphor source, in this case it is the sun, with what we know about its target, Juliet, and metaphor gives us a much more vivid understanding of Juliet than Shakespeare has literally described what she looks like."

In the speech above, the speaker first provides some examples of metaphor: Elvis Presley's song and then introduces the definition of metaphor. After that another example, Shakespeare's Juliet, and then explains the formula of metaphor, which is actually an example of many analogies.

The following speech is given by a 12-year-old boy, who has achieved outstandingly in making apps. The purpose of the speech is to inform about his thoughts, ideas and experience.

(Thomas Suarez: How do I make apps)

"I've always had a fascination for computers and technology, and I made a few apps(应用程序)for the iPhone, iPod touch and iPad. I'd like to share a couple with you today. My first app was a unique fortune teller(算命先生), called Earth Fortune, that will display different colors of earth depending on what your fortune was. My favorite and most successful app is Bustin Jieber(Justin Bieber 的搞笑版) which is a Justin Bieber Whac-A-Mole("打地鼠"游戏). I created it because a lot of people at school dislike Justin Bieber a little bit, so I decided to make the app. So I want to work programming it. And I released it just for the holidays in 2010.

A lot of people asked me, how did I make these? A lot of time it's because the person who asks this question also wants to make an app also. A lot of kids these days like to play games. But now they want to make them. And it's difficult, because not many kids know where to go to find out how to make a program. I mean, for soccer, you could go to a soccer team; for violin, you could get lessons for a violin. But what if you want to make an app? Because parents could have done one of these things when they were young. But not many parents have made apps. Where do you go to find out how to make an app? Well, this is how I approached it, this is what I did. First, I have been programming in multiple other programs, just to get the basics down, such as Python, C, Java, etc. and then the Apple released the iPhone, and with it, the iPhone software development kit(套件). And the software development kit is a suite of tools for creating and programming an iPhone app. This opened up a whole new world of opportunities for me. And after playing with the software development kit a little bit, I made a couple of apps, and made some test apps. One of them happened to be Earth Fortune. I was ready to put Earth Fortune on the App Store. And so I persuaded my parents to pay the 99-dollar fee to be able to put my apps on the App Store. They agreed, and now I have apps on the App Store. I heard a lot of interesting encouragement from my family, friends, teachers and even people from the App Store. That's been a huge help to me.

I've got a lot of inspirations from Steve Jobs. And I've started an app club at school, and a teacher at my school is kindly sponsoring my app club. Any student at my school can come and design or learn how to design an app. This is how I can share my experiences with others.

There is this program called iPad pilot program, and some districts have them. And fortunately I could be part of one. A big challenge is how should the iPads be used, and what apps should we put on the iPads? So we are getting feedbacks from teachers at the school, and to see what kind of apps they like. When we design the app, we sell it. It would be free to local districts, and other districts that we sell to. All the money from that goes to the local Ed-foundations.

These days, students know, usually know a little bit more than teachers with the technology. So, sorry. So this is resource to teachers. And educators should recognize these resources and make good use of them.

I like to finish up by saying what I'd like to do in the future. First of all, I'd like to create more apps, more games; I'm working with a third party company to make an app. I'd like to get into Android(安卓系统) programming and development; and I'd like to continue my app club. And find other ways for students to share knowledge with app groups. Thank you."

3.1.3 Tips on delivering a good informative speech

For many speakers, delivery is the most intimidating aspect of public speaking. Although there is no known cure for nervousness, we can make ourselves much more comfortable by following a few basic delivery guidelines as below:

1) Speak to the right audience

If too technical for the audience, our speech is beyond their understanding, then they are easily discouraged from listening. To relate our topic to the audience, a speech is measured by its impact on a particular audience. Once, the British dramatist Oscar Wilde arrived at his club after the disastrous debut of his new play.

"Oscar, how did your play go?" asked a friend.

"Oh," Wilde quipped, "the play was a great success, but the audience was a failure."

2) Do not overestimate the audience's knowledge

We're the researcher of a particular area or subject if we talk on it, so believe our speech will bring some valuable information to the audience.

3) Speak clearly

Use sentences of clear and simple structure. Try to use simple, concrete words, vivid images and details. Limit the number of jargons and complex vocabulary. Do not make the speech too long. No one likes to listen to dragging speeches. Make our speech focused on reasonable length.

4) Sound enthusiastic

Make listeners curious and involved, and help them see, hear, feel, taste and smell. We have to use our voice and facial expression to convey our enthusiasm.

5) Practice from the outline

Become comfortable and familiar with our keywords and clues from the outline to the point that what we say takes the form of an easy, natural conversation. Practice in front of an audience or tape record our practice. We are looking for feedback on rate of delivery, volume, pitch, non-verbal cues (gestures, card-usage, etc.), and eye-contact.

6) Use tools and aids if necessary

Be sure to incorporate as many elements as possible, especially visual aids and concrete objects which can help us a lot in describing and explaining, either it's a picture, a video clip, a model or the real object.

7) Cope with anxiety

Once we know the content, we will find the way that is most comfortable for us. Do a dress rehearsal of the speech under conditions as close as possible to those of the actual presentation.

3.2 Speaking Persuasively

Speaking to persuade always happens in our daily lives without our awareness: persuading others to accept our opinions or plans, urging others to buy some product, or asking the boss to raise our salary, to cite just three examples. So speaking persuasively doesn't just fall onto the roles of a politician or a business man. The goal of an informative speech is to share information, but a persuasive speech is aimed at changing others, their attitude, belief and behavior.

3.2.1 Types of persuasive speech

Generally, we have three purposes in this speech, to convince, to actuate and to inspire. But these purposes often overlap if ours is to influence the attitude and belief of the audience.

1) Speaking to convince

For such topics as convincing the audience about the moral implications of death penalty, the harm of the Internet games to the children, our primary purpose is to change people's attitude and belief, but alongside with that, there is usually the natural outgrowth of urging for their action, since no proposal or appeal of further action will frustrate the audience. In this case, a suggestion of a simple action, an urge is appropriate, thus, the speech becomes one to actuate.

Here is an example where the student speaker who has violated the school rules persuades the school committee to let him stay at school to graduate.

(Van Wilder, 2002)

"(Principal:) We're now in session(开庭). Mr. Wilder. You were found to be in violation of Article 2, sections B of Coolidge's bylaws(校规), soliciting(引诱) of alcohol to extreme minors(未成年人) which is grounds(证据) for immediate expulsion(开除). You have opted to appeal(申辩). The floor is yours.

(Wilder:) Ladies and gentlemen, as you know, um, I've been a student here for seven years, and I've, I've learned a lot here at Coolidge. Let the record show that when I attended class, I did receive exemplary(优秀的) marks. However, it was only when I met a special someone that I realized what I was doing—hiding. See, after this is real life, and I wasn't ready for that. I don't know why exactly. I do know that I don't wanna end up like my father whose whole life revolves around work. But I see that now. And I'm ready to move on.

I can't argue against the infraction(犯规). I was responsible for that party, so what happened was my fault. I'm here to lay myself at the mercy of this court and suggest an alternative(变更) punishment. Make me graduate. If you'll kindly take a look at my transcript(成绩单), you'll see I'm 18 units shy(缺少) from graduating with a degree of leisure studies(娱乐学业). I'm pleading to this committee, reinstate(恢复) me. Let me audit my last six classes, take the necessary finals and leave Coolidge with a degree(文凭).

God, I've bled, crimson and blue(遍体鳞伤) for nearly a decade. This school has given me so much. Let me repay Coolidge by parting ways(离开) as a graduate."

The speaker begins by a sincere apology, and then continues with pleading and urge, attempting to convince the committee to let him stay and graduate.

(*Lean on Me*, 1989)

"Alright people, here we are. This is the day. In one hour, you are going to take an exam administered by the State to test your basic skills and the quality of education at East Side High. And I want to tell you what the people out there are saying about you and what they think about your chances. They say you are inferior(低等的). You are just a bunch of Negroes(对黑人的蔑称) and spics(对说西班牙语的人的蔑称) and poor white trash(对白人的蔑称)! Education is wasted on you. You cannot learn. You're lost! I mean all of ya.

I want all the white students to stand up. All my white students, stand up, right now. Stand up. C'mon, all my white students, stand up. Stand up. That's it. C'mon, stand up. These are my white children. And they're the same as all of you. They've got no place to go. If they had, they would have abandoned(抛弃) us a long time ago like everybody else did, but they couldn't; so here they are at East Side High, just like the rest of us. You can sit down. [to the white students] Are you getting my point, people? (Students: Yeah.) Is it beginning to sink in(听懂)? (Students: Yeah!)

We sink. We swim. We rise. We fall. We meet our fate together! Now, it took the help of a good, good friend make me know and understand that. And I do understand it, and I'm grateful. I'm eternally grateful. And now I've got a message for those people out there who've abandoned you and written you off(取消,遗忘)! Can you hear me?! Can you hear me?!! Good!

You are NOT inferior! Your grades may be. Your school may have been. But you can turn that around and make liars out of those bastards in exactly one hour when you take that test and pass it and win!

So, here's what I want you to do. When you find your mind's wandering(走神), I want you to knuckle back down(开始认真做事) and concentrate — concentrate! Remember what's at stake(危险)! And show them what East Side High is all about: a spirit that will not die!"

As the principal newly appointed to head the school which suffered a bad reputation for mismanagement and a degenerated student body, the speaker's first day speech to the students is focused on convincing them that they are not inferior, and they can pass the test well to prove that the spirit will not die.

2) Speaking to actuate and urge

It is the natural extension of the process of a convincing effort, such as, to donate to charity, to join the campaign for a special purpose, and to fight bad habits that will pollute our environment. The most frequent words in this speech are "urge", "we must", "you must", etc.

Let's look at a great speech by former Secretary General of the UN Kofi Annan.

(Former UN Secretary General Kofi Annan commemorating World Water Day)

"Dear friends, water is essential for life. Yet many millions of people around the world face water shortages. Many millions of children die every year from water-borne (水传播) diseases. And drought (干旱) regularly afflicts (使受苦) some of the world's poorest countries. The world needs to respond much better. We need to increase water efficiency, especially in agriculture. We need to free women and girls from the daily chore of hauling (拖，拉) water, often over great distances. We must involve them in decision-making on water management. We need to make sanitation a priority. This is where progress is lagging most. And we must show that water resources need not be a source of conflict. Instead, they can be a catalyst (催化剂) for cooperation. Significant gains have been made. But a major effort is still required. That is why this year marks the beginning of the 'Water for Life' Decade. Your goal is to meet the internationally agreed targets for water and sanitation by 2015, and to build the foundation for further progress in the years beyond.

This is an urgent matter for human development, and human dignity. Together, we can provide safe, clean water to all the world's people. The world's water resources are our lifeline for survival, and for sustainable development (可持续发展) in the 21st century. Together, we must manage them better."

In this speech, Annan first convinces us that water shortage is a serious problem worldwide, and then urges us to take measures. So this speech is a combination of convincing and actuating.

Another speech is made by Edgar Hoover in the movie *J. Edgar* (2012, *Leonardo Dicaprio*). The FBI creator in the US is urging the Senate to pass the Lindbergh Law to protect the citizens from being abducted and kidnapped illegally in the country.

(*J. Edgar*, 2011)

"*President Hoover*(胡佛总统) *called me the morning the child was taken and asked me to do whatever was in my power to solve this crime. But do you know what all the power of the Bureau means without federal laws, without arms, without the ability to make arrests? It means nothing.*

Mr. Chairman, I urge passage(通过) *of the Lindbergh Law, making kidnapping a federal offense*(触犯联邦法律的罪行), *to immediately deliver all the fingerprints in this country to my office, so that we may create a central file, to help arm our agents so that they have a fighting chance against the submachine guns of some of the most dangerous characters in the history of American criminality. And I urge you to do this in the name of Little Lindy. Because if he can be taken, then what child is safe? And if we cannot aid in his safe return, then what use are we? (Applause in the audience)*"

The key word "urge" appears twice followed by a series of acts.

3) Speaking to inspire

The slight difference from the first two is that speaking to inspire is usually for a noble cause, for the fact that there is no detailed supporting material or complex argument, with the purpose to change how the listeners feel, on such topics as to devote to our nation, to cherish the time in university, to protect our environment, the animals and so on. The following speech is made by Nelson Mandela, former South African President, in court of law, to defend himself against the accusation made by the government for the charges of "being responsible for acts of sabotage and facilitating violent revolution and armed invasion of this country with the intention of overthrowing the government".

Chapter 3 Varieties of Public Speaking 演讲的种类

(*Long Walk to Freedom*, 2014)

> "*My name is Nelson Mandela. I'm the first accused*(第一被告). *I do not deny that I had planned sabotage*(破坏活动). *I did not plan it in the spirit of recklessness*(莽撞), *nor because I have any love for violence. The hard facts*(残酷的事实) *of that 50 years of non-violence*(非暴力抵抗运动) *have brought the African people nothing but more and more repressive*(压迫的)*legislations*(立法) *and fewer and fewer rights. Africans want a just share in the whole of South Africa. We want equal political rights: one man, one vote. I've dedicated myself to this struggle of the African people. I have fought against white domination*(统治地位). *I have fought against black domination. I have cherished the ideal of a free democratic society, where all persons live together in harmony with equal opportunities. It is an ideal which I hope to live for and achieve, but if needs be*(如果有必要), *it is an ideal for which I am prepared to die.*"

Mandela speaks in a measured and composed, yet very compelling way, strongly defending himself and the African National Congress's noble cause of fighting for black people's freedom and equal right. Firstly, he points out the fruitless result of non-violence movement; then he states firmly the purpose of this campaign: one man, one vote. At last, he's determined that he does not fear to lose his life for this ideal.

3.2.2 How to make a good persuasive speech

Aristotle put forward three aspects in the persuasive effort: ethos, logos, and pathos. They deal respectively with three areas of a speaker: the credibility, logical reasoning, and emotional appeals. To be specific, a good persuasive speech must observe the following points.

1) Reveal our competence

Including our special experience or training we have received in this area, our sources of research and our effort that qualify us to speak.

2) Reveal our moral character and good intentions

Try to avoid unnecessary attack on strongly held belief and attitude, show our concern for them, and sound fair-minded, avoid being too absolute or extreme. W. B. Yeats says that all empty souls tend to extreme opinions.

3) Avoid reasoning fallacies

Most fallacies result from inadequate evidence, irrelevancy or inappropriateness, but sometimes they happen because of carelessness. It's the speaker's ethical responsibility to support his argument with logical reasoning and sound evidence.

4) Combine rational appeal and emotional appeal

Being emotional does not mean being sensational, so a good speaker knows how to motivate both the audience's mind and heart.

5) Apply vivid experiences

A specific experience, hypothetical or real, will always be appealing and satisfying to the audience.

Speaking from Manuscript

3.3.1 Definition

To put it simply, speaking from manuscript is reading the manuscript. There are two varieties: one is reading the paper in hand, the other, reading the teleprompter. Speaking from a manuscript is necessary and happens in two situations: one is when on a formal occasion where absolute accuracy is required and no misinformation resulting from misstatement is allowed; the other, obviously, is the speaker's insufficient preparation of the speech.

3.3.2 Advantages and disadvantages

Reading from the manuscript will convey the speaker's idea accurately and completely, but the speaker's body language and facial expression will not look natural for lack of adequate eye contact and emotional appeal. If the speaker stands or sits behind the microphone and the podium, it will look even more awkward. Using a teleprompter for this kind of speech compensates for the loss which results from reading the manuscript, for there is somewhat eye movement and communication with the audience. The United States President's State of Union Address and other formal speeches made by head of state are usually delivered in this way.

3.3.3 Tips on how to read the manuscript

It is the least advised way for us to speak in public, but usually it happens when the speaker couldn't afford enough time to prepare. However, when there are no other alternatives, we have to pay attention to the following points.

1) Do not just read it to our audience

Many people just "read" the speech in the literal sense, sounding routine, dry, matter of fact and uninteresting. Lifting our eyelids from time to time and glancing at the audience is essential to get feedback and interaction.

2) Pay attention to vocal factors

Try to avoid reading in a flat monotone, faltering over words, pausing in the wrong places, reading too quickly or too slowly.

3.4 Speaking from Memory

Having a good memory is one thing, but speaking from memory in the moment is another, so a good memory doesn't guarantee a good delivery of speech. The reason is simple: speaking in the public can be influenced by many factors, which are often complicated. Except in the case of speaking competition, or a short speech, not many people will try to memorize the whole speech from the manuscript word for word. The disadvantage is that if confronting all the glaring eyes of the audience and other distracting elements on the spot, the speaker is prone to get stuck suddenly and have a short-fused memory, which will look embarrassing. For many students, it happens frequently that the speaker goes back to the previous sentences again, or repeats the stuck sentences back and forth. That is really a disaster for a public speaker. We should memorize it thoroughly so that we concentrate on communication rather than on trying to recall what we have memorized.

So a good and experienced speaker always has something else up his sleeve, which is to speak extemporaneously.

3.5 Speaking Extemporaneously

3.5.1 Definition

It's also called extemp. There are two varieties. The first type of extemporaneous speech is very popular in United States high schools and colleges, where students speak persuasively or informatively about current events and politics. In an extemp, a speaker chooses a question out of 3 offered, and then prepares for 30 minutes with the use of previously prepared articles from magazines, journals, newspapers, and articles from news web sites, before speaking for 7 minutes on the topic.

The second type of extemp happens in our daily lives when a speaker has prepared the speech a little before hand, so he/she can speak with the help of a few cue cards or notes in hand. Extemporaneous speech is recognized by employers as one of the most critical job skills for those who must frequently give presentations in both industry and academia. It is even difficult for experienced speakers; some good extemporaneous speakers can give a professional, intelligent, and smooth speech almost off the top of their heads. Most people, however, have difficulty doing that well even with weeks of preparation, copious notes and plenty of slides on which to rely.

3.5.2　Tips on how to do an extemp well

1) Decide the main points

Think of some main points which we need to address in our speech. Focus on as few topics as possible.

2) Decide the three parts and plan a good beginning

Think quickly about the three parts of our speech: introduction, body and conclusion. And think of something to grab the audience's attention at the beginning: a quote, joke, or any other attention-grabbing statements will work well for the beginning of our extemporaneous speech.

3) Write down key points

List the main points on a card or slip of paper, and in a numbered way, so it's clear for us to follow the order and we can reference them one last time before our speech.

4) Conclude with a solid, definitive conclusion.

5) Practice

If we have time, practice the speech. Practicing will make us more confident and comfortable with the timing and flow.

Speaking Impromptu

3.6.1　Definition

There are two varieties. The first one is popular in US colleges and high schools: It is a speech that involves a 5 or 8-minute speech. The speaker receives a slip of paper, which provides three choices for their speech. The topics can be abstract or concrete nouns, people, political events, quotations or proverbs. Or the speaker is given an envelope with slips in it, and he/she draws three slips of paper, chooses one, and then puts two back. He/she then has five minutes to prepare a five minute speech on the subject.

While the format is simple, it takes time to construct a speech in that time and talk on your feet. Mastery of this event is difficult, but many enjoy it, because one does not have to prepare for the event beforehand. Similar in theory to extemporaneous speaking, however unlike that category, impromptu speeches need not be factual and are indeed encouraged to be humorous. The second one is popular in our daily lives when we are asked to speak on the spot, last minute and in a random way of response, without any preparation or expectation, such as telling a story, proposing a toast, and answering a question, and other similar occasions, where we can't just refuse to do it, for we'll look ungraceful, stiff, uncooperative, awkward and thus become the killjoy.

3.6.2　How to do an impromptu speech

If we are known as an experienced presenter or as an expert on a particular subject, we will possibly be asked to give an impromptu speech at one time or another. Rather than declining, being uncooperative or becoming tongue-tied, we should view this with enthusiasm as a great opportunity to shine as a speaker. How can we make sure that this will be the successful outcome?

1) Do not apologize

Never, never apologize or make excuses. The minute a presenter starts to apologize and make excuses, he or she robs him or herself of credibility, and the audience prepares to reject the speech as a mediocre or average one. Think of ourselves as the hero or heroine who appears to save the day, and give the very best speech we can on such a short notice. We wouldn't have been asked if we weren't up to it. Furthermore, many Chinese think it might sound honest and polite to apologize at the beginning, but the opposite effect will be achieved. The audiences know that we're unprepared. Keep it in mind that they are forgiving. Beginning by

"Well, this is unexpected."

"Well, this is too much. I'm overwhelmed."

"This is embarrassing. I know Mr. Johnson is not going to make it easy for me this time, but I'll try my best." will suffice to project to the audience a graceful and generous image.

2) Give ourselves time to organize our thoughts

Hopefully, we will have some time to organize our presentation before we are "on the stage". If it is not too obvious, take a walk to a secluded area where we can think through our opening remarks (usually a good story that we've told many times); what three major points we will make (there are different structures that work well, for example, the past, present, and future); and what will be our conclusion (a strong closing story or a call for action will both work to our advantage). If we can't slip away, think of these while sitting in the audience.

3) Decide the main point and avoid the common blunders

If we haven't had sufficient time to prepare, we must be careful not to ramble or stray from the main subject. A good practice before giving any presentation, impromptu or not, is to decide what our main point is, and support it with facts and arguments, and then stick to it. We've all heard speakers who talk on and on without saying anything material.

4) Take the floor with enthusiasm, stay calm and look natural

Take a deep breath, look at the audience, and smile. Even though it is understandable that we will feel some apprehension in an impromptu experience, we can visualize ourselves as a confident speaker and feel excited about the opportunity to present to a group, who will be so happy that we have agreed to "save the day". Remember that, on the whole, most audiences want us to succeed, and if the introducer has done his or her job we will be greeted with relief and pleasure. Take a moment to breathe and establish rapport. Once we start and have the audience with us, our nerves will vanish.

5) Smile and speak slowly

We have the time to speak and think at the same time, so don't rush. Smile, look around and use such vocal pauses and stock words as "um", "ah", "so", "uh", "you know", "well", "okay", or opening with a greeting like "How is everyone?", "Hello, everybody.", "Mr. President is giving me a really hard time here." Pause and buy us some time. We can take our time and begin a little bit slower, and even pause for a while before speaking. Think quickly to collect the points and plan our speech. Remember, we don't have to start immediately: a hasty start usually leads to awkward stumbling and stops.

6) Keep our speech conversational and enjoy the appreciation

Once we are finished, let the audience have time to sink in, clap their hands and show their appreciation for a job well done. We have seen many speakers so eager to slip back to their seats that they don't give the audience time to let them know how happy they are that they have shared their knowledge with them. And, appreciate ourselves, too! If we forgot to say something we planned to say, or think of something we should have said, no one else knows that. Be happy with what we did! Don't be too hard on ourselves!

7) Be prepared

Mark Twain said that it usually took him three weeks to prepare a good impromptu speech. But how can we prepare if it is impromptu? Before going to join in some activity where there is a speech making possibility, and if you feel that you are going to be invited to give a speech because you're an important guest or have knowledge in the area with regard to the activity, start preparing. And this advanced preparation works well for your speech.

3.7 Answering Questions

Q&A session happens in the course of a speech or comes at the end of the speech. The occasions can be a press conference, a business presentation, a public hearing or for students, a classroom presentation. Such a session is usually confrontational: we are meeting the questions, doubts and even challenges directly from the audience.

3.7.1　How to prepare for the session

1) Formulating answers to possible questions

Prepare the questions in advance. A prepared mind always prevails.

2) To be brief is the best policy

Keep it in mind and practice the delivery of the answers.

3.7.2　How to manage the session

1) Confront the question with a positive attitude

Smile and be graceful. Use such sentences as "I seem to have discussed the point in my speech, but I would like to explain that again." as a tactical method to communicate our ideas, rather than consider it as a challenge to our competence or personhood and feel offended about it.

2) Listen carefully

Look at the questioner directly, and nod in encouragement, and then rephrase the question.

3) Direct the answers to the entire audience

Don't forget that it's not enough to have eye-contact with the questioner only, but simultaneously with the whole room. One good method is to throw the question back to the whole room, i.e. to ask an audience to answer the question from the audience. For instance, "The answer seems obvious. Anyone among the audience would like to answer the question?"

4) Buy us time

Rephrase the question and repeat it to give us time to formulate an answer.

5) Be honest and straightforward

Say "no" and then apologize for the answer we don't know. Don't evade; don't bluff. Offer to check the answer and provide it in the future and as soon as possible.

6) Stay on track and control the situation

The speaker is responsible for keeping the session on track, for he is not only a speaker on the stage, but also a moderator sometimes when there isn't anyone to host the occasion.

a. Prevent a single questioner from dominating the session by asking question one after another.

b. Don't be dragged into a personal debate with a questioner. A tactical way to deal with that can be, "This is an interesting line of questioning, but sorry, we need to give other people a chance to ask questions too."

President: Now I'll take a few questions. Ms Lerner?

Lerner: Jenny Lerner, MSNBC. Mr. President, why wasn't the announcement made sooner?

President: Well, until we knew we could build the rocket and the comet could be intercepted(拦截), we saw no reason to alarm the planet. Do you have another question, Ms. Lerner?

(*Deep Impact*, 1998)

Lerner: Yeah. Is there a connection between the comet and the recall of American troops from abroad?

President: Our fighting men and women are coming home because we felt it prudent (谨慎), in light of (鉴于) domestic security concerns, to have them available. Although I certainly hope we don't need to use them. Next question.

Lerner: Actually, Mr. President, if... just one final question, Sir. MSNBC has learned that Secretary Rittenhouse did not leave for the reasons announced by your administration. In fact, isn't it true, Sir, that not everyone in your administration(政府)is convinced that the "Messiah" will save us?

President: Secretary Rittenhouse served his country with full devotion. He resigned for personal reasons. Now I can promise you this, Ms. Lerner, all of you, everyone in this room and everyone listening to my voice that at some point over the next 10 months, all of us will entertain our worst fears and concerns. But I can also promise you this, life will go on. We will prevail(胜利).

The movie tells us that the President has specially arranged the first question at the press conference to be asked by Ms Lerner, who asks three questions in a row, as required by the plot development.

Topics for One-Minute Speech Practice

1. Tourism and eco-environment.
2. What do you think of the phenomenon that more Chinese students are applying for foreign universities instead of the domestic ones?
3. What do you think of the mobile phone culture among students?
4. Can money buy happiness?
5. Where do you want to live? In a big city or in the countryside?
6. Would you own a private car in the future, if possible?
7. If you had a second life, would you like to be a girl or a boy? Why?
8. What do you think of being a full-time housewife?
9. Would you prefer to get married early or late? Why?
10. What is your ideal marriage? Would a naked marriage be acceptable for you?

Chapter 4

••• Language in Delivery •••
演讲的语言因素

You'll never move others heart to heart, unless your speech comes from your heart. —Goethe
如果你说的话并非发自你的内心,你就不可能触动别人的心弦。□ 歌德

The difference between the right word and the almost right word is the difference between lightning and the lightning bug. —Mark Twain
正确的用词和几乎正确的用词之间的区别就像闪电和萤火虫的区别。□ 马克·吐温

● 本章要点 ●

- 如何克服演讲中的恐惧症
- 修辞与演讲的关系及运用
- 演讲与日常交流的区别

4.1 Conquering Speaking Anxieties

We have feelings of fear, worry, uneasiness, and dread in either presence or absence of psychological stress, which is called anxiety, and considered to be a normal reaction to a stressor. When anxiety becomes excessive, it may fall under the classification of an anxiety disorder. In public speaking, the stressor is facing the audience and expressing one's self. The anxieties are revealed in various symptoms.

Although panic attacks are not experienced by every person who has anxiety, they are a common symptom. Panic attacks usually come without warning and although the fear is generally irrational, the subjective perception of danger is very real. A person experiencing a panic attack will often feel as if he or she is about to die or lose consciousness. Between panic attacks, people with panic disorders tend to suffer from anticipated anxiety—a fear of having a panic attack may lead to the development of phobias.

4.1.1　Symptoms of speaking anxieties

There are common physical, emotional and cognitive reactions to a speaking apprehension, though they may vary from person to person.

1) Physical signs

This includes chest pain, shortness of breath, stomach aches, or headaches. As the body prepares to deal with a stress, blood pressure, heart rate, perspiration, blood flow to the major muscle groups are increased. External signs of anxiety may include sweating, trembling, flushed skin, light-headedness, and verbal disfluencies including stuttering and vocalized pauses ("well", "like", "you know", "ah", and "um").

2) Emotional signs

This includes the feelings of apprehension, worry, or dread. The speaker has trouble concentrating, feeling tense or jumpy. Sometimes we feel like our mind's gone blank and trapped.

3) Cognitive signs

Such as fear of being ridiculed or laughed at, thus, such self-devaluating and self-underestimating thoughts may occur such as "I'm going to make a fool of myself", "My speech will be boring", "My mind will go blank", etc.

4.1.2　Fear of public speaking

In an investigation conducted amongst Americans on what is the biggest fear in their lives, about 3,000 respondents' reply was "speaking before a group". (Stephen Lucas, 2007). Here is the list of their fears:

Greatest Fear	Percentage
A party with strangers	74
Giving a speech	70
Asked personal questions in public	65
Meeting a date's parents	59
First day on a new job	59
Victim of a practical joke	56
Talking with someone in authority	53
Job interview	46
Formal dinner party	44
Blind date	42

According to the survey, giving a speech is the second common fear, so it is understandable that we fear public speaking so much. With so many eyes glaring, our mind may go blank, thinking the audiences can be judgmental and other factors such as biologically based temperament, previous experiences and level of skills. Ancient Roman orator Cicero said, "I turn pale at the outset of a speech and quake in every limb." However, it is unrealistic to eliminate speech anxiety. Instead, we should manage to get over it.

4.1.3 Managing our anxiety

To overcome anxiety, the most important thing to remember is to recognize that it can be controlled, reduced, accepted and lived with. And we can learn to cope with it with accumulation of experience. Lenny Laskowski (1996), a famous professional public speaker, said in his book *Overcoming Anxiety in Meetings and Presentations* that proper preparation and rehearsal can help to reduce speaking anxiety by about 75%; breathing techniques can further reduce another 15%; our mental state accounts for the remaining 10%. Here are the practical methods for us to overcome anxiety in speech.

1) Give ourselves enough time to prepare fully

Remember that it accounts for as much as 75% of our success.

2) Remember that audiences are with us

Understand that the audiences are generally forgiving and they want us to succeed. They have mutual feelings that it is not easy to confront a big audience, and they are our supporters, not enemies.

3) Don't apologize for being nervous

Chinese people like to start with the sentence "I'm sorry. I'm nervous." which, otherwise, will worsen the situation, for the audience will turn their attention to our anxiety.

4) Do some relaxing exercises

Before speaking, have a bath, read aloud, listen to some music or do a deep breathing exercise.

5) Confidence counts

Visualize ourselves succeeding. If we visualize ourselves as a successful speaker, we'll feel more confident. Look at our audience and look around. The more we turn our eyes on the audience, the better we will feel. It only gets worse when we feel otherwise.

6) Manage a good beginning

Concentrate on the beginning, for a good beginning is half done.

7) Have a backup up our sleeve

It helps greatly when we prepare some pictures, handouts and visual aids. Using these things in the speech helps a lot to turn away the audience's attention and lessen our anxiety.

8) Don't expect perfection

Audiences are focusing on our message, not looking for mistakes in our speech.

Making mistakes make us seem more human. Understand that speech is an act of communication, not performance.

4.2 Rhetoric and Public Speaking

According to the definition given by Longman Dictionary, rhetoric is the art of speaking and writing in order to influence and persuade. Rhetoric is the art of discourse that aims to improve the facility of speakers or writers who attempt to inform, persuade, or motivate particular audiences in specific situations. Aristotle considers it a counterpart of both logic and politics, and calls it the faculty of observing in any given case the available means of persuasion (George Q. Xu, 2004). He identifies three integrated parts of a speech: ethos, logos and pathos. Ethos: how the character and credibility of a speaker can influence an audience to consider him/her to be believable, i. e. the speaker must establish the strong credibility. Logos: the use of reasoning, either inductive or deductive, to construct an argument. Pathos: the use of emotional appeals to alter the audience's judgment. This can be done through various rhetorical devices: metaphor, amplification, storytelling, or presenting the topic in a way that evokes strong emotions in the audience. In the perspective of pathos, public speaking and rhetoric are inseparable.

4.2.1 Rhetoric is human

John Locke, the English philosopher of the 17th century defined rhetoric as the art of speaking properly, elegantly and forcefully. American neo-rhetoric scholars hold that rhetoric is the tool of connecting isolated people. From these definitions, rhetoric is human nature. When we use language, rhetoric happens. So Bryant said, "We need rhetoric, voluntarily or involuntarily." (1998) Therefore, the conclusion drawn by them can be: Humans are creatures of rhetoric.

4.2.2 Rhetoric and public speaking

1) Etymologically

The origin of rhetoric dates its meaning back to public speaking. In ancient Egypt, the approach to rhetoric was a balance between convincing argument and wise silence. In ancient Greece, the earliest mention of oratorical skill occurs in Homer's *Iliad*, where heroes like Achilles, Hector, and Odysseus were honored for their ability to advise and exhort their peers and followers (the army) in wise and appropriate action. Many of the great thinkers and political leaders performed their works before an audience, usually in the context of a competition or contest for fame, political influence, and cultural capital. The western classical rhetorical study places the top priority on the art of speaking, and those notable rhetoric scholars were at the same time orators themselves, such as Aristotle and Cicero. Aristotle referred to rhetoric as the art of ruling the minds of men. His iconic book *Rhetoric* deals with five aspects of speaking: ① Invention (creating); ② Disposition (planning); ③ Elocution (styling); ④ Memory (memorizing) and ⑤ Delivery(speaking). This traditional way of public speaking study is still the area of modern rhetoric. Another great orator Cicero (106 BC—43 BC) in Rome, in his masterpiece *De Oratore*, comprehensively deals with what qualities an orator should have. In this book, he specifically refers to the rhetorical devices of sentence organization, sound effects and such figures of speech as rhetorical question, simile, irony, etc. He contended that the goal of a speech is not only to reason with sound judgment, but to move the heart of the audience by designing a series of effective rhetorical devices. In ancient China, rhetoric dates back to the Chinese philosopher, Confucius (551 BC—479 BC), and continues with later followers. The tradition of Confucianism emphasized the use of rhetoric in speaking.

2) Functionally

Rhetoric and speaking share the same roles socially and politically. The ultimate purpose of rhetoric is not just passing on the information, but also educating people and reaching consensus. The objective of public speaking also is to evoke emotionally in the audience, to form an attitude, to reinforce an attitude and to change an attitude.

Socially, over the past century, people studying rhetoric have tended to enlarge its object domain beyond speech texts. Kenneth Burke(1995) asserted humans use rhetoric to resolve conflicts by identifying shared characteristics and interests in symbols. There are also those who classify rhetoric as a civic art, believing that rhetoric has the power to shape communities, form the character of citizens and greatly impact civic life. It regulates people's relations, promotes understanding and cooperation, and achieve social harmony.

Politically, the ancient Greeks highly valued public political participation, rhetoric emerged as a crucial tool to influence politics. Consequently, rhetoric remains associated with its political origins. It serves the purpose of inspiring, encouraging, persuading, guiding and leading, and ultimately, governing. Aside from the great thinkers and educators in ancient Rome and Greece and the roles they have played in their political and social life, China has also produced a large number of such great orators as Su Qin, Zhang Yi in the Spring & Autumn and Warring States Periods. With their great persuasive power in speech, they played a significant role in Chinese history. Comparatively, though, speaking art in ancient China stressed more on the combination of speaking and debating, indicating the philosophy of putting scholarship into practical use, while appearing to be weak in the theoretical research.

To sum up, rhetoric evolved as an important art, one that provided the orator with the forms, means, and strategies for persuading an audience of the orator's arguments. Today the term rhetoric can be used at times to refer only to the form of argumentation, often with the pejorative connotation of a means of obscuring the truth. Classical philosophers believed quite the contrary: the skilled use of rhetoric was essential to the discovery of truths, because it provided the means of ordering and clarifying arguments. A speech is a tool for idea communicating, emotion conveying, and information sharing. Above all, the language of a good speech must be accurate, clear, and appropriate. The ultimate desired level of language is touching, interesting, natural and vivid.

4.2.3 Use language accurately

The first rule for an English speaker is to speak correctly. It includes the right choice of words and the collocation of them. For Chinese speakers, the accuracy problem happens frequently in the following areas:

- The choice of words with similar denotations but different connotations;
- The use of prepositions and conjunctions;
- Subject-verb agreement;
- Misplaced modifiers;
- Tense agreement in a sentence or a passage;
- Passive voice;
- "There be" structure, and;
- Idiomatic use of English etc.

These errors can catch the attention of the audience immediately, and when this happens, they will not pay attention to what we'll say, but how we'll say it, thus miss or misunderstand the message conveyed in the speech. So when we prepare a speech and are not so sure about the grammar and idioms, we should refer to a dictionary, grammar book or a teacher. Secondly, don't forget to rehearse it in front of friends and ask them to point out the mistakes. These strategies will help us detect and correct errors.

(*Iron Man*, 2008)

"*Gentlemen, what is <u>at stake</u> here? I want you to think about this. Civilization <u>has been preserved</u> because the right people have had the right idea at the right time. This technology—it <u>comes along</u> once in a generation. And, It's a gift—that <u>has been put</u> in* *our hands.*

And why is that? It's because we have a vision, <u>a vision for</u> the future of this <u>country</u>, of this <u>nation</u>, of the WORLD ORDER! Because make no mistake: This tool that you're creating in the wrong hands would end civilization <u>as we know it</u>. Think about what's at stake, here!"

Here in the speech above, the Chinese English learners must pay attention to the following.

☆ Choice of words of denotation and connotation: country, nation.
☆ Idiomatic expressions: at stake, a vision for, comes along, as we know it.
☆ Passive voice of present perfect term: has been preserved, has been put.

4.2.4　Use language clearly

Using language clearly requires that the language must be specific and familiar, not too abstract, general or obscure. If you say somebody "does well in study", it is too general, but "gets all A+'s and A-'s" would be specific. Picking rare words for the purpose of showing off only compounds the problem and inconveniences everyone. When having to use technical terms like "melamine", the speaker had better explain it and when facing Chinese audiences, the speaker may have to use a Chinese equivalent to translate it. For instance, when you talk about "Naked Marriage" in China, you may have to give the Chinese equivalent *luo hun* to explain it.

(*The Iron Lady*, 2011)

"We congratulate the men and women of the armed forces for their <u>skill, bravery and loyalty</u> to this country. We were faced with an act of unprovoked aggression(无端挑起的入侵)and we responded as we have responded in times past: <u>with unity, strength and courage</u>, sure in the knowledge that though much is sacrificed, in the end, right will prevail(战胜)over wrong. And I put it to the right on(澄清)the gentlemen opposite, that this is not a day for him to <u>carp</u>(吹毛求疵), <u>find fault, demand inquiries</u>. They will *happen I can assure him of that, for we have nothing to hide, no! This is a day <u>to put differences aside, to hold one's head high, and take pride in being British</u>!"*

Margaret Thatcher uses four sets of words and phrases to strengthen her expression of similar ideas: skill, bravery and loyalty; with unity, strength and courage; to carp, find fault, demand inquiries; to put difference aside, hold one's head high, and take pride in being British. They are specific, concrete, similar yet contrasting and compelling.

4.2.5 Use language appropriately

Using language appropriately requires us to use the right words suitable for the occasion, our audience, our topic and at the same time, for the speaker. In a formal setting, formal words and expressions, correct grammatical structures are required. Slangs and clichés are to be avoided; profanity, swear words and foul language are forbidden. Try to avoid sexism, ageism and racism, to avoid using words which are offensive, harsh and displeasing in these aspects, e.g. "fat, stupid, negro, old people". The following two examples tell us the difference of uses between two delicate choices in propriety.

1) Student: Sir, I've got something to ask.

Teacher: Ok. Let's (Let me) see what problem we've (you've) got.

2) Away-out for homeless (houseless) couples

(*Air Force One*, 1997)

"The dead remember our <u>indifference</u>. The dead remember our silence. I came here tonight to be congratulated. But today when I visited the Red Cross camps, <u>overwhelmed</u> (震撼) by the flood of refugees <u>fleeing</u> from the horror of Kazakhstan, I realized I don't deserve to be congratulated. None of us do. Let's speak the truth. And the truth is, we acted too late. <u>Only when our own national security was threatened did we act.</u> Radek's <u>regime</u>(政权) murdered over 200 000 men, women and children and we watched it on TV. We let it happen. People were being <u>slaughtered</u> for over a year and

> we issued economical sanctions(制裁)and hid behind a rhetoric of diplomacy(外交辞令). How dare we? The dead remember. Real peace is not just the absence of conflict; it's the presence of justice.(真正的和平并不是消除冲突,而是匡扶正义)
>
> And tonight, I come to you with a pledge(宣誓)to change America's policy. Never again will I allow our political self-interests to deter(制止)us from doing what we know to be morally right. Atrocity(残暴)and terror are not political weapons and to those who would use them: Your day is over. We will never negotiate. We will no longer tolerate and we will no longer be afraid. It's your turn to be afraid."

The speaker uses all the formal words and expressions, such as "indifference, overwhelmed, flee, regime, slaughter, sanctions, rhetoric of diplomacy, deter and atrocity". And the formal sentence structures: "Only when our own national security was threatened did we act.", "Never again will I allow our political self-interests to deter us from doing what we know to be morally right." "Real peace is not just the absence of conflict; it's the presence of justice." The choice of words and sentences fit the occasion where the president of a nation speaks in a diplomatic gathering.

4.2.6　Use language vividly

Grammar is the law of language; rhetoric is the art of language. Apart from the appeal to logic, integrity and passion, the speaker's success in making an effective speech depends largely on the effective use of language. This art of using language is rhetoric. Rhetorician Wool Helen commented that Grammar tells what is correct; rhetoric tells what is effective and pleasing. The difference between using rhetoric and not using it results in the difference "from language to speech, from expression to confront, from communication to persuasion, from explanation to contention".

Language being correct, clear and appropriate is the fundamental requirement of a good speech. Colorfulness and vividness is another essential element that makes our speech impressive and forceful. The effective way is to use figures of speech to appeal to the audience's senses and imagination. The word "figure" suggests other terms such as "form" or "shape". We have a long history of naming and classifying figures of speech based on their unique "forms" or "topographies". Different forms can be achieved through repetitions, juxtapositions, contrasts, and associations, by violating expectation, by evoking echoes of other people, places, times, and contexts and through novel, provocative imagery (McArthur, 1992). Specific figures can clarify, emphasize, exaggerate, amuse, or surprise. Using figurative speeches can make our language more interesting, lively, impressive, touching, romantic, and ultimately more persuasive and effective.

1) Simile

A simile makes an explicit comparison between two things that are essentially different but have something in common. We use words such as "like" or "as" to make a comparison between two things which are fundamentally unlike.

<u>Politeness is like an air cushion.</u> There may be nothing in it, but it eases the jolts wonderfully.

<u>Marriage is like a cozy, calm harbor</u> where you are protected from the storms of the outside world.

This momentous decree came <u>as a great beacon light</u> of hope to millions of Negro slaves who had been seared(灼烧)in the flames of withering injustice. It came <u>as joyous daybreak</u> to end the long night of their captivity(囚禁). (Martin Luther King)

We will not be satisfied until justice rolls down like waters, and righteousness like a mighty stream.(公正似水奔流,正义如泉喷涌)(Martin Luther King)

Today, we dumped another 70 million tons of global-warming pollution into the thin shell of atmosphere surrounding our planet,<u>as if it were an open sewer</u>(下水道). (Al Gore)

Setting aside a section of a restaurant for smoking is <u>like</u> setting aside a section of a swimming pool for peeing. (author unknown)

I was born in Texas. In Texas they say an old judge is <u>like</u> an old shoe. Everything is all worn out except the tongue. (Sandra Day O'Connor)

2) Metaphor

A metaphor compares two things without using words "as, like". For example:

All the world is <u>a stage</u>,

And all the men and women <u>merely players</u>.

They have their <u>exits</u> and their <u>entrances</u>,

And one man in his time <u>plays many parts</u>. (Shakespeare)

The Royal Navy, with the help of countless merchant seamen, and using nearly 1,000 ships of all kinds, have carried over 335,000 men out of <u>the jaws of death and shame</u> to their native land. (Winston Churchill)

In Martin Luther King's speech *I Have a Dream*, there are lots of metaphors:

But one hundred years later, the Negro still is not free. One hundred years later, the life of the Negro is still sadly <u>crippled</u>(奴役)by the <u>manacles of segregation</u>(种族隔离的锁链)and the <u>chains of discrimination</u>(种族歧视的羁绊). One hundred years later, the Negro lives on <u>a lonely island of poverty</u> in the midst of <u>a vast ocean of material prosperity</u>.

In a sense we've come to our nation's capital to <u>cash a check</u>(兑现支票).

Instead of honoring this sacred obligation,<u>America has given the Negro people a bad check, a check which has come back marked "insufficient funds"</u>(资金不足).

But we refuse to believe that <u>the bank of justice is bankrupt.</u> We refuse to believe that there are insufficient funds in the great vaults(金库)of opportunity of this nation. And so, we've come to cash this check, a check that will give us upon demand <u>the riches of freedom and the security of justice.</u>

Now is the time to rise from the dark and desolate valley of segregation to the sunlit path of racial justice.

Now is the time to lift our nation from the quicksands(流沙)of racial injustice to the solid rock of brotherhood. Let us not seek to satisfy our thirst for freedom by drinking from the cup of bitterness and hatred.

Let us not wallow(打滚)in the valley of despair, I say to you today, my friends.

I have a dream that one day on the red hills of Georgia, the sons of former slaves and the sons of former slave owners will be able to sit down together at the table of brotherhood. I have a dream that one day even the state of Mississippi, a state sweltering with the heat of injustice, sweltering with the heat of oppression, will be transformed into an oasis of freedom and justice.

With this faith, we will be able to hew out of the mountain of despair a stone of hope. (从绝望之山中凿出一颗希望的宝石)

With this faith, we will be able to transform the jangling discords(争吵的噪音)of our nation into a beautiful symphony of brotherhood(兄弟之情的交响乐).

Listed above are examples from *I Have a Dream* by Martin Luther King. Other examples:

Terrorist attacks can shake the foundations of our biggest buildings, but they cannot touch the foundation of America. These acts shatter steel, but they cannot dent the steel of American resolve. (George Bush)

America was targeted for attack because we're the brightest beacon(灯塔)for freedom and opportunity in the world. And no one will keep that light from shining. (George Bush)

We are nothing but sheep, being herded to the final slaughterhouse. I will not go down that way. (*City Hall*)

This green field right here was painted red, bubbling with the blood of young boys, smoke and hot lead pouring right through their bodies. (*Remember the Titans*)

Television is chewing gum for the eyes. (author unknown)

What is life? It is the flash of a firefly in the night. It is the breath of a buffalo in the wintertime. It is the little shadow which runs across the grass and loses itself in the sunset. (*Crowfoot*)

3) Hyperbole

A hyperbole is an exaggerated way of statement, or overstatement. For example:

Hamlet: I loved Ophelia; forty thousand brothers could not, with all their quantity of love, make up my sum. (Shakespeare, *Hamlet*)

Helen, your eyes had wounded me to death. (Ronsard)

In the spring, I have counted one hundred and thirty-six different kinds of weather inside of four-and-twenty hours. (Mark Twain)

I have a dream that one day every valley shall be exalted(抬升), every hill and mountain shall be made low; the rough places will be made plain; and the crooked places will be made straight(Martin Luther King).

4) Alliteration

Alliteration adds the effect of rhythm and movement to verbal expression by using the same initial sound in a series of words.

Don't let fate forecast our future.

Good team members have commitment, communication and competitiveness.

Even though large tracts of Europe and many old and famous states have fallen or may fall into the grip of the Gestapo(纳粹秘密警察), and all the odious apparatus of Nazi rule, we shall not flag(投降)or fail.(Winston Churchill)

I have a dream that one day, our sons and daughters will not be judged by the color of their skin but the content of their character. (Martin Luther King)

Let every nation know, whether it wishes us well or ill, that we shall pay any price, bear any burden, meet any hardship, support any friend, oppose any foe, to assure the survival and the success of liberty. (J. F. Kennedy)

Let's go forth to lead the land we love. (John F. Kennedy)

It'll be the ballot or it'll be the bullet; it'll be liberty or it'll be death. And if you are not ready to pay that price, don't use that word in your dictionary. (Malcolm X)

In a nation founded on the promise of human dignity, our colleges, our communities, our country should challenge hatred wherever we find it. (Hillary Clinton)

5) Pun

A pun plays with the sameness of sound of different words which are called homophones; or the same words with different meanings called homonyms. e. g.

Claudius: My son, Hamlet, how is it that the clouds still hang on you?

Hamlet: Not so, my lord, I am too much in the sun. (Shakespeare, *Hamlet*)

We must all hang together, or we'll hang separately. (Benjamin Franklin)

When Dan told me the girl he was gonna marry, I didn't believe it. Only a few short years ago, he was throwing rocks at girls, now he is putting one on her finger. (*I Hope They Serve Beer in Hell*)

(*Leap Year*, 2010)

> "I don't want to interrupt a good party, um, but I want to say thank you to my husband. I want to say, may you never steal, lie or cheat. But if you must steal, then steal away my sorrows (悲伤); And if you must lie, *lie with me all the nights of my life*, and if you must cheat, then please cheat death, because I couldn't live a day without you. Cheers!"

The bride is skillfully using the pun of "lie", a homonymy, i.e. the same pronunciation but different meaning.

6) Personification

Personification is a figure of speech attributing human's quality to an inanimate object, an animal or an idea, that is, treating them as if they were human beings. e.g.

Love is a <u>naked child</u>. Do you think he has pockets for money?

Conscience is the <u>inner voice</u> that <u>warns</u> us that someone may be looking. (H. L. Mencken)

Sometimes, without warning, the future <u>knocks on our door</u> with a precious and painful vision of what might be. (Al Gore)

The future is <u>knocking at our door</u> right now. Make no mistakes, the next generation will ask us one of two questions. Either they will ask, "What were you thinking; why didn't you act?" (Al Gore)

7) Zeugma

A zeugma is a way of expression putting two or more unrelated things together and correlate to still another unrelated thing, just like two horses drawing a cart. This use creates a sense of humor and vividness. For example:

(1) <u>Make up</u> your mind before you <u>make up</u> your face.

(2) We <u>suck</u> our <u>mother</u> when we are young and our <u>father</u> when we grow up.

(3) He <u>opened</u> his <u>door</u> and his <u>heart</u> to the poor girl.

(4) My father came back from his fishing trip, having <u>caught</u> a big trout and a <u>bad cold</u>.

(5) Do you think I speak <u>in an accent</u> that I think <u>in an accent</u>?

(6) When I was young, I used to <u>organize</u> my father's <u>tools</u>, my mother's <u>kitchen ware</u>, and my sister's <u>boyfriends</u>.

(7) He <u>picked up</u> his <u>hat</u> and his <u>courage</u>.

(In her Presidential nomination campaign speech in 2008, Hillary Clinton said so)

As we gather here today in this historic, magnificent building, the 50th woman to leave this Earth is orbiting overhead. If we can <u>launch</u> <u>50 women into space</u>, we will someday <u>launch</u> <u>a woman into the White House</u>.

(Again, in her speech meeting with Russian foreign minister Lavrov on Oct. 15,

2009, Hilary Clinton said so)

I unfortunately was not able to come during the Summit between our two presidents because I broke my elbow. Now both my elbow and our relationship are reset(矫正) and we're moving forward, which I greatly welcome.

(Steve Jobs said to his wife)

We've been through so much together and here we are right back where we started 20 years ago—older and wiser—with wrinkles on our faces and hearts.

(Helen Mirren said so in the 79th Oscar Award)

For fifty years, and more, Elizabeth Winsor has maintained her dignity, her sense of duty and her hair style.

8) Rhetorical Question

A rhetorical question needs no answer from the audience or the speaker answers the question himself/herself.

e. g.

Well, if no one among us is capable of governing himself, then who among us has the capacity to govern someone else? (Ronald Reagan)

This is the most important topic on earth: peace. What kind of peace do I mean and what kind of peace do we seek? I'm talking about genuine peace, the kind of peace that makes life on earth worth living. Not merely peace in our time, but peace in all time. Our problems are man-made, therefore, they can be solved by man. For in the final analysis, our most basic common link is that we all inhabit this small planet. We breathe the same air, we all cherish our children's future. We are all mortal. (J. F. Kennedy)

We were great once. Can we not be great again? Now I put that question to James Bone, and there is only silence. Yet, could not something pass from this sweet youth to me? Could he not empower me, to find in myself the strength? To have the knowledge, to summon up the courage, to accomplish this seemingly insurmountable task of making this city livable? Just livable? (*City Hall*)

In a court trial, when the counsel is debating on behalf of his/her client, he/she uses a lot of rhetorical questions.

(*The Accused*, 1988)

"Ladies and gentlemen, the State has charged these three men with a crime. And the State supported that charge with the testimony of two witnesses. Sarah Tobias, who told you how three men raped her, and she told you how she heard other men shouting encouragement to her attackers. <u>Did she name these other men?</u> No. <u>did she describe these other men?</u> No. <u>Could she tell you what these other men shouted?</u> No. Her sworn testimony(证词)—her poignant(心酸的), heart-rending(悲痛的) sworn testimony—was an appeal to your pity. And if her story is true, you should pity her. But even if her story is true and you do pity her that has nothing to do with this case, because those three men did not rape her. Her sworn testimony is <u>nothing</u>, and you must treat it as <u>nothing</u>. Now if you wish, you can also treat as nothing the testimony of her lover, Larry, who told you what kind of woman she is. And you can treat as <u>nothing</u> the testimony of the bartender, Jesse, who told you that she was so drunk, she could barely stand. And you can treat as nothing the testimony of her friend, Sally, who told you what Miss Tobia's intentions were when she first saw our clients. Our case does not depend on those witnesses, just as the People's case(公诉人) does not depend on Sarah Tobias'. The People's case depends on Kenneth Joyce. If you believe him, you'll convict(判决有罪) those three men. And if you don't, you'll acquit them. <u>Do you believe him?</u> Why did Kenneth Joyce testify(作证)? Every day for months, he said to himself, "I'm guilty. I'm guilty." Finally he was offered a way to purge(净化,消除) that guilt, and he took it. Kenneth Joyce told you he watched a rape and told you that everyone else in that room watched a rape. <u>How did he know that? Did he read their minds?</u> To solicit(引诱) a crime, you must first know that it is a crime. <u>Who knew it? Kenneth Joyce. Do you think it matters to Kenneth Joyce who shouted?</u> In his mind, every person in that room was guilty. He told you that. And Kenneth Joyce—who is guilty, who did watch a rape and do nothing, will purge himself by bringing down(拉下水) anyone who was in that room. And of course, at no legal cost to himself, while those three men face prison. <u>Do you believe him?</u> If you do, convict him. And if you don't, and I know you don't, acquit."

The underlined questions one after another asked by the council sound very compelling and even intimidating.

Woodruff: Ladies and gentlemen, it is my honor to introduce this year's valedictorian(毕业告别演讲者), Jack Charles Howell.

Eric: Yo, Jack, go get 'em.

(*Jack*, 1996)

Howell: I got it, Eric. I'm cool... my speech. I don't have very much time these days, so I'll make it quick—like my life. You know, as we come to the end of this phase (阶段) of our life, we find ourselves trying to remember the good times and trying to forget the bad times. And we find ourselves thinking about the future. We start to worry, thinking, "What am I gonna do? Where am I gonna be in ten years?"

But I say to you, "Hey, look at me." Please, don't worry so much, 'cause in the end none of us have very long on this earth. Life is fleeting (飞驰). And if you're ever distressed, cast your eyes to the summer sky, when the stars are strung across the velvety (丝绒般的) night, and when a shooting star (流星) streaks through the blackness turning night into day—make a wish, think of me. And make your life spectacular. I know I did.

I made it, Mom. I'm a grown-up. Thank you.

The speaker asks two questions at the end of the first part of the speech, and then he answers the questions himself in the second part of the speech.

9) Antithesis

Antithesis uses parallel construction to contrast ideas. Examples in speeches:

Ask not what your country can do for you; ask what you can do for your country. (J. F. Kennedy)

Let us never negotiate out of fear. But let us never fear to negotiate. (J. F. Kennedy)

United, there is little we cannot do. Divided (分裂), there is little we can do. (J. F. Kennedy)

Not that I love Caesar less, but that I love Rome more. (Brutus)

As Caesar loves me, I weep for him; as he was fortunate, I rejoice at it; as he was valiant (勇敢), I honor him; but as he was ambitious, I slew him. (Brutus)

Your success as a family, our success as a society, depends not on what happens in the White House, but on what happens inside your house. (Laura Bush)

The world will little note what we say here, but they will never forget what they did here. (Abraham Lincoln)

10) Anaphora

Anaphora, the repetition of a phrase at the beginning of sentences, is a rhetorical tool employed in a speech. Repeating a phrase or a sentence can be a very emphatic way of expression, adding to the tension and force.

One of the easiest and most effective ways of developing parallelism is to repeat the same words, phrases, or clauses at the beginning or end of successive lines. For example:

The enlightenment is dead, Marxism is dead, the working-class movement is dead, and the author does not feel very well either. (*Harvey*)

Repeating can happen inside a paragraph:

Never give in! Never, never, never, never, never, never. In nothing great or small, large or petty—never give in except to convictions of honor and good sense. (Winston Churchill)

Yesterday, the Japanese government also launched an attack against Malaya. Last night, Japanese forces attacked Hong Kong. Last night, Japanese forces attacked Guam. Last night, Japanese forces attacked the Philippine Islands. Last night, the Japanese attacked Wake Island. And this morning, the Japanese attacked Midway Island. (Franklin Roosevelt)

In 1931, ten years ago, Japan invaded Manchukuo—without warning. In 1935, Italy invaded Ethiopia—without warning. In 1938, Hitler occupied Austria—without warning. In 1939, Hitler invaded Czechoslovakia—without warning. Later in 1939, Hitler invaded Poland—without warning. And now Japan has attacked Malaysia and Thailand—and the United States—without warning. (Franklin Roosevelt)

We shall go on to the end. We shall fight on the seas and oceans. We shall fight with growing confidence, and growing strength in the air. We shall defend our island, whatever the cost may be. We shall fight on the beaches, we shall fight on the landing grounds, we shall fight in the fields, and in the streets. We shall fight in the hills. We shall never surrender. (Winston Churchill)

Repetition can also happen in the whole speech, working as the thread stitching the whole structure of the speech. A classic example of anaphora is found in Martin Luther King's *I Have a Dream*. He urges his audience to seize the moment: "Now is the time..." is repeated four times in the sixth paragraph. The most widely cited example of anaphora is found in the often quoted phrase "I have a dream..." which is repeated eight times as King paints a picture of an integrated and unified America for his audience. Other occasions when King used anaphora include "One hundred years later" "We can never be satisfied" "With this faith" "Let freedom ring" and "free at last".

I say to your today, my friends, that in spite of the difficulties and frustrations of the moment, I still have a dream. It is a dream deeply rooted in the American dream.

I have a dream that one day this nation will rise up and live out the true meaning of its creed: "We hold these truths to be self-evident: that all men are created equal."

I have a dream that one day on the red hills of Georgia the sons of former slaves and the sons of former slave owners will be able to sit down together at a table of brotherhood.

I have a dream that one day even the state of Mississippi, a desert state, sweltering with the heat of injustice and oppression, will be transformed into an oasis of freedom and justice.

I have a dream that my four children will one day live in a nation where they will not be judged by the color of their skin but by the content of their character.

I have a dream today.

...

Go back to Mississippi, go back to Alabama, go back to Georgia, go back to the slums and ghettos of our northern cities, knowing that somehow this situation can and will be changed. Let us not wallow in the valley of despair. (Martin Luther King)

(In her speech *On Women's Rights*, Hillary Clinton said so)

The voices of this conference and of the women must be heard loud and clear:

It is a violation of human rights when babies are denied food, or drowned, or suffocated, or their spines broken, simply because they are born girls.

It is a violation of human rights when women and girls are sold into the slavery of prostitution.

It is a violation of human rights when women are doused with gasoline, set on fire and burned to death because their marriage dowries are deemed too small.

It is a violation of human rights when individual women are raped in their own communities and when thousands of women are subjected to rape as a tactic or prize of war.

It is a violation of human rights when a leading cause of death worldwide along women ages 14 to 44 is the violence they are subjected to in their own homes.

It is a violation of human rights when women are denied the right to plan their own families, and that includes being forced to have abortions or being sterilized against their will.

What we are learning around the world is that if women are healthy and educated, their families will flourish. If women are free from violence, their families will flourish. If women have a chance to work and earn as full and equal partners in society, their families will flourish.

In defending Caesar and accusing Brutus of murdering him, Mark Antony delivered his world famous speech at Caesar's funeral. Threading throughout the whole speech, he repeats the phrase "Brutus is an honorable man" and another sentence "Brutus says he

(Caesar) was ambitious", creating a sharp contrast and irony.

"Friends, Romans, countrymen, lend me your ears. I come to bury Caesar, not to praise him. The evil that men do lives after them. The good is oft interred(埋葬)with their bones. So let it be with Caesar. <u>The noble Brutus</u> hath told you <u>Caesar was ambitious.</u> If it were so, it was a grievous fault, and grievously hath Caesar answered it.

(*Julius Caesar*, 1953)

Here, under leave of Brutus and the rest — <u>*for Brutus is an honorable man*</u>; *so are they all, all honorable men* — *He was my friend, faithful and just to me*; <u>*But Brutus says he was ambitious, and Brutus is an honorable man.*</u> *He has brought many captives home to Rome, whose ransoms*(战利品)*did the general coffers*(国库)*fill; Did this in Caesar seem ambitious? When that the poor have cried, Caesar has wept;* <u>*Ambition should be made of sterner*(坚强)*stuff. Yet Brutus says he was ambitious; And Brutus is an honorable man.*</u> *You all did see that on the Lupercal Ⅰ thrice*(三次)*presented him a kingly crown, which he did thrice refuse. Was this ambition?* <u>*Yet Brutus says he was ambitious; and sure he is an honorable man.*</u> *I speak not to disprove what Brutus spoke, but here I am to speak what I do know. You all did love him once, not without cause; what cause withholds you, then, to mourn for him? My heart is in the coffin there with Caesar, and I must pause till it come back to me.*

But yesterday the word of Caesar might have stood against the world: now lies he there, and none so poor to do him reverence(瞻仰). *O masters, if I were disposed to stir your hearts and minds to mutiny and rage, I should do Brutus Wrong, and Cassius wrong,* <u>*who, you all know, are honorable men.*</u> *I will not do them wrong; I rather choose to the wrong the dead, to wrong myself and you, than I will wrong such honorable men. But here's a parchment*(羊皮纸)*with the seal of Caesar; I found it in his closet — it's his will. Let but the commons hear his testament, which, pardon me, I do not mean to read, and they would go and kiss dead Caesar's wounds, and dip*(沾上)*their napkins in his sacred blood; yea, beg a hair of him for memory. And, dying, mention it within their wills, bequeathing*(遗传)*it as a rich legacy onto this issue."*

The repetition of "Brutus is an honorable man" "Brutus says he was ambitious" strengthens the speaker's tone of irony each time.

11) Parallelism

Parallelism is most frequently used in speeches. It is a structural arrangement of parts of a sentence, sentences, paragraphs, and larger units of composition by which one element of equal importance with another is similarly developed and phrased. Parallelism is usually used in the following forms.

Parallel words

We think of those whom death in this war has hurt, taking from them <u>fathers</u>, <u>husbands</u>, <u>sons</u>, <u>brothers</u> and <u>sisters</u> whom they loved. No victory can bring back the faces they long to see. (Harry Truman)

I have nothing to offer but <u>blood</u>, <u>toil</u>, <u>tears</u> and <u>sweat</u>. (Winston Churchill)

Today, <u>our fellow citizens</u>, <u>our way of life</u>, <u>our very freedom</u> came under attack in a series of deliberate and deadly terrorist acts. The victims were in airplanes and offices: <u>secretaries</u>, <u>businessmen and women</u>, <u>military and federal workers</u>, <u>moms and dads</u>, <u>friends and neighbors</u>. Thousands of lives were suddenly ended by evil, despicable acts of terror. (George Bush)

Parallel phrases

With this faith we will be able <u>to work together</u>, <u>to pray together</u>, <u>to struggle together</u>, <u>to go to jail together</u>, <u>to stand up for freedom together</u>, knowing that we will be free one day. (Martin Luther King)

Let every nation know... that we shall <u>pay any price</u>, <u>bear any burden</u>, <u>meet any hardship</u>, <u>support any friend</u>, <u>oppose any foe</u>, to assure the survival and the success of liberty. (John F. Kennedy)

There are <u>tears for his love</u>; <u>joy for his fortune</u>; <u>honor for his valor</u>; and <u>death for his ambition</u>. (Brutus)

And the government <u>of the people</u>, <u>by the people</u>, <u>for the people</u>, shall not perish from the earth. (Abraham Lincoln)

Parallel clauses

I met good, honest, and hard-working people, <u>people that want to raise their families here</u>, <u>people who want to do business here</u>, <u>who want to have jobs here</u>, <u>who want to educate their kids here</u>, <u>people that want to enjoy the clean air and the clean water</u>. (Arnold Schwarzenegger)

What we are learning around the world is that <u>if women are healthy and educated</u>, their families will flourish. <u>If women are free from violence</u>, their families will flourish. <u>If women have a chance to work and earn as full and equal partners in society</u>, their families will flourish. (Hillary Clinton)

Parallel sentences

<u>There is no Negro problem.</u> <u>There is no Southern problem.</u> <u>There is no Northern problem.</u> <u>There is only an American problem.</u> And we are met here tonight as Americans — not as Democrats or Republicans. We are met here as Americans to solve the problem. (Lyndon Johnson)

<u>This is what</u> <u>I hope for China.</u> <u>This is what</u> <u>I hope for the world.</u> <u>This is what</u> <u>I hope for you</u>, the new generation of China, whose task it is to help to build and to meet those goals. (Richard Nixon)

Parallel paragraphs

The examples from section 10) Anaphora *I Have a Dream* by Martin Luther King's and *On Women's Rights* by US Secretary of State Hilary Clinton are both examples of parallel paragraphs. The following is a defendant counsels' opening speech in the court:

(*Philadelphia*, 1993)

<u>Fact</u>: Andrew Beckett's performance on the job varied from competent, good to oftentimes mediocre(平庸), to sometimes flagrantly(臭名远扬的) incompetent(无能). <u>Fact</u>: He claims he's the victim of lies and deceit(欺骗). <u>Fact</u>: It was Andrew Beckett who lied going to great lengths(极尽手段) to conceal his disease from his employees. <u>Fact</u>: He was successful in his duplicity(奸诈). The partners at Wyant Wheeler did not know that Andrew Beckett had Aids when they fired him. <u>Fact</u>: Andrew Beckett is dying. <u>Fact</u>: Andrew Beckett is angry, because his lifestyle, his reckless(不计后果的) behavior has cut short his life. And in his anger, his rage, he is lashing out(放肆出击), and he wants someone to pay. Thank you.

In this movie, an employee Andrew Beckett with Aids is fired by his firm because of his disease, so he accuses the firm of discrimination. This is the speech by the counsel defending the law firm. The uniqueness of the speech lies in the 6 repetitions of "Fact", which introduces the argument. The 6 pieces of evidence in the parallel structure sounds neat, incisive and even intimidating.

4.3 Public Speaking and Daily Conversation

Public speaking and daily conversation share both common ground and differentiate each other. For common grounds, they both involve the speaker and the listener's involvement in the process; both use verbal and nonverbal ways to communicate; both apply the same technical approaches to achieve maximum effect in using language in terms of accuracy, clearness, appropriateness and vividness. But the differences are so striking that recognizing them can help us speak better.

1) Level of language

Level of language in a speech is higher or more formal. Slang, jargon, bad grammar have little place in public speaking, and such colloquial uses of words as "gonna, wanna, high (the enjoyment of using drugs), cool, dig (like)" are rarely seen in a formal speech. There was a TV host speaking such English in a talk show with a guest, "So great have you here!" "We just have three question want to ask you." "Today we know the share markets slump heavily, plunge over 100 points." In these sentences, broken English, or Chinese English is obviously too rough to be acceptable in a speech, but doesn't cause much trouble in daily conversation.

2) Sentences and textual structure

A public speech is highly structured in syntactical form and textual arrangement. A good speech is just a good article in the oral form. The accuracy of grammar, appropriateness of expression, vivacity in diction are all presented in a polished and elegant way, while, in daily conversation, no such standards are required, with the purpose chiefly to pass on the information.

(*Gandhi*, 1982)

"Since I returned from South Africa, I have traveled over much of India. And I know that I could travel for many more years and still only see a small part of her. And yet, I already know that what we say here means nothing to the masses(人民群众)of our country. Here, we make speeches for each other, and those English liberal magazines that may grant(赠予) us a few lines.

But the people of India are untouched. Their politics are confined to bread and salt. Illiterate(文盲) they may be, but they're not blind. They see no reason to give their loyalty to rich and powerful men who simply want to take over the role of the British in the name of 'freedom'.

This Congress tells the world it represents India. My brothers, India are 700,000 villages, not a few hundred lawyers in Delhi(德里) and Bombay(孟买).

Until we stand in the fields with the millions that toil(辛劳) each day under the hot sun, we will not represent India—nor will we ever be able to challenge the British as one nation."

The speech is characterized with complete sentence structure, accurate choice of words, and coherence with smooth transitions.

3) Nonverbal aspects

In daily conversation, we use a lot of stall phrases, or fillers, such as "OK, yeah, like, kind of, you know, stuff, got, or something like that, big deal, I mean, I guess, I figure" etc. and vocalized pauses such as "ah, oh, er, um, ahem, mmm, well". Whereas, in a speech, these phenomena are to be avoided.

The following is a dialogue between a boy and a girl:

(*Bart Got a Room*, 2008)

Boy: So, um, I'm not really good with these kinds of things. I, uh...
Girl: You need a date for the prom(高中毕业舞会).
Boy: How did... yeah.
Girl: Yeah, I'll go with you.
Boy: You will? Uh, are you serious? What... Really?
Girl: I had a feeling you were gonna ask that. I think we are gonna have a good time.
Boy: Yeah, totally. Totally, yeah, yeah.
Girl: I do have to keep a secret though, since my parents would never want me to go.
Boy: No, I totally understand, yeah. You know, we could sneak out(偷偷溜出去)

or something.

    Girl: And this really isn't a big deal, but I do have this kind of long-distance relationship, so we couldn't, like, get intimate on the dance floor or anything.

    Boy: No, right, yeah, of course.

    Girl:... 'cause that could always get back to him.

    Boy: In case people might see that and tell him, yeah. On the dance floor.

    Girl: And I wouldn't want to take any pictures 'cause they could always get in the wrong hands. I mean if he saw that...

    Boy: Yeah, right, that's...oh, well, if you held the negatives (底片) and...

    Girl: And actually, in general, I wouldn't want to be seen walking together. In fact, I'd rather not be seen walking around at all, just in case.

    Boy: So, like, umm...

    Girl: But, I mean, we could always meet up afterwards, at some post-party in someone's room. 'cause I think Bart got a room...

In this conversation, nearly all the stalk phrases and vocal pauses are found. In a speech, it is obviously unwise to use them.

4) Way of delivery

In modern days, public speaking depends more on a hall, lectern, microphone and mobile equipment; while a daily conversation can happen anywhere and less formal.

In our daily life, around 30% of our time awake is taken up in engaging in conversing with people or giving a speech. But talking to people and giving a speech differentiate each other in manners, tactics, content, sound and tones.

Topics for One-Minute Speech Practice

    1. How would you imagine your life ten/twenty years later?
    2. What do you think of students wearing cosmetics?
    3. Do you believe in doomsday? Do you think human beings can survive it?
    4. Should smoking be banned among teenagers?
    5. How important are individuals in environment protection?
    6. What qualities make a good teacher in your mind?
    7. Please name the teacher/family/friend that has influenced your life the greatest.
    8. There has been a widespread criticism on the moral decay of such professions as teachers and doctors in China. What is your opinion?
    9. What is your ambition in your life?
    10. How important is outside appearance to job hunting? What is your opinion on some people having cosmetic surgery in order to stand out in a job interview?

Chapter 5

••• Vocal Factors in Delivery •••
演讲的声音因素

A speech is more than ideas. It is sound! It is music! It is rhythm! It is poetry! It is performance!
—Klepper Flaherty
演讲不仅仅是思想表达,它是声响! 是音乐! 是节奏! 是诗歌! 是表演! □ 克莱普·弗拉迪

The language of the lips is easily taught; but who can teach the language of the heart? —Mohandas Gandhi
教人用嘴皮子说话很容易,但谁能够教人用心说话? □ 甘地

● 本章要点 ●

● 如何理解声音各因素在演讲中的作用及如何掌控和发挥这些因素的积极作用,包括发音、发声、音量、音高、语调、速度、语气和停顿,等等。

5.1 A Perfect World of Sound

The human voice is the instrument we all play. It's the most powerful sound in the world, probably the only sound that can start a war, or say "I love you". And yet many of us have the experience that when we speak, people don't listen to us. Why is that? A perfect world will be we are speaking powerfully to people who are listening consciously in environments which are actually fit for the purpose. To put it in another way, a perfect world will be we are creating sound consciously and consuming sound consciously and designing all our environments consciously for sound. That would be a world that does sound beautiful and one where understanding would be the norm and that is an idea worth spreading. How can we speak powerfully, to make change in the world? Now what we say is one thing, but how we say it is another. What matters is also the way we say it. We have a few tools which can help increase the power of our speaking. They are pronunciation, articulation, volume, pitch, tone, rate, pause, register, timbre, prosody.

5.2 Pronunciation: Say the Words Correctly

Except many comedians who use mispronounced words to get a laugh, we are required to pronounce the words in a generally accepted way so that everyone can understand. There is nothing worse than listening to a speaker who mumbles and mispronounces words. This sloppiness projects an unprofessional image. There are various ways for us to mispronounce a word: accenting the wrong syllable (e. g. exercises, obvious, important, promising, always, economic), shortening the vowel when it should be long or vice versa (e. g. memorize) or totally messing up the word entirely (e. g. enthusiasm, curiosity). There are many causes for this problem: unfamiliar or multisyllabic words; words and names from abroad; technical and new words; the interference of mother tongue, and a die-hard bad habit, e. g. pronouncing /v/ as /w/ among many speakers. And there are some people having physical problems with their tongues or impact of local dialect which gives out too strong accents for others to understand. For example, when we are getting lazy, we drop letters, and slur syllables and even the whole words together, such as gonna—going to, doin'—doing, wanna—want to, gotta—got to, didja—did you; But with adequate practice, mispronunciation can be diminished as much as possible.

5.2.1 Don't be conscious of our accents

We all have our accents; it's natural to be this way, of which nothing is to be ashamed. Everyone has an accent, the British Queen's accent is British accent, and the American president speaks in an American accent. And there are numerous local accents owing to regional differences. And remember we don't have to pronounce like the Americans or the English, but we must pronounce it right. The golden rule is articulation: to pronounce correctly, clearly and loudly.

5.2.2 Manage the vowels and the consonants well

Vowels must be pronounced fully and consonants clearly. Many speakers will have problems giving out the sound forcefully because when they let out the consonants, the air does not come from the medium pubic region (Zhong Dantian in Chinese: the area around the chest), or lower pubic region (Xia Dantian in Chinese: the area below the bellybutton), especially when we pronounce the fricative and explosive sounds like /h/, /r/, /p/, /b/, /k/, /g/, /t/, /d/, /f/, /v/, /tr/, /dr/ etc. More practice can improve our vowels and consonants.

5.3 Articulation: Speak Clearly

Articulation is about the clarity and forcefulness of a sound, about producing sounds clearly and distinctly. Few people have vocal organs problem, but many of us make mumbling sounds in the following cases.

5.3.1 Omit the sounds that shouldn't be omitted, and shorten the sounds that should be extended

Especially the suffixes of "-es", "-ed" and non-accentuated syllables. For example, in this sentence, "*Ladies and gentlemen, I present the graduates of Harvard Law School, class of* 2004", many speakers will leave out "/iz/" in ladies, /tl/ in gentlemen, /ts/ in graduates, /v ə d/ in Harvard. Some will pronounce the vowels in "ladies", "graduates", "class", "thousand", "law" too short, which will certainly cause blurring sounds.

5.3.2 Make sure of the pronunciation

When we are not so sure of the pronunciation of a word, go and look it up in a dictionary. Many people take things for granted and risk making a fool of themselves. E.g. celebrity, senile, economy, loser, fragrance, etc.

5.3.3 Don't speak too fast!

When we speak too fast, omitting the unnecessary sounds and syllables may happen. Whenever the incomplete pronunciation happens because we swallow them, we are producing unclear sounds.

5.3.4 Tongue twists practice

Tongue twists are good for us to practice pronouncing correctly and clearly. Here are some classic ones:

(1) A big black bug bit a big black bear and made the big black bear bleed blood.

(2) Never trouble trouble until trouble troubles you!

(3) All I want is a proper cup of coffee made in a proper copper coffee pot. You can believe it or not, but I just want a cup of coffee in a proper coffee pot. Tin coffee pots or iron coffee pots are of no use to me. If I can't have a proper cup of coffee in a proper copper coffee pot, I'll have a cup of tea!

(4) A writer named Wright was instructing his little son how to write Wright right. He said: "It is not right to write Wright as 'rite'—try to write Wright aright!"

(5) Bob bought a big bag of buns to bait the bears' babies.

(6) Bill's big brother is building a beautiful building between two big brick blocks.

(7) Elizabeth has eleven elves in her elm tree.

(8) Elizabeth's birthday is on the third Thursday of this month.

(9) How many cookies could a good cook cook if a good cook could cook cookies? A good cook could cook as many cookies as a good cook who could cook cookies.

(10) How may saws could a see-saw saw if a see-saw could saw saws?

(11) I thought a thought. But the thought I thought wasn't the thought I thought I thought. If the thought I thought I thought had been the thought I thought, I wouldn't have thought so much.

(12) I wish to wish the wish you wish to wish, but if you wish the wish the witch wishes, I won't wish the wish you wish to wish.

(13) I wish you were a fish in my dish.

(14) If two witches would watch two watches, which witch would watch which watch?

(15) If you notice this notice, you will notice that this notice is not worth noticing.

(16) If a woodchuck could chuck wood, would a woodchuck chuck wood?

How much wood would a woodchuck chuck if a woodchuck could chuck wood?

A woodchuck would chuck all of the wood if a woodchuck could chuck wood.

A woodchuck would chuck as much wood as a woodchuck could chuck wood.

If a woodchuck could chuck wood, he would and should chuck wood. But if a woodchuck couldn't chuck wood, it shouldn't and wouldn't chuck wood.

If I were a woodchuck, and I chucked wood, I would chuck wood with the best woodchucks that chucked wood.

(17) She sells seashells on the seashore. The shells she sells are seashells she is sure.

(18) Three thousand thinkers were thinking how the other three thieves went through.

(19) What noise annoys an oyster most? A noisy noise annoys an oyster most.

(20) Can you can a can as a canner can can a can.

(21) How many cans can a canner can, if a canner can can cans?

(22) A canner can can as many cans as a canner can, if a canner can can cans.

(23) Canners can can what they can can but cannot can things can't be canned.

(24) How much dew would a dewdrop drop if a dewdrop could drop dew?

(25) The driver was drunk and drove the doctor's car directly into the deep ditch.

(26) He thrusts his fists against the posts and still insists he sees the ghosts.

(27) A snow-white swan swam swiftly to catch a slowly-swimming snake in a lake.

(28) Peter Piper picked a peck of pickled pepper prepared by his parents and put them in a big paper plate.

(29) Peter Piper picked a peck of pickled peppers. Did Peter Piper pick a peck of pickled peppers? If Peter Piper picked a peck of pickled peppers, where's the peck of

pickled peppers Peter Piper picked?

(30) A flea and a fly were trapped in a flue, and they tried to flee for their life. The flea said to the fly "Let's flee!" and the fly said to the flea "Let's fly!" Finally both the flea and fly managed to flee through a flaw in the flue.

5.4 Volume: We Must Be Heard

Volume refers to the loudness of our voice, which depends on the size and shape of the setting and the microphone performance. Most of the times, we are speaking too softly, which may project an unconfident, insincere image; on the contrary, too loud voices create harsh and unpleasant noise. If there is a microphone, we must know how to use and adjust it; if there isn't, we must be prepared to speak loud enough so everyone in the audience can hear us. To speak loud enough, we must remember the following points. We can get really excited by using volume. Or we can have the audience really pay attention by getting very quiet. Some people broadcast the whole time, imposing our sound on people around us carelessly and inconsiderately, which is bad.

5.4.1 Learn to use our vocalization

To produce a sustained volume, we need to use our diaphragm and abdominal muscles, try not to use the throat to project our voice. Take a deep breath, store a supply of air, and then produce a sustained tone.

5.4.2 Don't go to extremes with our voice

Some people will speak on top of his/her lungs, and then find his/her voice hoarse and exhausted in a short time. Some others speak in a soft voice all the time and lose the interest and attention of the audience, for they can't hear us.

(*Deep Rising*, 1998)

"*Ladies and gentlemen*! *Ladies and gentlemen. Mesdames et Messieurs. If I could have your attention for just one moment, please. On behalf of myself, Captain Atherton and his crew, welcome to the maiden voyage(首航)of the Argonautica! Each and every one of the hundreds of men and women in service upon this vessel(船只)has but one objective: to make your dreams come true. As for myself, my entire life, I have had but one dream: to create the greatest, most luxurious(豪华的), most expensive ship ever built. And tonight, seeing all of you here so beautiful, so elegant, so rich, I realize that my dream has come true. And I thank all of you from the bottom of my heart for making it so. To the Argonautica! Good times forever!" (Audiences shout: Forever! Forever!)*

Practice this speech, and pay special attention to the pronunciation, articulation and volume.

Pitch & Intonation: Make Our Voice Varied

Pitch refers to how high or how low our voice is and creates intonation. It's different from volume, which is the loudness of the voice. With the regular interval of lows and highs in our voice, we have a varying intonation, that is to say, it fluctuates, as against a monotone. A monotone can both be a loud one or a soft one, neither of which is desirable. By varying our pitch with personal emotion and tone, we can hold the audience's attention and help them understand our message better. Reading poems is an effective way to train our intonation. Here is Robert Frost's *Stopping by Woods on a Snowy Evening*. Please pay attention to the variety of intonations while reading aloud.

Whose woods these are I think I know.
His house is in the village though;
He will not see me stopping here
To watch his woods fill up with snow.

My little horse must think it queer
To stop without a farmhouse near
Between the woods and frozen lake
The darkest evening of the year.
He gives his harness bells a shake
To ask if there is a mistake.
The only other sound's the sweep
Of easy wind and downy flake.

The woods are lovely, dark and deep.
But I have a promise to keep,

And miles to go before I sleep,

And miles to go before I sleep.

The rising-falling intonation pattern: an unstressed syllable is followed by a stressed syllable, called a meter, four in a row. (Or in terms of poetics, iambic tetrameter, four beats per line.) When we recite these lines, feel the regular patterns of intonations.

Tone: Be Consistent with the Subject Matter

The tone of voice tells a lot about our feelings towards our audience and the topic: a tone of modesty, affability and friendliness is preferred to that of arrogance or condescension, but more importantly, the tone must be consistent with the subject matter. A tone of solemnity is required in a eulogy; a tone of light heartedness is required in a company picnic or a jovial social gathering. it's also called prosody(韵律). This is the sing-song of our voice, the metal language that we use in order to impart meaning. People who speak all on one note are really quite hard to listen to, if they don't have any prosody at all. That's where the word "monotonic" comes from, or "monotonous, monotone". Also, we have repetitive prosody now coming in, where every sentence ends as if it were a question. When it's actually not a question, it's a statement. And when you repeat that one over and over again, it's actually restricting your ability to communicate through prosody, which is a shame. So let's try breaking that habit.

Rate: Don't Speak Too Fast

It is the speed at which we speak. Two obvious faults occur that we speak either too slowly or too quickly. As beginning speakers, we probably want to leave the podium quickly, or want to show off our fluency of the language, or we're too overwhelmed emotionally, so we tend to rush through our speech. When we speak too slowly, the audience gets bored; conversely, when we speak too quickly, our ideas cannot sink in and the audience lose track of our ideas. A fast rate is adopted to express happiness, fear, anger and surprise. A slow rate: sadness, disgust, complex information and emphasis. Slowing down our rate can mean seriousness, calmness or sadness. Quickening our rate can mean a burst of passion, excitement and urge, and very often, when we are approaching the climax of our speech or relating an anecdote.

We can get very, very excited by saying something really, really quickly, or we can slow right down to emphasize, and at the end of that, of course, a little silence. There is nothing wrong with a bit of silence in a talk, for we don't have to fill it with ums and ahs. Silence can also be very powerful.

5.8 Pause: Let It Sink in

Pauses mean temporary stops in a speech. It is a major challenge for most speakers. Pauses can signal the end of a thought unit; give an ideal time frame to sink in; lend a dramatic impact to a statement, etc. Martin Luther King said, "The right word may be effective, but no word is ever as effective as a rightly-timed pause." Mark Twain said again, "when the pause was right, the effect was right." Rightly timed pauses not only let our words sink in, but also exert powerful influence. It doesn't count as a pause, however, when we fill in meaningless words to break the embarrassing silence with "uh, er, um, you know, I mean, it's like". Generally speaking, good pauses serve the following purposes.

5.8.1 Transition from one point to another

It's natural and necessary to pause between topics to give the audience time to think and let the words sink in.

5.8.2 For the audience's attention

To emphasize and draw the attention of the audience, at the same time, provoke their thoughts.

(*Legally Blonde*, 2001)

Woods: On our very first day at Harvard, a very wise Professor quoted Aristotle, "The law is reason free from passion." Well, no offense (得罪) to Aristotle, but in my three years at Harvard I have come to find that passion is a key ingredient (关键因素) to the study and practice of law—and (pause) of life. It is with passion, courage of conviction (信念), and strong sense of self that we take our next steps into the world, (pause) remembering that first impressions are not always correct. (pause) You must always have faith in people. (pause) And most importantly, (pause) you must always have faith in yourself. (pause) Congratulations class of 2004 — (pause) we did it!

The pauses used by the speaker are for the purpose of transitioning to the next point, and at the same time, emphasizing the points.

When listening to the part of the video, please try to imitate the voice elements: pronunciation, articulation, volume, pitch, rate, and pause.

5.8.3　For creating a suspension

In the movie *Wall Street 2*, the speaker ends his speech this way:

"Speculation is mother of all evils. Leveraged debt, bottom line, it's borrowing to the hilt. And I hate to tell you this, but it's a bankrupt business model. It won't work. It's systemic, malignant(恶性的), and it's global, like cancer. It's a disease, and we got to fight back. How are we gonna do that? How are we gonna leverage(控制)that disease back in our favor? Well, I'll tell you. (pause) Three words (pause): buy my book. (audience laughs)

(*Dead Poets Society*, 1989)

"...*Seize the day.* '*Gather ye rosebuds while ye may.*' *Why does the writer use these lines?* (*a student answers*) *Because he's in a hurry.*

No! Ding! Thank you for playing anyway. Because (*pause*) *we are food for worms, lads*(小伙子们). *Because,* (*pause*) *believe it or not, each and every one of us in this room is one day going to stop breathing, turn cold and die. I would like you to step forward over here and peruse*(细看)*some of the faces from the past. You've walked past them many times. I don't think you've really looked at them. They are not that different from you, are they? Same haircuts. Full of hormones*(荷尔蒙), *just like you. Invincible* (无所不能), *just like you feel. That world is their oyster*(牡蛎). *They believe they're destined for great things, just like many of you. Their eyes are full of hope, just like you. Did they wait until it was too late to make from their lives even one iota*(微小)*of what they were capable? Because, you see, gentlemen, these boys are now fertilizing*(施肥)*daffodils*(水仙花). *But if you listen real close, you can hear them whisper their legacy to you. Go on, lean in. Listen.* (*pause*) *Do you hear it?* (*pause*)*Carpe. Hear it? Carpe. Carpe diem. Seize the day, boys. Make your lives extraordinary.*"

The pauses used here by the teacher are suspenseful and dramatic, arousing the interest and curiosity of the students.

5.8.4　For bottling the speaker's overwhelming emotion

It's a good method to bottle our emotion when we are too excited, angry or get carried away.

(*New Year's Eve*, 2011)

"Hello, I'm Claire Morgan of the Times Square Alliance(纽约时代广场联盟会), and, (*pause*) as you all can see, the ball has stopped halfway to its perch(柱子). (*pause*) It's suspended there to remind us before we pop the champagne and celebrate the new year, to (*pause*), stop, and reflect on the year that has gone by, to remember both our triumphs(胜利) and our missteps(失败), (*pause*) our promises made and broken, (*pause*) the times we opened ourselves up to great adventures (*pause*), or closed ourselves down for fear of getting hurt, because that's what New Years is all about: getting another chance, a chance to forgive, to do better, to do more, to give more, to love more, and to stop worrying about 'what if…', and start embracing 'what will be…' (*pause*) So when the ball drops at midnight, and it will drop, let's remember to be nice to each other, (*pause*) kind to each other. (*pause*) And not just tonight, but all year long. (*pause*) Thank you."

In the movie, to welcome the New Year as an annual traditional event, the speaker is in charge of the Times Square crystal ball, which goes up to the top of the building and then drops with the countdown to welcome the New Year with the witness of millions of people in New York and America and all over the world. But because of some unexpected technical problem, the ball is stuck halfway, coinciding with what the characters have experienced or are experiencing in their life: made and broken promises, closed hearts, unspoken love, missed chances, strong desires, regrets, etc. and the speaker herself is one of those characters who are experiencing the same things, so she pauses several times in the speech to show her bottled emotions.

5.9 Timbre(音色)

Timbre is about the quality of our voice, and the way our voice feels. A research shows we prefer voices which are rich, smooth, warm, like hot chocolate. Well, we can't all be blessed with such a beautiful voice. So if that's not you, that's not the end of the world, because we can train. Go get a voice coach. And there are amazing things we can do with breathing, with posture, and with exercises to improve the timbre of our voice.

5.10 Register(音域)

Register is about the sound we give when we locate our voice chord in a different position. Falsetto(假声)register might not be very useful most of the time, but there is a register in between. We can locate our voice when we can talk up in our nose; we can hear the difference if we go down in our throat, which is where most of us speak from most of the time. But if we want weight, we need to go down to the chest. We can hear the difference. We vote for politicians with lower voices. It's true, because we associate depth with power and with authority.

Where and when we can use this tool most of all is when we've got something really important to do. It might be standing on a stage giving a talk to people. It might be proposing marriage, asking for a raise, a wedding speech. Whatever it is, if it's really important, we owe it to ourselves to look at this toolbox and the engine that it is going to work on, and no engine can work well without warming up. So do a little warm-up exercise on our voice before we are all set to take the stage.

Topics for One-Minute Speech Practices

1. What do we learn from such liberal courses as history, philosophy and literature?
2. What do you think of euthanasia (assisted-suicide)?
3. Make comments on Generation Gap: the causes and how to deal with it.
4. How should we select our majors? Of our own will or parent's will?
5. What is true friendship? How can we get it?
6. Reading books and E-books, which one to choose?
7. Western Valentine's Day and Chinese Qi Xi, which one do you prefer?
8. Depression: how do we cope with it?
9. To go for a job or go for further study? That is a question.
10. Are you for the idea that students can keep pets at schools?

Body Language in Delivery
演讲的体态语因素

Words may be false and full of arts; sighs are the natural language of the heart. —Thomas Shadwell
词语有虚假伪饰的一面,但叹息声是发自内心的自然的语言。□ 托马斯·萨德韦厄

Eloquence resides as much in the tone of voice, in the eyes, and in the expression of the face, as in the choice of words. —François
口才不仅仅体现在出口成章,还体现在说话者的声音腔调,目光交流和面部表情。□ 弗朗索瓦

● 本章要点 ●

- 体态语在交流中的作用
- 体态语在演讲中的作用
- 如何把握体态语

6.1 Body Language and Nonverbal Communication

Communication is something so simple and difficult that we can never put it in simple words. It is a complicated process, which, for one thing, involves both verbal communication and nonverbal factors. Verbal communication is the expression through words; while nonverbal communication is usually understood in the process through sending and receiving wordless messages between people. Messages can be communicated through gestures and touch, body language or posture, facial expression and eye contact and even the space that we use when communicating with others. Nonverbal messages could also be communicated through material expression, i.e. objects or artifacts (such as clothing or hairstyles).

Nonverbal communication strengthens the impression in common situations as well as on a public speaking occasion. The wrong message through these gestures and signals we send to others, however, can happen at a conscious or unconscious level, and thus give rise to misunderstandings if the body language conveyed does not match the verbal message.

6.1.1　Definition and functions of body language

Body language or body behavior refers to the facial expression or movement of body parts to pass on information and emotion. Physical expressions like waving, pointing, touching and slouching are all forms of nonverbal communication. Humans move their bodies when communicating because, as research has shown, it helps ease the mental effort when communication is difficult. Physical expressions reveal many things about the person using them. For example, gestures can emphasize a point or relay a message, posture can reveal boredom or great interest, and touch can convey encouragement or caution. Verbal communication also requires body language to show that the person we are talking with is listening. Body language can show feelings to other people, which works in return for other people. The study of body movement and expression is known as kinesics, which provides us the technique of "reading" people, who show their body language to us and reveal their feelings and meanings. It is important to note that some indicators of emotion are largely universal (e.g. smiling/laughing when happy, frowning/crying when sad). Other similar examples are: eye contact and nodding our head showing we understand; yawning (sleepiness), showing lack of interest (sexual interest/survival interest), etc. We share the universal emotions and feelings as follows:

☆ Contempt
☆ Contentment
☆ Embarrassment
☆ Excitement
☆ Guilt
☆ Amusement
☆ Pride in achievement
☆ Relief
☆ Satisfaction
☆ Sensory pleasure
☆ Shame

This universal nature of body language among human beings can help facilitate our message conveying and understanding in both cross-cultural and intra-cultural communication. An English speech conducted either by a speaker of Chinese or any other ethnics is an occasion where, whatever the audience's nationality or ethnicity, a proper use of body language is always appreciated and better understood.

6.1.2 Universal interpretations of body language

In cross-cultural communication, verbal message is not enough; it should be aided with proper body language, which is heavily loaded with cultural contents, value orientation and conduct codes. But despite the barriers of language and culture, we share a universal perception of body language in the following aspects:

1) Crossing arms across the chest

As one of the most basic and powerful body languages, it signals that a person is putting up an unconscious barrier between themselves and others. It can also indicate that the person's arms are cold, which would be clarified by rubbing the arms or huddling. When the overall situation is amicable, it can mean that a person is thinking deeply about what is being discussed. But in a serious or confrontational situation, it can mean that a person is expressing opposition. This is especially so if the person is leaning away from the speaker.

2) A harsh or blank facial expression

It often indicates outright hostility and confrontation.

3) Consistent eye contact

It can indicate that a person is thinking positively of what the speaker is saying. It can also mean that the other person doesn't trust the speaker enough to "take their eyes off" the speaker.

4) Lack of eye contact

It can indicate negativity. On the other hand, individuals with anxiety disorders are often unable to make eye contact without discomfort. Eye contact can also be a secondary and misleading gesture because cultural norms about it vary widely.

5) Eye contact and arms-across-chest

The eye contact could be indicative that something is bothering the person, and that he wants to talk about it. Or if while making direct eye contact, a person is fiddling with something, even while directly looking at you, it could indicate the attention is elsewhere. Also, there are three standard areas that a person will look, which represent different states of being. If the person looks from one eye to the other, then to the forehead, it is a sign that they are taking an authoritative position. If they move from one eye to the other, then to the nose, that signals that they are engaging in what they consider to be a "level conversation" with neither party holding superiority. The last case is from one eye to the other and then down to the lips. This is a strong indication of romantic feelings.

6) Averted gaze, touching the ear or scratching the chin

Disbelief is often indicated by this. When a person is not being convinced by what someone is saying, the attention invariably wanders, and the eyes will stare away for an extended period.

7) Head tilting to one side, slightly unfocused eye contact

Boredom is indicated. A head tilt may also indicate a sore neck or amblyopia, and unfocused eyes may indicate ocular problems in the listener/speaker.

8) Touching the face

It indicates deceit or the act of withholding information during conversation.

9) Blinking

It is a well-known indicator of someone who is lying. Recent evidence has surfaced that the absence of blinking can also represent lying as a more reliable factor than excessive blinking.

10) Distances between people

The distance between people in a social situation often discloses information about the type of relationship between the people involved. The study of this behavior is called "proximity", which may also reveal the type of social setting taking place. There is an intimate zone reserved for lovers, children and close family members. This zone is between six and eighteen inches. 1.5 to 4 feet is the distance that friends or associates will generally be within. That is, people that are close but not necessarily on a regular touching basis. Between 4 and 12 feet is the zone for more social environments. These are familiar people such as co-workers or someone else that is seen occasionally throughout the week. The outer end of this zone is reserved for newly formed groups, and new acquaintances. The last zone between 10 and 25 feet is known to be public distance. This area of space is used for speeches, lectures and theater; essentially, public distance is the range reserved for larger audiences or for people that are not familiar.

11) Unintentional gestures

Such as making an eye rub, a chin rest, a lip touch, a nose itch, a head scratch, an ear scratch, crossing arms, and a finger lock have also been found conveying some useful information in specific context.

Understanding body language in its universal perspective helps us succeed in communication.

Functions of Nonverbal Factors

Some studies show that facial communication is believed to be 4.3 times more often than verbal meaning. Another investigation about the importance of using body language in speech said that the result is only 7% of the audience's comprehension of the speech comes from the content of the speech, while 38% comes from the vocal effect and 55% comes from the speaker's body language (Isa Engleberg, 2006). Regardless of the discrepancy of the survey, we can find that nonverbal factors weigh heavily in a speech.

Before we speak—utter the words to the audience, we stand before the audience and "speak" with our appearance, accompanying actions, gestures and facial expressions. And even before that, the way we sit in the chair before getting up, how we walk to the lectern, and arrange our notes is quickly spotted by the audience. Our hostility, sincerity, or phoniness and vitality are exposed to them, so bodily actions can support and contradict the speakers' way of using words. To be exact, there are the following 4 advantages by using appropriate body language.

1) Facilitating the message conveying

Different accompanying gestures and facial expression work differently on the effect of passing across the message.

2) Obtaining the feedback from the audience

The audience may feedback with head-shaking, smiling, frowning, folding arms across the chest or fidgeting around, which is good indication for us to adjust ourselves.

3) Establishing rapport with the audience

When it is either a formal or informal speech, the speaker can stand behind the lectern or walk around in the audience. Think about the difference in establishing rapport with the audience.

4) Strengthening our credibility and competence

The vocal variety, eye-contact can work well on that.

6.3 Managing Our Body Language

A speaker's body language includes firstly, etiquette, which includes outfits & accessories, appellation and at last, bearing & manners. And secondly, body movement, which includes eye contact, facial expression, posture and gesture, etc. They play the role that no verbal expressions can take the place of; on the contrary, they are more important in a successful speech in the sense that it's an advance opportunity for the speaker to bond with the audience. The look on our face, the general stance, the way we carry our arms, the angle of our head and shoulders, the position of our feet all carry a message and transmit an image.

6.3.1 Etiquette

Etiquette is how we present our manners and bearings in a public place. Shakespeare said that the soul of a man is in his clothes. A speaker should tend to his/her outlook, clothing fitness, act and appellation as well.

1) Appearance

Physical appearance leaves a direct impression of a speaker to the audience. We shouldn't judge a book by its cover, but a fine and pleasant appearance always brings a delightful enjoyment to others. To improve our appearance, we should bear in mind the following three points.

a. Natural beauty

A healthy body, well-balanced figure always reveals the natural beauty and vivacity of a speaker. Do not feel bad for your physical disadvantage if there is any, and be proud of yourself as you are.

b. Decorative beauty

A good speaker will be conscious of his/her polished side of beauty as well as his/her natural beauty. What's more, what we lack of in natural beauty, a polished part of our outlook will make up. The best policy is to look neat, appropriate, lovely, elegant and graceful, and most importantly, confident.

c. Composure

A speaker's inner beauty and quality is cultivated through a long history all his/her life. Every gesture, motion, eye movement suggests the speaker's inner charm, kindness and warmth.

2) Appellation

This is what we say to address the audience (or judges). An appropriate appellation is necessary in spite of its function of being only a polite formula, which some people might consider it redundant. But as a very important way to warm-up ourselves in a speech, it's always necessary to address the audience in the beginning, then with a short pause before our speech. To do well in this part, we need to pay attention to the following points.

a. Keep guard against Chinese way of using English

Such expressions as Teacher Wang, Comrade Li, respected leaders, etc. must be avoided, for it's not the English way of addressing people. The most common way is to say, "Honorable judges, distinguished guests and my dear friends", of which a simpler version can be, "Good morning/afternoon, ladies and gentlemen".

b. Accompany our addressing with a smile

Always present yourself as a sincere, modest and kind person. Smiling is the best policy! As a saying goes, a smile is a curve that makes everything straight.

c. Speak in a loud and clear voice

Speak in a determined and confident tone.

6.3.2 Body movement

1) Facial expression

Aside from physical appearance and clothing, people initially judge a person by their facial expression. As a form of nonverbal communication, facial expression is one or more motions or positions of the muscles in the skin. They are a primary means of conveying social information amongst human beings, and are closely tied to emotion. A friendly, relaxed expression will create a positive atmosphere for communicating. Again, as we look at our audience, smile at them. A quick smile and a bright eye indicate to the audience a quick wit and a sharp mind, and reveal sensitivity and perception. In the same way, a speaker will be judged by the audience to a great extent on his/her facial expression. To do it better, we must follow these points.

a. Avoid extremes when using our facial expression

We tend to either exaggerate it or have trouble using it. Too exaggerated facial expression will look awkward and even absurd, but on the other hand, too little spells no feeling, boredom and misplaced tension.

b. Avoid unnecessary facial expression

Such as a furrowed brow or a raised brow—unless they reinforce our points: incredulity, horror, surprise, urgency and disapproval.

c. Try not to make a funny face

Such expression as a disgruntled face will send a negative message to the audience.

d. Practice by using a mirror or asking a friend to be our guide

Some of us tend to use too much facial expression, and sometimes we find little and inadequate expression on our face. We should try to adjust or restrain it according to the emotion expressed in our speech.

e. Do some exercises

Before the speech, do some facial massaging and rubbing to relax and loosen up, then we will feel easier on our face.

f. Be natural

The best policy is to look natural and spontaneous.

2) Eye contact

Eye contact is a meeting of the eyes between two individuals. The term defines the act as a meaningful and important sign of confidence and social communication. Though customs and significance of eye contact vary widely between cultures, with religious and social differences often altering its meaning greatly, eye contact and facial expressions provide important social and emotional information. In human beings, eye contact is a form of nonverbal communication and is thought to have a large influence on social behavior. We, perhaps without consciously doing so, probe each other's eyes and faces for positive or negative mood signs. So in public speaking, a proper amount and way of eye contact always comes first in confronting an audience. Here are the reasons.

a. Speaking is interactive

It is an important feedback device in a two-way communication process. How they are responding to our message—this feedback will make us a better speaker.

b. Eye contact eases nervousness

Eye contact can help reduce nervousness and overcome it. When we depend on our notes, cards or outlines, we still need to look up at the audience from time to time.

c. Eyes are the mirror to the soul

Our sincerity, attentiveness and assertiveness are all revealed in our eye contact with the audience. No matter how large the audience may be, each listener wants to feel that we are talking to him or her.

How can we do it well in eye contact? The following tips may help:

☆ Scanning from left to right, from middle to the two sides, at least 90% of our speech time.

☆ Overcome physical barriers. Try not to stand behind the lectern, which might be conceived as a refuge by the audience, and a psychological obstruction to communication. So abandon the platform if we can and shorten the gap between us and the audience. The lawyers in a court of law always set up a good example by speaking standing in front of the jury or even walking to and fro in front of them.

☆ Do not fix our eyes at one person or one area for a long time. Misunderstanding and uneasiness may occur.

☆ Do not look over the heads of our audience at the ceiling or look down at the floor for a long time.

3) Posture

In humans, posture can provide important nonverbal communication. Posture deals with how the body is positioned in relation to another person or group of persons (e.g. leaning stance, posture, standing, sitting, etc.) It tells the following information of us: how our body looks like physically, our attitudes in interpersonal relations, our social standing, current emotional states and our temperament.

People with an open posture (e.g. slightly bending forward, head raised, shown palms are read as openness, friendliness, willingness to contact) are perceived as friendly and of having a positive attitude. People with a closed body posture (e.g. attaching feet, clinching the legs, arms crossing the closure body, showing the back of our hand, gripping them, hiding the thumb) is a signal closure which gives the impression of detached, uninterested contact and even hostility. In a speech, we should try to present us in an open posture: standing and sitting essentially to convey our poise, confidence, dignity, comfort, energy and alertness. To have a proper posture, we must observe the following do's:

a. Stand still

Avoid shifting foot to foot and swinging from side to side. Otherwise, it will look absurd. The old saying is stomach in, chest out, shoulders back, and head up.

b. Where to place our arms and hands?

Control our hands and arms in a composed and comfortable way. Do not move our hands and arms aimlessly, distractingly and desperately.

c. Sit straight

When speaking in a sitting posture, don't cross our legs or lean backward. Sit straight.

d. Don't lean on the lectern

Do not lean on anything else to support our lazy weight.

4) Gesture

Gestures include movement of the hands, face, or other parts of the body. A gesture is a form of non-verbal communication in which visible bodily actions communicate particular messages, either in place of speech or parallel with spoken words. Gestures are a crucial part of everyday conversation and allow individuals to communicate a variety of feelings and thoughts, from contempt and hostility to approval and affection, in addition to words when we speak.

A gesture, for a speaker, is always purposeful. Think of a conductor using hands or a baton to control an orchestra. A gesture always reflects a speaker's individual personality and reinforces the verbal message in two ways: for emphatic purpose, that is to emphasize an important point; for demonstrative purpose, that is to refer to presentational aids.

For the first purpose, the general gestures are: throwing out a hand, pounding on the lectern, throwing a smack into the other hand, fluttering of fingers, gripping the lectern, clenching a fist. These gestures are quick, tense, graphic and timed to coincide with the words and emotion.

For the second purpose, the general gestures are: a cutting move with a hand, pointing a finger, raising a hand and using hands to form and describe. E. g. When describing the thickness of a book, the distance between two things, we use hands to make it more graphic and easily visualized. And above all, they are spontaneous.

Let's look at the following situations, and try using our hand/arm gestures.

☆ A sudden hand gesture to show anger/passion/determination

☆ Describing the relationship between the speaker and the audience

☆ Indicating the whole loss of love or something else

☆ Expressing two opposite ideas

To use gestures well, we must pay attention to the following points.

☆ A gesture should be natural and spontaneous. Do not make it awkward and pretentious.

☆ If there is a podium, we might place our hands on either side.

☆ Do not overdramatize it. It's only an aid to our speech, not the other way round.

☆ Do not fuss, toy and play with keys, pens, a watch band, coat button, belt buckles, rings and other accessories.

☆ When using a prop or a tool aid in hand, do not play with it too dramatically or else it will be a distraction.

☆ Pacing back and forth is a distraction for the listeners.

In the following speech, we have a speaker who is speaking at a company gathering to the employees in welcoming the New Year. Let's see how his clothes, facial expression, body language, use of voice, etc. work well together to serve his speech.

(*New Year's Eve*, 2011)

"Hi, I'm Sam Ahern Jr. I won't give a long speech. (laughter) Socrates(苏格拉底) gave long speeches and his friends killed him. (laughter) In the past, my father would always kick things off(放下手头的事情) and then turn it over to the vice presidents, but as you know, Dad's not with us anymore. I think that anybody that knew him knows that he was a great man. And we're thinking about you tonight, Pops(父亲). He always ended with a quote. He would say, 'What would you do today if you knew you would not fail?' and then he'd say, 'Now go out and do it!' You know where he got that from? My mother, Rose Ahern. All right, let me finish with this. As we move forward into this New Year, let's try to remember that sometimes it's okay to listen to your heart. I know it's risky. Take that leap of faith. Happy New Year, everybody!"

Please watch the video and find out the features of the speaker's body language.

Topics for One-Minute Speech Practices

1. Confronting myself to understand myself.
2. The future is now.
3. Global citizenship begins at home.
4. Patience is bitter, but the fruit is sweet.
5. We don't see things as they are, but see things as we are.
6. It's the eye that makes the horizon.
7. To exist is to co-exist.
8. The world is a book, and those who don't travel only open one page.
9. When pleasure is the business of life, it ceases to be pleasure.
10. We get so much information all day long that we lose our common sense.

Chapter 7

••• Using Humor in Delivery •••
演讲中的幽默

Humor is the finest outfit people are wearing on a social occasion. —Thackeray
诙谐幽默是人们在社交场上所穿的最漂亮的服饰。□ 萨克雷

A sense of humor is part of the art of leadership, of getting along with people, of getting things done.
—Dwight D. Eisenhower
幽默感是领导艺术的一部分,是待人处事能力的一部分。□ 艾森豪威尔

• 本章要点 •

- 幽默的定义和文化理解
- 幽默在演讲中的功能
- 演讲中使用幽默的方法
- 演讲中使用幽默的误区

7.1 The Importance of Humor in Our Speech

7.1.1 Definition of humor

Humor is the tendency of a particular cognitive experience to provoke laughter and provide amusement. The term derives from the humor medicine in ancient Greece, which teaches that the balance of fluids in the human body, known as humors (Latin: humor, "body fluid") which control human's health and emotion.

7.1.2 Humor and culture

People of all ages and cultures respond to humor, though to a different extent.

Different cultures have different expectations of humor, so comedy shows are not always successful when transplanted into another culture. Two well-known sayings in Britain are "Americans don't do irony" and "Germans don't have a sense of humor" simply on account of the fact that there is a different response people from one culture give to a humor which is considered humorous in another culture.

The majority of people are able to experience humor, i.e., to be amused, to laugh or smile at something funny, and thus they are considered to have a sense of humor. The hypothetical person lacking a sense of humor would likely find the behavior induced by humor to be inexplicable, strange, or even irrational. Though ultimately decided by personal taste, the extent to which a person will find something humorous depends upon a host of variables, including geographical location, culture, maturity, level of education, intelligence and context. Satire may rely more on understanding the target of the humor and thus tends to appeal to more mature audiences. Non-satirical humor can be specifically termed "recreational drollery", i.e. comical in an odd or whimsical manner with a tongue-in-cheek kind of humor frequently. This provides good advice for us that a successful humor delivery depends on not only the occasion, but also on the target audience themselves, and also explains why a side-splitting joke-cracking among the American and British audience would seem strange and incomprehensible to Chinese, and vice versa.

7.1.3 Functions of humor in a speech

Many theories focus on what humor is and what social function it serves. The prevailing types of theories attempting to account for the existence of humor include psychological theories, the vast majority of which consider humor-induced behavior to be very healthy; spiritual theories, which may, for instance, consider humor to be a "gift from God". In a public speech, a well-timed humorous act or remark can work magically as a lubricant. The effects can be summarized as in the following.

1) Lightening the atmosphere in the setting

Laughing and laughter always bring people joy and happiness. Humor displays both a social etiquette and certain intelligence. In an international conference, when US President Obama was addressing the audience, the plate glued to the lectern, which marked the speaker's name, title and nationality, suddenly came off and banged onto the floor. There was a little commotion in the audience and they looked at President Obama, who shrugged his shoulders and said, "I didn't do anything." Then after he looked around for the plate a while and dismissed the necessity of picking it up, he said, "Well, you all have known me already." The audiences laughed twice. We can imagine the awkwardness if he didn't do anything and say anything. Another speaker did the opposite, when he discovered that he delayed the speech too much and said sorry to the audience excusing himself, "My watch is broken, I didn't know how to control the time." Listening to this, one of the audiences replied, "It doesn't matter. There is a calendar behind you on the wall." We can imagine the embarrassment.

In the movie *Up in the Air*, Ryan Bingham spends all year around flying everywhere and sacking people on the spot cold-heartedly in their workplaces. As a highly decorated and over-achieved man in the company, he speaks in front of his colleagues on his work:

(*Up in the Air*, 2009)

"*This is how I start everyday in my life. Now this is going to be a little difficult, so stay with me. You have a new backpack. This time I want to fill it with people. Start with casual acquaintances, friends of friends, folks around the office. And then you move in the people that you trust with your most intimate secrets, your cousins, your aunts, your uncles, brothers, your sisters, your parents, and finally your husband, your wife, boyfriend, your girlfriend. Get them into that backpack. <u>Don't worry; I'm not going to ask you to light that on fire.</u> (laughter) Feel the weight of that bag. Make no mistake; your relationships are the heaviest components（成分）in your life. Do you feel the straps cutting into your shoulders? All those negotiations and arguments, and secrets and compromises（妥协）. You don't need to carry all that weight. Why don't you set that bag down? Some animals are meant to carry each other, to live symbiotically for a lifetime. Star-crossed（命运多舛）lovers, monogamous（一夫一妻制的）swans. We're not those animals. The slower we move, the faster we die. We're not swans, we're sharks.*"

In the speech, Ryan has come to understand some more important things in life: love and commitment. Nothing else is more important. The tone of the speech is heavy and serious, but the one underlined sentence lightens up the air.

2) Attracting the attention of the audiences and bonding with them

Good humor can quickly shorten the distance, break the ice and reduce the tension, at the same time, grabbing the attention and interest.

George W. Bush Jr., former outgoing US President was speaking in Iraq in 2008. Suddenly, an Iraqi journalist took off one of his shoes and threw it at him. Bush was quick to duck it. After the security controlled the situation, the president said, "I can be sure that was a size 10." All the people around laughed.

In a speech, an old man in his 90s has to mount the stage first, but the stairs are too high for him to go up. When he finally makes it to the stage on his own, refusing any help from others, and meets the admiring and sympathetic eyes from the audience, he pauses for a while, pointing at the stairs, begins his speech like this:

"Thank you, thank you. I'm... I'm absolutely overwhelmed (pause) that I could climb those stairs..."

The audiences all laugh heartily. Of course, this long pause has worked very well in creating suspense, at the same time, shortening the distance between the speaker and the audience.

3) Revealing the healthy mind and charming personality of the speaker

Speech is a mirror of the soul. We can pretend to be serious, but cannot pretend to be humorous. The 18th century German scholar Georg Lichtenberg says that the more we know humor, the more we become demanding in fineness.

When Queen Victoria knew that she was going to die, she said calmly, "I did my best." She knew that she wasn't perfect, and when she said that she had tried her best all her life, this humility and sincerity is obviously charming in a person. In the movie *R.V.*, the speaker (Robin Williams) has experienced all kinds of ordeals and accidents on his way to the meeting. When he finally makes it to the meeting, messy and dirty all over, he begins his speech:

"Sorry, I came down the mountain. Next time, I'll take the road. I guess you haven't received the memo(备忘录)of extreme nature. I love your wilderness(自然生态) so much that I decided to wear it."

Comparing with another version of explaining and justifying in vain, like "I'm sorry I look so messy and terrible because I had a terrible experience on the way here", we can find the difference of personality charm with and without using humor.

Here is a speech at the 84th Academy Awards in 2012, the winner of the best actor in the supporting role Christopher Plummer, who is 82 years old and it's his first Oscar Award, gives an acceptance speech as follows.

(Christopher Plummer giving his Academy Award acceptance speech)

"(Looking at the Oscar statue) *You are only two years older than me, darling! Where have you been all my life?* (laughter) *I have a confession to make. When I first emerged from my mother's womb*（子宫）, *I was already rehearsing my Academy thank-you speech.* (laughter) *That was so long ago, most of the speech I've forgotten it. But I haven't forgotten who to thank, the Academy, of course, for this extraordinary honor and my fellow nominees. I'm so proud to be in your company. And my screen partner, of course, Ewan McGregor, that superb artist, whom I would happily share this award with if I have some decency*（大方）, *but I don't.* (laughter) *And lastly, my long suffering wife, Elaine, who deserves a Nobel Peace Prize, for coming to my rescue in every day of my life.* (laughter) *Thank you. Thank you so much.*"

This is a speech we hear from an actor who wins his first Oscar Award in his nearly 60 years of acting career. From this speech, we see not only a charming, charismatic elderly man of quick wit and sound mind, but also great optimistic and cheerful attitude towards life.

4) Criticism and education through humor are more acceptable and effective

The nature of humor reveals the kindness of a person, so people say that humor is the real form of democracy. Criticism and education through humor can be more effective and acceptable. American writer Frank Clark points out that criticism, like rain, should be gentle enough to nourish a man's growth without destroying his roots. When George W. Bush Jr. was addressing the Yale University commencement, he teased his Vice President Dick Cheney who also went to the same university but only for a short while without graduation, and said to the students, "I would like to congratulate you on graduating today, and for those who have performed well, I would say well done, for those only got C, I think you could also be president of the US one day. Yale University degree is valued a lot. So I would like to remind those hard working students here, if you make your way through college here, you can be President of the United States, and if you quit halfway, you can be Vice President." (laughter)

The lighthearted teasing amuses the students, and at the same time, the instructive and inspiring effect sinks in with the help of a good humor.

5) A surprising effect can be achieved

A well-timed sense of humor is always charming and surprising. E. g. A newly-appointed executive opened his inauguration this way: "Hello, I'm Jerry. I was born to be a leader, because I am the son of the former president of this company." He was actually suggesting that he is determined to prove himself worthy of his title and opportunity, so his opening remarks received kind chuckle from the employees. Lao She, a Chinese writer was giving a speech. He opened his speech with a brief introduction that his speech would cover six topics. But when he went on to the sixth point he realized that the audience might have been bored and tired, then he suddenly said, "And the sixth point is: the meeting is over." The audiences were all surprised and gave him a round of loud applause.

As president of Columbia University, Eisenhower once attended a banquet and was scheduled to be the last one to give a speech. The speakers before him all gave long speeches and when it was finally his turn, he went to the platform and started without his manuscript, "Punctuations are essential in every speech. And today I use only a stop." Then, he bowed out with thanks and won loud applauses.

(*Serendipity*, 2001)

"*Thank you, I take it very seriously. It's a gift to be the best man*(伴郎). *They say that once in your life time, someone comes along, whom are absolutely meant to be with, everything feels great: stars are lined*(星辰排列), *body and spirit are in balance. For my friend, Jonathan Trigger, <u>that person was me.</u> (laughter) But as you know, Jonathan and I were some particle*(微粒); *we were brothers from another mother; we were friends since freshmen year. I watched him go out with woman after woman, he would always come crawling*(爬回来). *He would come crawling back to me (laughter). It was embarrassing. But then one night, he came home, and things were different. His adolescent dream to be a documentary filmmaker was a thing of the past. He hardly even responded to my playful yet tormenting flexing*(挠)*of my finger, against the soft part of the skull as he studied for finals*(期末考试)(*laughter*). *And that is because he had found her, the woman he is meant to be with. And if anyone is qualified to know when he met his soul mate, <u>it would be me, his first wife.</u> (laughter)She is smart, she is funny, she is beautiful. In short, she is kind of woman that any man would dream about. I think we all have. So it is with sadness, and fond, fond*(甜美的) *memories that I raise my glass to the new Mrs. Jonathan Trigger. I tell you what, my friends, <u>if I had to lose John to</u>*(托付)<u>*anyone,*</u> (*laughter*) *I can't imagine a more perfect woman than Halley. Cheers to both of you!*"

In this wedding engagement toast, the speaker pokes fun at his best friend—the would-be groom with lots of warm memories and surprising jokes. The three underlined places collaborate with each other to form an integrated wholeness: I was the person for him, I was his first wife and at last, I lost him to a perfect woman.

7.2 How to Be Humorous in Public Speaking

As the English saying goes, a healthy mind is housed in a healthy body. Humor is not something to be born with. As a part of intelligence, but more of a personality trait, it is closely linked to one's attitude towards life. There are some methods and skills to improve one's sense of humor, combining the right ingredients of time and place, as well as a quick wit.

1) Self-deprecation

Teasing oneself is a safe way to be humorous. It is a sense of humor of mocking oneself. The 27th American President William Howard Taft (1909—1913) was considered the heaviest President in the US history. He joked about his own corpulence a lot, and people loved it, which took nothing from his inherent dignity. Lincoln eased tense moments with bawdy stories, and often laughed at himself. History honors him for this human quality. Generally speaking, a speaker should impress the audience as a generous, gracious and confident person. Former US President G. W. Bush Jr. was well-known for his slip of tongues and wrong uses of words. When Elizabeth Ⅱ, Queen of England visited America, he was speaking to welcome her in front of 7 000 people including US congressmen, senior officials and British diplomats, "The American people are so proud to welcome Her Majesty here. You've had dinners with 10 American Presidents. And with your help, our nation celebrated the 200th National Day in 17... in 1976." The President once again, mispronounced 19 as 17, which caused all the audiences to laugh. Bush stopped to look at the Queen, and then went on,"She gave me just now a look that only a mother will give to her child who made mistakes." Another round of laughter rose from the audience.

The following sentences are selected from some good opening remarks in self-deprecation:

"At the very start, let me just say that we both have something in common. You don't know what I'm going to say—and neither do I."

"While a majority of people will be a little nervous standing on the stage, I belong to the minority part, because I am very nervous."

"As a speaker, I've received only two complaints: one, I speak so loud that they can't go to sleep; and the other, I speak so long that they can't wake up."

"You can choose to sleep or not to sleep, but I will continue my speech only if you don't snore."

"I would like to tell you a story. If you've already heard this story, please don't stop me because it's the only one I know."

"With your permission, I'm going to read this paper. I'm going to read it for three reasons: one, I have a very poor memory—and the other two I can't remember."

The following is the beginning part of former US Vice President Al Gore, which is a typical example of mocking the speaker himself.

(Al Gore speaking on the Harvard commencement)

"Before I begin, I would like to bring your attention to a small item on the inside cover of the June 4th issue of The Boston Globe magazine. Correction(更正启事): The May 29th cover story on Vice President Al Gore suggested he is funny. He is not. The Globe regrets the error. (Burst of laughter) I'm used to that. (laughter) It's no secret that I ran for President in 1988 although it seemed like one at the time. (laughter) It was a character building experience. (laughter)

I learned a lot of new jokes: Al Gore is so boring. (audiences laugh) His Secret Service code name is Al Gore. (laughter) If you use a strobe light(聚光灯), it looks like Al Gore is moving. (laughter) Al Gore is so stiff(僵硬), racks(衣架) buy their suits off him. (laughter) Al Gore is an inspiration to the millions of Americans who suffer from Dutch elm disease(榆树枯萎病). (laughter) How can you tell Al Gore from a roomful of Secret Service agents(特工)? He is the stiff one. (laughter)

I've heard most of them, but every time I hear a new one, I always have the same reaction: very funny, Tipper(戈尔夫人). (loud laughter) In order to escape that demeaning(损人的) ridicule and reclaim(找回) my dignity, I decided to run for Vice President of the United States of America." (laughter and clapping)

Using his early year failure of running for President of the US, Al Gore urges the young graduates to have faith in America and believe in themselves.

A teacher was invited to speak at a student's English drama club, after the performance, he gave a speech, stressing the importance of this activity, and said,

"We have some cynics among us as English learners, who think it's childish to take part in this kind of activities like the English drama club and the English speaking club, who don't want to join others to learn English, who spend their whole time reading on their own, writing in the back corner of the classroom. They look so lonely. Can we learn English well without joining others, communicating with others? Can we learn English well the way we learn mathematics by doing exercises all the time? Learning English should be fun, just like what we did today. Learning English should be enjoyable and relaxing, just like what we did today. Learning English should be a social activity to meet people and to talk to people, just like what we did today. But unfortunately many students haven't realized that they are making a big mistake in their way of learning in college study. In my opinion, you spending one night here learning English is probably worth one week in the teacher's class, at least in my class."(laughter)

In the movie *Man of the Year*, Tom Dobbs, who turns overnight from a household name of a comedian into a presidential nominee and successfully gets elected, still he doesn't forget his old trade: satirizing and mocking with bitter humor.

(*Man of the Year*, 2006)

"Thank you very much. I guess we should get this over at the beginning because you've all heard this bit of rumor going around right now. So I'll share the big scoop (独家新闻) with you because Oprah (奥普拉, 美国著名主持人) was booked. (laughter) I'm not even president of the United States yet, and I'm involved in a scandal with a woman. I did not have sex with that woman. I wanted to. I'm single. And you've elected a man as president who is probably the unluckiest man in the world in that area. In high school, most of my dates was with myself. (laughter) I would take myself out for dinner, bring myself home, put on music that I like, have my way with myself and then go, 'Should I drive myself home now?' Pretty much like that. I guess if I was in Italy, and I got lucky, and they elected a porn star to their senate, which is wonderful, there is no sex scandal there, just great posters, and incredible downloads. I think that's the bottom

> *line. It's democracy, we can have a certain sense of humor about ourselves if we have to. You're allowed to make fun of those in power. But in the face of terrorism, there was comedy. There were two old Jews sent to kill Hitler. They waited in the alley where they were supposed to kill Hitler at 12:30. They were there with guns, bombs, knives. 12:30, no Hitler. 12:45, no Hitler. One o'clock, no Hitler. Finally one turns to the other and goes, 'My God, I hope nothing happened to him.' It's good to see you back again. The fact that we could laugh again last few years, we've been divided though. Red states, blue states. There are no red states, blue states, there is only the United States. That's all is about. That's why I say you can't spend 2 hundred million dollars on a campaign and not be owing people something. And the next thing you know, you'll have to deal with their special interests, and the next thing you know, you'll do special favor for special people, and not dealing with what you need: education, health care, environmental issues. They have to deal with oil companies, chemical companies, drug companies, and they owe them. In the process, people get neglected."*

The speech gabbles on and on explicitly mocking and demeaning himself on his sexual experience, and creates bursts of laughter. In the end, he points out the nature of American election system: the elected only works for the rich and power class.

2) Teasing others

George W. Bush's act of teasing Vice President Dick Cheney is surprising, but the effect is good, and at the same time, he showed the students his humility by suggesting that he could be President of the US only because he studied hard in college. Another example is related to former Vice President Dick Cheney too, regarding the accident where he shot his friend on a hunting trip mistaking his friend for a running animal in the woods. And this incident is used by Jon Steward, a famous TV presenter and comedian in the US to amuse the audience. At the opening remarks of 80th Academy Award ceremony, he said, "I've some bad news to announce today. Bjork (a singer from Iceland, fond of wearing furs of various bizarre styles and colors) can't come today. Dick Cheney shot her."(burst of laughter)

The audiences were overwhelmed with this humor and wild with laughter. Another example is from British actress Helen Mirren who talks about Queen Elizabeth II in her Oscar Award speech when she slightly mocks her hair style.

"You know for fifty years and more, Queen Elizabeth of Windsor has maintained her dignity, her sense of duty and her hair style."(laughter)

3) Improvising

To improvise means we do or say something on the spot, spontaneously without any preparation. Of course, being part of a person's quick wit, most humors are improvised. A speaker's improvisation is actually not just a whim, for he/she must have done a lot of homework collecting information and paying attention to those jokes and witty remarks in daily life, so he/she could dispatch them at the right time and in the right place, and again, humor reveals a person's healthy mental state. There was a send-off party for a young government official, a man who was leaving to head another new office, and the incumbent office director gave a farewell speech in honor of him. The director was standing on the platform when he gave his speech. When it was the young officer's turn to speak, he opened his speech this way, "I'm leaving this office, which means I have stepped down, so I'd better come down from the platform and speak." Actually, he had meant to stand closer to the audience when he was speaking so that they could hear him better. The audience gave him an understanding chuckle.

Abraham Lincoln is a role model of quick wits for us. One day in the middle of his speech, a note was passed on to him with only one word "idiot" on it, obviously insulting him. Lincoln not only opened the note in front of the audience and read it out, but also then raised the note above his head, saying, "I had all the notes with questions and without signatures, but this one is the contrary, with only a signature but without a question." All the audience gave him a warm applause for his quick response.

In the movie *Keeping Mum*, the speaker (Rowan Atkinson), a vicar stands by the lectern and begins to speak, but accidentally bumps into the microphone, causing unpleasant noise and he is panicked subsequently, and then he stumbles his speech beginning like this: "The title of my speech today is Cod's Mysterious Ways". He mispronounces God as Cod, which is a kind of fish. The audiences are stunned. But after a brief moment of effort to compose him, he corrects himself and says, "*I'm sure cods have their mysterious ways too, but they will have to wait for their own meetings.*" All the audience laughs heartily.

No one likes long speeches, especially when the speech is nothing but dragging bureaucratic red tape. Lin Yutang said it well: a speech is just like a girl's mini skirt, the shorter the better. When an official came to address a meeting for the writers' association conference, he had prepared for it a long speech, but when he realized that this speech wouldn't be welcomed, he opened his speech in this way, "<u>First,</u> on behalf of my colleagues of the municipal government, I would like to extend my warm welcome to all of you present at this conference. (pause) <u>At last,</u> I wish the meeting a great success. (pause) <u>My speech is over.</u>" (loud applause)

There came a burst of applause among the audience. The suspense created by the two pauses are very important.

4) Using overstatement

From the speech of famous Hollywood film director Woody Allen at the 74th Academy Awards in 2002, we find the charm of humor by using overstatement.

Speech at the 74th Annual Academy Awards
By Woody Allen

"*Thank you, thank you very much, that makes up for the strip search*（入场的搜身安检，9·11事件后第二年的奥斯卡典礼加强安检措施；伍迪·艾伦认为自己被搜身有失尊严，但观众的热情鼓掌让他感到安慰，得到了补偿）!（audience laughs）*Let me tell you why I'm here exactly: about four weeks ago, I was sitting home in my apartment in New York, and the phone rang, and a voice on the other end said: this is the Academy of Motion Picture Arts and Sciences*（美国电影艺术与科学学院；奥斯卡评奖颁奖机构）; *and I <u>panicked</u> immediately, because I thought that they wanted their Oscars back, 'cause I've won a few Oscars over the years, and I thought they, you know, that they were calling to get them back, and I <u>panicked</u>, because the pawn shop*（典当行）*has been out of business for ages, you know, and I have no way of retrieving*（取回）*anything, and they said: no, this was not it, that, and I couldn't figure out, 'cause my movie, The Curse of the Jade Scorpion*（《玉蝎子的诅咒》）*was not nominated for anything this year, nothing, no category*（奖项）*, and then, it suddenly hit me, maybe they're calling to apologize, you know. And I remembered during the course of the year I had been walking on 5th Avenue in Manhattan*（曼哈顿第五大道）*, and a homeless man came up to me and asked me if I would buy him lunch, and I didn't buy him lunch but I gave him 50 cents, and I thought, maybe certain members of the Academy had witnessed this and they were gonna give me a Jean Hersholt Humanitarian Award*（人道主义奖）*. 'cause that's what goes through your mind, you know, I, I thought maybe Adora Thalberg or something, <u>you know, 'cause you start calculating, you know I'm 66 years old, a third of my life is over now, and, you know, start to think, maybe they want to honor me</u>. But they said no. They said that, here's what the story is: in view of the terrible events that have occurred in New York over the last year, the Academy wanted to show support and make a nice gesture, and put together a little film paying tribute to movies that had been shot in New York over the years, and they wanted someone to introduce it. So, I, you know for New York City, you know I'll do anything, got my tux*（礼服）*, I came out here. The film you're about to see now, the clips, were lovingly put together by a terrific New York filmmaker, Nora Ephron, and you can roll this any time you want now. Thank you!*"

From the verb "panicked" twice used in an exaggerated way about the Oscar Awards and joking about his age, we see a very lovely character.

The Pitfalls of Using Humor in Public Speaking

Using humor is a powerful weapon, but humor is hard. if wrongly used, the weapon can backfire. Humor done badly can destroy the speech and ruin a speaker's credibility. To be specific, humor to a large extent can be a situation-bound, culture-bound and language-bound. So first, most often, none of us are as funny as we think we are. Second, much humor requires a native understanding of English, and there will be a number of members of our audience who do not use English as a first language. What's more, there will be a number of people in our audience who do not share our cultural upbringing. So there is only one safe and suitable style of humor: light and subtle self-deprecation. In other words, we as speakers are the only really safe subject for humor.

1) Spoil the plot

When we are going to say something we think is a humor, don't foretell the audience that we're going to do it, or else we will spoil it. Even though the joke is funny, the humor is spoiled.

2) Irrelevant

People say we can pretend to be serious, but we can't pretend to be humorous. In order to lighten the atmosphere, the speaker pushes out with a joke, which will be of no value, even if it's funny. Remember: do not pretend to be humorous merely for the sake of it. The best way to do it is at the right time, in the right place and in the right way.

3) Laugh with your own joke

The best humor teller is one who looks innocent and calm all the way as if nothing happened when he tells the joke but the audiences split their sides with laughter.

4) Put the cart before the horse

Be it a joke or humor, it mostly is only an ingredient, just like sauce is for the fish to taste better, not the other way round, so if the whole speech is all jokes, the audiences get nothing valuable, then the speech is degraded to a failure.

5) Don't repeat what is just said

Repeating ruins the humor, no matter how funny it is.

6) Tell or act without pauses

Some speakers may find it a good idea to do a humor fast and rush it on all the way to the end without giving any pauses. This is wrong, for pauses create tension, and tension creates suspense, which is a moment created by the speaker on purpose to prepare for his punch line. The pause will reinforce the effect. Sometimes pauses themselves make the audience laugh. So we must dare to pause and give the audience enough time to react, then our punch line will hit the target really hard.

7) When teasing and touting others, be careful

Avoid offending and insulting people. Helen Mirren won the 79th Oscar for the best actress in the leading role, in her acceptance speech, she salutes the British Queen Elizabeth Ⅱ in owe and with a joke: *"You know for fifty years, and more, Elizabeth Winsor has maintained her dignity, her sense of duty and her hair style."* This lighthearted way of ridiculing others works quite well on the occasion.

8) Protect our credibility

Using self-deprecating humor will not offend others, but unless we can do this with a light and subtle touch, we may be harming our credibility rather than creating a connection between ourselves and the audience.

7.4 Enjoy a Speech

At last, let's enjoy the speech by Helen Mirren again and enjoy her humor in the Golden Globe Awards of 2012, when honoring Life Achievement to Morgan Freeman, an American actor.

(Helen Mirren paying homage to Morgan Freeman)

"Well, I'm really sorry, that after Sydney, I'm going to lower the tone(降低档次) somewhat, because I've had a couple of glasses of wine. And this may not seem like an appropriate time to bring this up(提起这事), but I do have a bone to pick with(找碴) Morgan Freeman. He's made over 50 films, and I've only been in only ONE of them, Red. I mean I was just complaining about this with Mr. Sydney. He said, Helen, join the club(我跟你有同感). At least you are in one of the films. I mean, there is no reason why Miss Daisy(黛西小姐,1989) couldn't be English. All you would have to do is drive on the wrong side of the road. Well, I mean, of course, in England, we think it is the right side of the road. Well, it's not actually on the right side of the road. It's on the left side of the road. 'cause left is right. Glad I cleared that up. Really, Morgan, just one movie? With you? For God's sake. I mean. I could have been a penguin(《帝企鹅日记》,2005,摩根配音). So let's have the pleasure of watching Mr. Freeman at work in many of the movies which I'm not in. Ladies and gentlemen, Mr. Morgan Freeman!"

In this speech, Hellen Mirren uses the humor about the difference of traffic rules between the US and England, which is hilarious.

Topics for One-Minute Speech Practices

1. Love makes people inventive.
2. Courage is pleasure under pressure.
3. You'll never have what you like until you like what you have.
4. If you don't rule your life, someone will.
5. Should college education in China be less academic and be more job-oriented?
6. You are your greatest enemy if you are a coward.
7. My idea of success.
8. My idea of hero in the new age.
9. What do you think is more important for a child? A happy childhood or top marks at school?
10. Has the Internet narrowed the distance or increased the distance between people?

Tools and Aids in Delivery
演讲中的辅助工具和手段

I used not only all the brains I have, but all I can borrow. —Woodrow Wilson
我不仅发挥我自己全部的思想,还充分调遣他人的。□ 伍德罗·威尔逊

Words should only be clothes, carefully custom-made to fit your thoughts. —Jules Renard
词语是为了表达思想而精心定制的衣服,仅此而已。□ 朱尔斯·雷纳德

• 本章要点 •

- 演讲工具和手段的作用
- 演讲有哪些辅助手段
- 如何使用演讲辅助工具和手段

8.1 Using Tools to Aid Our Speech

Such things as books, newspapers, pamphlets, film, television, drawings, graphs, photographs, posters, video and audio clips, and slides are all visual mediums, which have become one of the most important means of conveying ideas from person to person, or from company to consumer. When creating a public presentation for an occasion, we ought to consider incorporating visual aids to enhance the effectiveness of communication.

8.1.1　Functions of tools and aids in our speech

Technological developments have diversified the types of communication available to speakers in order to activate different ways of understanding. Interactive computer software and the internet have provided important avenues of communication that we interact with on a regular basis, and have made it possible for us to integrate several different types of display in addition to conveying information orally. Whether we plan to enter the workforce, go into business, or enter the teaching profession, in this media-saturated age, the use of visual aids performs a number of important functions as a part of a public presentation, and familiarity with using visual materials must be an essential part of our education. To be specific, visual aids have the following functions in our speech.

1) Increase understanding

Phrases like "seeing is believing" and "a picture is worth a thousand words" tell us the truth. In some cases, showing something to an audience can be much more effective than describing that same event. What may take us several minutes and require significant forethought to keep attention of the audience, a single image or set of images can accomplish the same goal in a matter of seconds. Visual aids can perform several different functions to increase understanding: they can review information already presented, and give the audience a second opportunity to absorb it; they can emphasize a certain point in the presentation, and finally, they can provide examples of material described in the speech. In our presentations, it would be wise to use visual aids in several different ways, depending on our needs and the capabilities of our audience.

2) Simplify complex procedures

A cooking recipe with either illustrations or a picture of the finished product will be more useful than thousands of words. Many processes, especially those that we normally learn through mimicking another person or through practice, are much easier to learn with visual aids. Besides, some issues can be much too intricate and complicated to describe in words.

3) Increase memory

Several studies have concluded that the use of visual aids in classroom teaching environments drastically increases knowledge retention. Several explanations for this data exist (Brumberger, E. R. 2005). First, the combination of speaking and seeing reinforces information by doubling audience exposure to it. Second, people learn differently, so using a combination of ways of presenting information increases the chances that the audience will be stimulated by the presentation. Third, images tend to linger in the memory much better than words.

4) Help decrease communication apprehension

Some scholars have found that visual aids help speakers overcome stage fright. The reasons are obvious. First, visual aids deflect the attention of the audience, taking some of the perceived public pressure away from the speaker. Second, using the visual aid as a focal point to deliver their message, the speakers feel less nervous about remembering the order of points.

5) Grab the attention of the audience

The audiences' attention is the reason we give a speech. Visual aids increase audience concentration on the message by diversifying the means by which their thinking is stimulated. The audiences see an aid with not only attention to the points we are trying to make, but also an effort to identify, for showing images of people doing good things, like exercising and recycling, can also promote audience identification with proposed solutions. Audiences can also identify with a speaker that looks like them in age, status, or appearance. So when choosing visual aids, we must think carefully about what is likely to interest our audience.

8.1.2　Categories of aids in speeches

The definition of visual aids has evolved over time, but their purpose has remained the same: to support and enhance the presentation. Several new types of media have been developed since the ancient orators began using visual aids. Most prominent is the advent of the computer and software applications available to create graphics and presentations.

1) Dynamic two-dimensional visual aids

Two-dimensional visual aids are visual representations that exist on a single plane, either physical or optical. We have the following dynamic visual aids like chalkboards, bulletin boards, video and audio clips, graphs, charts, diagrams, maps, sketches, posters, etc., which can help the viewers understand and absorb the information more quickly. Since they require us to move physically around during the speech, i.e. writing on the board, flipping the board to the blank side, turning, playing, etc. A word of advice is that we can prepare it in advance, lest we block our visual and eye contact with the audience in the process.

2) Static two-dimensional visual aids

Computer generated graphics are also static two-dimensional visual aids. Using computer software and electronic media is an effective and convenient way to convey information. Today, electronic two-dimensional visual aids are the most commonly used for the professional speaking occasion. With a typical software application such as PowerPoint, we are able to create drawings, organizational charts, and diagrams. Combined with other multi-media software, a presentation of vivid sound, color, image and animation is available. However, creating computer-generated visual aids can become a time-consuming task depending upon the skill level of the individual developing them and the type of visual aids created.

3) Actual objects: three dimensional visual aids

Audiences like real things, which can be seen, smelled, touched, and even tasted. The most common three-dimensional visual aids include physical objects, models, people, and animals. Each has its own advantages and limitations. Physical objects can be helpful when used as an aid to an informative speech. For example, a ripened piece of fruit, or a pair of running shoes. Sometimes people and animals can also be used in our presentations, in the case of talking about a dance, for example, two people can easily show the new steps by working together.

4) Models

Models are representations and prototypes of other objects and can be important aids when our presentation involves something that is too large, too small, unavailable, or impossible to present physically. Using a model while giving a persuasive speech or sales presentation can help argue our case, increase customer sales, or boost investor support. For instance, a skeleton is a good example of using a model to illustrate human structure by a doctor.

The following speech is an example of using posters and pictures:

(*13 Going on 30*, 2004)

"*I know it's different, I mean, from everything we've ever done. And I know you might hate it, and think I'm completely crazy, but I won't care, even if I get fired. I don't mean that disrespectfully. It's just that I've realized something. Who are these women? Does anyone know? I don't recognize any of them. I want to see, my best friend's big sister, and the girls from soccer team. My next door neighbor, real women who are smart, pretty and happy to be who they are, these are the women to look up to*(敬仰). *Let's put life back into the magazine, in fun, in laughter and silliness. I think I think we all, all of us want to feel something that we forgot or turned our backs on*(置之不理). *Cause maybe we didn't realize how much we're leaving behind. We need to remember we used to be good. If we don't, we won't recognize it even if it hit between the eyes*(出现)."

In this speech, the presenter uses pictures and posters of people in their daily life. The effect is vivid, refreshing and impressive.

(*Dinner for Schmucks*, 2010)

"A thousand years ago, the only people on Earth were monkeys. And they said, 'We'll never walk erectus(直立行走). We'll never use tools. We'll never talk.' And then one monkey said, 'Oh, yeah? Well, I'm talking right now.' That monkey was a dreamer. Fast-forward(快速向后推进) 500 years. The Wright brothers decide to make themselves a flying machine. 'You fools! You idiots! What's your problem?' everyone shouted. 'That will never work because plywood(胶合板) weighs more than air!' To which the Wright brothers responded, 'No, it doesn't.' The Wright brothers were dreamers. The Earl(伯爵) of Sandwich and Sir(爵士) Francis Bacon. Had it not been for them, the BLT would merely be lettuce and tomato. They were dreamers. And sandwich makers. Vincent van Gogh(凡·高). Everyone told him, 'You only have one year. You cannot be a great artist.' And you know what he said? 'I can't hear you.' Vincent van Gogh was a dreamer. Louis Pasteur turned cheese into medicine. Benjamin Franklin. People said, 'You can't fly a kite in a rainstorm.' And Ben Franklin said, 'Yes, you can. If you have an electric kite.' A man who broke more bones than any man in history, Eve Knievel. And who might this handsome young lad be? Tim Conrad. He believes that someday he will marry the girl of his dreams, even though every time he asks, she says no. and even though, as we speak, she is probably having sex with a handsome artist. Tim Conrad is a dreamer. So dare to dream. Dream your wildest dreams. You can climb the highest mountain. You can drown in a teacup, if you find a big enough teacup. And if somebody tells you that you can't do something. You say, 'Yes, I can. 'cause I'm doing it right now!'"

The most amazing thing about the speech is that the speaker can accompany his narration with a number of mimic statuettes of mice, portraying people in real life.

8.2 Advice on Handling Aids and Tools

Despite the audience size, topic, or setting, using an appropriate visual aid during a presentation can help us communicate our message more succinctly. As such, each speaker should consider the following strategies when choosing or preparing a presentation aid.

1) Prepare in advance

We must firstly, prepare the visual aid as early as possible, which will enable us to choose an aid that is simple, appealing, and relevant to the speech content. And the benefits are twofold: first, earning the appreciation from the audience with our thoughtful preparation and effort, and thereby their positive response to both the speaker and the presentation. Second, early presentation allows the speaker to practice using the visual aid, including the setting-up and transitioning, etc.

2) Keep it simple

In a presentation, it is the content that counts. Aids are an only aid, which means they are only a minor part of our work, not the major part. Keeping it simple also means that the time we spend explaining each visual aid must be limited. Specifically, in a Powerpoint demonstration, a no more than one-minute time allocation to each slide is suggested.

3) Select the right aids

Considering our speaking situation, the content, and our own creativity, we can decide on the aids accordingly. Pictures, graphs or charts, drawings, objects, computer-generated documents such as pictures, drawings, posters, graphs, and charts, which appear professional without needing a lot of artistic talent to produce. We should also consider the difference of our own response to those aids from other people, so it is necessary to ask for advice from colleagues and friends before making up our mind.

4) Avoid overuse of aids

Visual aids we use should be aesthetically pleasant, in case it doesn't turn off the audience. At the same time, how much aid is appropriate depends on the specific occasion, the content and the purpose of our presentation. Some presenters will overwhelm the audiences with too much aid, and too fancy and ostentatious aid. Specifically, in a Powerpoint document, a speaker sometimes adds graphical application without regard to the topical relevance of the imagery. Some develops complex visual designs which distract the audience from speech content and hinder the effectiveness of presentations. We must keep in mind that the visual aids will only enhance our presentation rather than overpower it.

5) Don't forget the audience

When using Windows Office software such as Powerpoint or Word to create graphic aids, we must not let it dominate our speech. Otherwise, the speaker will be only busy operating the machine, turning over the pages and fixing the eyes on the screen rather than paying attention to the audience, and thus losing eye contact with them.

6) Do not turn our back at the audience

When we use a tool or aid, try not to turn our back to them and talk at the same time! Pay attention to the audience in the far back of the room. Make sure that they can also see it well.

7) Don't break things

The object we choose to demonstrate must be large enough for the audience to see without passing it around. When we need to move a heavy or bulky object, ask someone from the audience for help. Any breaking up or ruining will reveal our carelessness, recklessness and even immaturity, which will spoil the occasion.

Topics for One-Minute Speech Practices

1. Modernity and tradition in China.
2. Better habits, better life.
3. What's your family legacy?
4. Technology makes us more intelligent or more foolish?
5. Make every day count.
6. Is modesty still a valued virtue?
7. Money is a good servant but a bad master.
8. The impact of Olympic Games on me as an individual.
9. The benefits of traveling.
10. Who would you talk to first with your problems in your life: your friends or your parents?

Speaking on Special Occasions
特殊场合的演讲

If you make yourself understood, you're always speaking well. —Moliere
如果能让人听懂,你就是成功的演讲者。□ 莫里哀

Great oratory needs not merely an orator, but a great theme and a great occasion. —Herbert Samuel
伟大的演讲并不仅仅需要一个能言善辩者,还需要一个伟大的主题和一个伟大的场合。□ 塞缪尔

● 本章要点

● 各种特殊场合的英语演讲介绍及赏析,包括开场、颁奖、受奖、祝贺、追悼、辩论、新闻发布、毕业典礼、竞选、就职仪式、商务报告、开幕闭幕、传经讲道、告别饯行、法庭演说和婚礼主持等场景。

  Having a set of presentation skills up our sleeve can go far in our life and serve us well in both professional and social environment, from pitching new business deals to addressing a conference, from participating speaking competitions to talking to a community group and so on. But in addition, there are many other occasions that require us to stand up and "say a few words" and present us gracefully in front of our guests. These special occasions include: weddings and anniversaries, funerals, awarding ceremonies, dedications, elections and debates, to name just a few. These little presentation gems are highly personalized and require a different approach from the straight-up presentation. The universal guideline is to always adapt our remarks to the audience and the occasion, as Nelson Mandela put it, "If you want to walk into one's heart, you must speak his language". Appreciating and getting immersed in the English culture and learning the language, English learners can get access to no better sources than watching movies. Equally, it's an ideal way to learn English speaking from the speech scenes in movies. Indeed, who can resist the charm of English movies with regard to the real atmosphere, the authentic language, and spontaneous acting with facial expressions and the body language? In this chapter, we will enjoy English speeches on various occasions typically set in the English culture from movies.

9.1 Introducing & Presenting

The responsibility of introducing a guest or another speaker usually falls to the host or emcee or the master of the occasion or ceremony. A good speech of introduction achieves the following three goals.

(1) It builds enthusiasm and expectation among the audience for the upcoming speaker.

(2) It generates interest in the speaker's topic.

(3) It establishes a climate that will boost the speaker's credibility.

There are several guidelines for speeches of introduction.

(1) Speeches of introduction should be brief. Long speeches of introduction irritate the audience and distract attention from the guest speaker. Under normal circumstances, a speech of introduction should be no more than two or three minutes in length.

(2) Speeches of introduction should be completely accurate. Errors in a speech of introduction embarrass both the introducer and the guest speaker in front of the audience. Nothing is more important in a speech of introduction than pronouncing the main speaker's name correctly.

(3) Speeches of introduction should be adapted to the occasion. Whether a formal or informal style is required depends on the occasion.

(4) Speeches of introduction style should be adapted to the guest speaker.

(5) Speeches of introduction should be adapted to the audience. A little explanation of the guest speaker about her/his achievements and qualifications is necessary if the audience don't know much about her/him.

(6) Speeches of introduction should try to create a sense of anticipation and drama. With a little suspension and drama, as well as sincerity and enthusiasm, a good introduction is at hand.

1) Valedictorian introducing

A valedictory is routinely hosted by the principal or president of a school and the invited guest speaker can be one of the students' favourite teachers or as a nice surprise, a celebrity speaker.

(*Legally Blonde*, 2001)

"Ladies and gentlemen. I present the graduates of Harvard Law School, class of 2004. I am, personally, very honored to introduce this year's class-elected speaker. After getting off to a quite interesting start here at Harvard, she graduates today with an invitation to join one of Boston's most prestigious(著名的)law firms. I am sure we are going to see great things from her. Ladies and Gentlemen: Elle Woods."

In this speech, the professor speaks in a succinct and smooth way with a fine rhythm, constrained enthusiasm and pleasant voice; at the same time, her solemn, yet elegant style goes according to her status as a well-respected professor.

2) Retirement Farewell

In the English culture, retirement is another important stage in a person's life worth celebrating. In this example, the ceremony master introduces Colonel Hutchins, who is about to retire from his army life.

(*Rules of Engagement*, 2000)

"Ladies and gentlemen, the reason we're all here, Colonel(上校)Haze Hutchins. He's calling it a career(结束生涯)after thirty-two years of distinguished service. And Colonel, we got you a gift and a surprise, so don't act like you are not coming up."

In this short introduction, the speaker gives a warm welcome to the guest.

3) Introducing a new employee

Head of a department or a company usually gives a speech to welcome the new comer, in such a way as mentioning his/her qualifications, experiences and achievements and ending with new hope for him/her in the new position. In this case, President of Sloane Curtis introduces the new Vice President of the marketing department.

(*What Women Want*, 2000)

"I'm very, very excited for you all to meet Darcy McGuire. I know Darcy's extraordinary reputation as a leader in the field precedes(走在……前面) her. At BBD&O, Darcy led a creative team that snagged(夺得) 500 million dollars in new business wins. And that was just last year alone. Here at Sloane Curtis, we've always prided ourselves on our strategic thinking(战略思维). Now it's time for us to step up and once again prove ourselves creatively in the marketplace. And I'm thrilled that Darcy has consented(同意) to move across town, join our team and lead us into the 21st century."

This speech follows the routine of welcoming new employees: past experiences and achievements, hope and good wishes for working in the new company. The speaker shows us a good speech sometimes needs a certain amount of "acting", i.e. facial expressions and the body language, which goes with the enthusiasm and tone.

The following is another example. A manager introduces to the company staff the newcomer and gives her a warm welcome.

(*Up in the Air*, 2009)

"I'm just... I'm thrilled that everyone's back under one roof(聚在一起). Welcome home, boys. I know there's a lot of whispering about why we are here, so... let me jump right in(直奔主题). Retailers(零售业) are down 20%. Auto industry is in the dump(疲软). Housing market doesn't have a heartbeat. It is one of the worst times on record for America. This is our moment. Now last summer, we received a dynamite(有活力的) young woman here from um... from Cornell(康奈尔大学). And she had some pretty big ideas that she challenged me with. And my first reaction was, "Who does this kid think that she is?" But after I gave it a listen, she really knocked me out(震住). So... With a peek into our future, Natalie Keener."

Casting a little suspension of the reason why they are gathered together, the manager introduces a girl whose new ideas challenged him.

9.2 Award Giving

As an essential part of an award ceremony, awarding speeches and receiving speeches add color and glamour to the event. Presenting an award or other special honor or title to someone, the speaker's primary focus should be on the achievements of the recipient and why he/she is receiving the award. Each year, the Oscar, Grammy, Emmy awards have given us numerous great speeches from the winners and the presenters in those ceremonies. From these speeches, we have learned the basic rules of an award-giving speech. Firstly, speeches of presentation should usually be fairly brief. At times, they can be only a few lines and focus on one particular detail or interesting point. And then the speech should point out the achievements for which the recipient is receiving the award. The speech should discuss the recipient's achievements in a way that will make them meaningful to the audience. At last, if the recipient won the award in a competition against other candidates, the speech of presentation should consider praising his/her peers or colleagues as well.

1) Lady Gaga giving a speech by honoring Brittany Spears an MTV award in 2011

(2011 MTV Award)

"When you're a struggling artist, literally(几乎) starving for your dream, you gotta live off inspiration. When I used to perform in open-mic nights(免费公开表演) for free in small clubs in New York, one of my biggest inspirations was Britney Spears. Britney taught me how to be fearless. She taught us all how to be fearless. She is a pop music legend. And the industry will not be the same without her. I used to hang posters of her on my wall and touch myself when I was lying in bed. Throughout the years, Britney has given some of us the most iconic(非凡的) music videos and stage shows of our time, and that's why tonight MTV and myself are honoring Britney and her influence on music videos and dance with the Michael Jackson Video Vanguard Award(迈克尔·杰克逊音乐录影先锋奖). Ladies, take it away!(电视播放信号语:开始播放)"

Lady Gaga spares no kind words in praising Britney Spears by first pinpointing her as an inspiration for herself, followed by how she looked up to her as an idol, and at last gives the reason why she deserves this award.

2) The 69th Golden Globe Awards in 2012 honoring Morgan Freeman Life Achievement (the Award presenter is Mr. Sydney Poitier, a highly respected actor in the US, who gives a speech to honor him)

(2012 Golden Globe Awards)

"Morgan Freeman, that you illuminate（照亮）your presence, that you infuse（注入）the characters you play with a real life, three dimensional（三维）aura（气质）. You become the character; the character becomes you. And so begins a process that captivates（迷住）your audience, even the likes of Spencer Tracy, Laurence Olivier, Marlon Brando and Canada Lee would applaud your process, were they still with us. In my humble opinion, sir, you are, indeed, a prince, in the profession you have chosen. We thank you, Mr. Freeman, for raising the level of excellence yet another notch（高度）. Welcome aboard, Morgan Freeman. May your journey be long, and your characters continue to multiply. Congratulations."

Quite the opposite of the one above by Lady Gaga in style, this speech is formal as is shown in its refined wording and polished style, as well as the speaker's facial expressions, body language and tone.

Award Receiving

It's customary that the winner of an award gives a speech after receiving the award. If one has been bestowed with an award or honor, an acceptance speech is usually expected from him/her. The purpose of the speech usually is to thank for the award and also acknowledge the people who helped the recipient on the way to winning the award. A good acceptance speech is marked by three traits:

a. Brevity—Keep it short and sweet.

b. Humility—This is not the time to brag.

Chapter 9 Speaking on Special Occasions 特殊场合的演讲

c. Graciousness—Accept with genuine gratitude.

1) Beauty Contest

The winner Kitty Helen gives a speech in the Spring Fling(春季狂欢节)in a high school.

(*Mean Girls*, 2004)

"Well. Thanks. Um, Well, half the people in this room are mad at me. And the other half only like me because they think I push somebody in front of the bus. So that's not good. To, uh, all the people whose feelings that got hurt by the Burn Book(传播他人绯闻和坏话的日记), I'm really sorry. You know, I've never been to one of these things before. And when I think about how many people wanted this, and how many people cried over this stuff... I mean, I think everybody looks like royalty(光彩夺目)tonight. Look at Jessica Lopez. The dress is amazing. And Emma Gerber, I mean, that hairdo you must have taken hours, and you look really pretty. So... why is everybody stressing over this thing? I mean, it's just plastic(指 crown). Really, just... (snaps it in half) share it. A piece for Gretchen Wieners, a partial Spring Fling Queen. A piece for Janis Ian, and a piece for Regina George. She fractured her spine(脊柱骨折), and she still looks like a rock star. And some for everybody else. (throws the remaining pieces into the crowd)"

The crown winner gives a dramatic speech in an unorthodox way, by first apologizing for the things she has done before, then out of expectation, she wants to share the crown with everyone in the party.

2) At the 79th Oscar, 2007, Helen Mirren giving an acceptance speech as the winner for Best Actress in the leading role in *The Queen*

(Oscar Award, 2007)

"I've got my purse in one hand, and my earring in the other. Thank you Academy, thank you so much. A huge honor. You know my sister told me, that all kids love to get gold stars. This is the biggest and the best gold star that I have ever had in my life. I want to share my gold star with my fellow nominees(提名人), those brilliant, brilliant actresses, who gave such amazing performances this year. I also share my gold star with the film makers, with Stephen Frears and Peter Morgan and with Andy Harries and all the producers and all the film makers and the cast. Thank you. Now you know for fifty years, and more, Elizabeth Winsor(伊丽莎白二世) has maintained her dignity, her sense of duty and her hair style. She's had her feet planted firmly on the ground(立场坚定), her hat on her head, her handbag on her arm, and she's weathered many many storms(经历无数风雨), and... and I salute her courage and her consistency(毅力). And I thank her, because, for her, if it wasn't for her, I most... most certainly wouldn't be here. Ladies and gentlemen, I give you the Queen!"

The speaker skillfully uses "gold stars" to base the speech on by paying respect to three sets of people: the fellow nominees, the producers and the queen. A little humor also works wonder when mentioning Queen Elizabeth's hair style.

3) Veronica Guerin, a brave woman who sacrificed her life in fighting against injustice, speaking after winning the Press Freedom Award

(Veronica Guerin, 2003)

C. P. J. President: *The Committee to Protect Journalists is proud to present this year's Press Freedom Award*(新闻自由奖)*to a reporter who has consistently resisted brutal, criminal attempts to silence her and subvert*(推翻)*the news. Despite the intimidation, she continues to defend the public's right to read the truth. Ladies and gentlemen, please salute a brave woman: Veronica Guerin.*

Guerin: *Thanks, John. Uh... Sadly, it's not unusual to hear that a reporter has been shot or intimidated. A number of reporters at home—not just myself—have been subjected to death threats and intimidation on a daily basis. This year alone the number*

Chapter 9 Speaking on Special Occasions 特殊场合的演讲

of journalists killed worldwide has reached fifty-one. The only thing that distinguishes me is that I survived to tell the story. <u>I hope that's not the only reason I'm receiving this award tonight</u>, but either way I'm very grateful to the C.P.J. for awarding an Irish, European journalist.

I really am both humbled and honored to receive this award, particularly because of the company that I'm keeping—the other recipients who I certainly feel are more deserving than myself. In doing so, I want to thank two people who have encouraged and supported me, despite an incredibly difficult last twelve months—and they are my husband, Graham, and my son, Cathal. Because I can assure you if they hadn't supported me, I wouldn't be doing it. Thanks very much.

The speech reveals the harsh reality for reporters and the danger they face in their line of work. The underlined sentence is a forced humor with tears and blood in it. It follows such a clue: raising people's awareness of the harsh environment of the journalists; singing high praise for the fellow nominees; giving thanks to her family.

Toasting

The occasions are birthday celebrations, engagement gatherings, wedding ceremonies, anniversaries, and so on. A toast is a salute with raised glasses to a person or persons marking some special event. It calls for brief, warm and personal remarks. For example, "Here's to Jake and Sarah's 50th Wedding Anniversary. Their 50 years together is a testimony to their love for each other, for their children and for life. May they have 50 more years together!"

To make it special, we could recite an appropriate quote or poem or relate an anecdote. And we want to wish the celebrant(s) good health, much joy, a smooth life, or many more years of good times.

A word of caution: we might want to observe temperance until toast time so over-imbibing does not negatively impact our salute.

1) Wedding

A woman toasts her younger sister's wedding.

(*What's Your Number*, 2011)

"Hi, everyone. Um...When Daisy and Eddie first got together, I have to admit I was a little bit nervous. I could tell that it was serious and I...I thought that the closer she got to him, the further away she'd get from me. But that didn't happen. Not only do I see more of Daisy, I see a happier, even better Daisy. It's like with Eddie, she is completely herself. When you're a big sister, it's your job to teach your little sister everything. You know, how to ride a bike, how to lie to your parents, how to kiss, not with tongues, settle down, Uncle Charlie. Uh...But I never thought about what my little sister can teach me until right now, so I wanna thank you, Daisy, thank you for teaching me that being in love means being yourself. To Daisy and Eddie!"

The speaker, as an older sister, feels happy for her sister's transformation in love. A little humor makes the audience laugh and lightens the sadness in herself when reflecting on her own state of failing to find her other half.

2) Anniversary

A man toasts his best friend's wedding anniversary.

(*The Change-Up*, 2011)

"For those of you who don't know me, my name is Mitch Planko. I was that nut sack's(蠢货) best man(伴郎) 10 years ago. You know when we were kids, Dave and I, we...uh...we had a lot of big plans. Dave, he...he was going to be an astronaut, and I...and I was going to sell dolphins on the black market. Astronaut! The reason I'm not selling dolphins—we live in Atlanta; they're tough to find. And those things, they don't sleep, which also makes it real hard to catch them. You know I think we all know that life doesn't always turn out exactly how you plan it. Sometimes, just sometimes, it turns out better. You know, Dave, I think there is a reason that...that you're not walking on the moon right now. It's because you belong here, in your life, with that incredible woman sitting beside you. Can we please raise our Kamikaze(日语:神风。此处指一种鸡尾酒) shots(少量饮料,尤指少量烈酒) to my two best friends, please? To Dave and Jamie! Happy anniversary!"

As it is often the case, a toaster may start the speech by recalling some heart-warming past events. Speaking as the die-hard buddy of the man of the hour, the speaker in his toast combines a humorous tone and a sincerity in expressing good wishes to his best friend.

 Tribute

Paying tribute to someone is to salute, show respect and admiration or give public recognition by singing high praise of the afore-mentioned person's achievements. The fundamental purpose of a tribute-paying speech is to inspire the audience — to heighten their admiration for the person. Two aspects of language use are especially important for this type of speech. The first is avoiding clichés and trite sentiments. The second is utilizing stylistic devices such as those to enhance the imagery, rhythm, and creativity of the speech.

1) Governor Gertrude Lang honoring Glenn Holland and his opus（大作，巨著）

(*Mr. Holland's Opus*, 1995)

"Mr. Holland had a profound influence on my life, on a lot of lives that I know. And yet I get the feeling that he considers a great part of his own life misspent（浪费）. Rumor had it he was always working on this symphony（交响乐）of his. And this was going to make him famous, rich, probably both. But Mr. Holland isn't rich and he isn't famous, at least not outside of our little town.

So it might be easy for him to think himself a failure. And he would be wrong, because I think he's achieved a success far beyond riches and fame.

Look around you. There is not a life in this room that you have not touched, and each one of us is a better person because of you. We are your symphony, Mr. Holland. We are the melodies and the notes of your opus. And we are the music of your life.

Mr. Holland, we would now like to give something back to（回馈）you, to you and your wife, who along with you has waited 30 years for what we are about to hear.

If you will, would you please come up here and take this baton（指挥棒）and lead us in the first performance ever of the American Symphony by Glenn Holland."

The speaker starts with her own personal salute to Mr. Holland and then extends it to others, followed by praising his accomplishments. The speech ends with a surprise, a performance to salute Mr. Holland.

2) Tim Robins saluting Morgan Freeman in his role as Nelson Mandela in the film *Invictus* (for which he is nominated the best actor in the leading role)

(2010 Oscar Award)

"Morgan, we became friends working together on The Shawshank Redemption (《肖申克的救赎》), for which you were nominated for an Academy Award. The film follows a trajectory(轨迹) of friendship, and that friendship was easily mirrored in real life on the set(片场). I'll never forget what you said to me about friendship on the last day of shooting. You said, 'Being a friend is getting the other a cup of coffee.' Can you do that for me, Ted? It is Ted, isn't it? We became so close. Honestly, <u>Morgan is an extremely giving actor, a master at his craft(表演大师), and an inspiration to all those lucky enough to have the chance to work with him.</u> Considering the dignity and integrity (尊严与正直) that he brings to all his work, I was not surprised to learn that he'd been nominated tonight for his role as the great Nelson Mandela. Morgan, <u>I salute you and your tremendous talent.</u> And I'm always proud to call you, my friend, when you take the call."

Recalling the past experience as his partner, the speaker, Tim Robins focuses on two points in the speech: their friendship and Morgan's acting achievement.

Eulogy

Eulogies may be given as part of a funeral service and usually delivered by a family member or a close family friend in the case of the deceased. Eulogies should not be confused with elegies, which are poems written in tribute to the dead; nor with obituaries, which are published biographies recounting the lives of those who have recently died; nor with obsequies, which refer generally to the rituals surrounding funerals. Presenting a eulogy, we keep the following in mind: first, speak with sincerity and solemnity; second, be generous and praise the departed person's good deeds and merits; third, show how he/she has inspired us and how we're going to remember him/her.

(*Four Weddings and a Funeral*, 1994)

"*Garry used to prefer funerals to weddings. He said it was easier to get enthusiastic about a ceremony one had no such a chance of eventually being involved in. In order to prepare the speech, I rang a few people, to get a general picture*(总体印象)*of how Garry was regarded by those who met him. Fat, seems to be the word people most connected with him. Terribly rude also rang a lot of bells*(回忆起来)*. So very fat and very rude seems to be the strangers' viewpoint. On the other hand, some of you being kind enough to ring me and let me know that you loved him, which, I know he would be thrilled to hear. You remembered his fabulous hospitality*(殷勤)*, his strange experimental cooking, the recipe*(菜谱)*for Duck a la Banana*(一道菜名)*, fortunately goes with him to his grave. Most of all, you tell me of his enormous capacity for joy, and when joyful, when joyful for highly vocal drunkenness*(酩酊大醉)*. I hope joyful as how you'd remember him. Not stuck*(困在)*in the box in the church, pick a favorite of his waistcoat and remember him that way. The most splendid, replete*(饱的)*, big hearted, weak hearted as it turned out, and jolly bugger*(同性恋者)*most of us ever met. As for me, you may ask how I will remember him, what I thought of him. Unfortunately there I run out of words. Perhaps you will forgive me if I turn from my own feelings to the words of another splendid bugger, W. H. Auden*(英国诗人)*. This is actually what I want to say:*

    Stop all the clocks, cut off the telephone,
    Prevent the dog from barking with a juicy bone,
    Silence the pianos and with muffled drum
    Bring out the coffin, let the mourners come.

    Let aeroplanes circle moaning overhead
    Scribbling on the sky the message He Is Dead,
    Put crepe bows round the white necks of the public doves,

> Let the traffic policemen wear black cotton gloves.
>
> He was my North, my South, my East and West,
> My working week and my Sunday rest,
> My noon, my midnight, my talk, my song;
> I thought that love would last forever: I was wrong.
>
> The stars are not wanted now: put out every one,
> Pack up the moon and dismantle the sun,
> Pour away the ocean and sweep up the woods;
> For nothing now can ever come to any good."

The speaker begins by recalling his best friend's life and the impression he left in other people's minds, and then gives his own comment on his death, followed by reciting a poem.

9.7 Debating

Debate is contention in argument, dispute, controversy, discussion, esp. the discussion of questions of public interest. In schools and colleges competitive debate often takes the form of a contest with explicit rules. It may be presided over by one or more judges. One team will propose and the other will oppose. Each side seeks to win, following the rules, either in favor of (for, pros, affirmative), or opposed to (against, cons, negative), a statement (proposition, moot or resolution). The "for" side must argue supporting the proposition; the "against" side must refute these arguments. Each speaker on both sides will speak in the order: 1st Proposition, 1st Opposition, 2nd Proposition, 2nd Opposition, and so on, in some cases, followed by free debating session and then a summary speech on each side. Emphasis is typically on analytical skills, entertainment, style and strength of argument.

Cher debates "Whether all oppressed people should be allowed refuge in America".

(*Clueless*, 1995)

Chapter 9 Speaking on Special Occasions 特殊场合的演讲

Mr. Hall: *Should all oppressed people be allowed refuge*(避难)*in America? Amber will take the con position*(反方). *Cher will be pro.*(正方)*Cher: 2 minutes.*

Cher: *So, OK, like right now, for example, the Haitians*(海地人)*need to come to America. But some people are all,* "*What about the strain*(紧张)*on our resources?*" *But it's like when I had this garden party for my father's birthday, right? I said R.S.V.P.*(法语:请答复)*because it was a sit-down dinner. But people came that, like, did not R.S.V.P. So I was, like, totally buggin'*(烦恼). *I had to haul my ass*(屁颠屁颠地)*to the kitchen, redistribute*(重新分配)*the food, squish*(挤压)*in extra place settings; but by the end of the day it was, like, the more the merrier! And so, if the government could just get to the kitchen, rearrange some things, we could certainly party with the Haitians. And in conclusion, may I please remind you that it does not say R.S.V.P. on the Statue of Liberty? Thank you very much.*

The debater uses a series of analogies in her arguing for the proposition that American government should take the Haitian refugees, i.e., her father's birthday party event, the government getting to the kitchen, and the statue of liberty. And she successfully did that, in a graceful way. Another striking feature is use of a number of colloquial words and phrases, such as "like", "bugging", "totally", "haul my ass to".

9.8 Press Conference

In a news conference, one or more speakers may make a statement, which may be followed by questions from reporters. Sometimes only questioning occurs; sometimes there is a statement with no questions permitted. A media event at which no statements are made, and no questions allowed, is called a photo opportunity. A government may wish to open their proceedings for the media to witness events, such as the passing of a piece of legislation. When the President of the United States holds a press conference, he takes questions from the press pool in a designated or random order.

President Andrew Shepherd is at the press conference on Bob Rumson and the Crime Bill.

(*The American President*, 1995)

Reporter: *Robyn, will the President ever respond to Senator Rumson's question about being a member of the American Civil Liberties Union*(民权自由协会)?

President Shepherd: *Yes, he will. Good morning.* [*Members of the White House Press Corps*(记者团)*are surprised and begin to rise*] *It's alright. Please keep to your seats. Good morning.*

For the last couple of months, Senator Rumson has suggested that being President of this country was to a certain extent about character. And although I've not been willing to engage in his attacks on me, I've been here three years and three days, and I can tell you without hesitation: being President of this country is entirely about character.

For the record, yes, I am a card-carrying member of the ACLU, but the more important question is "Why aren't you, Bob?" Now this is an organization whose sole purpose is to defend the Bill of Rights(人权法案)*, so it naturally begs the question, why would a senator, his party's most powerful spokesman and a candidate for President, choose to reject upholding the constitution*(维护宪法)*? Now if you can answer that question, folks, then you're smarter than I am, because I didn't understand it until a few hours ago.*

America isn't easy. America is advanced citizenship. You've gotta want it bad, 'cause it's gonna put up a fight(展开斗争)*. It's gonna say, "You want free speech? Let's see you acknowledge a man whose words make your blood boil*(热血沸腾)*, who's standing center stage*(中央舞台)*and advocating at the top of his lungs*(声嘶力竭)*that which you would spend a lifetime opposing at the top of yours." You want to claim this land as the land of the free? Then the symbol of your country cannot just be a flag. The symbol also has to be one of its citizens exercising his right to burn that flag in protest. Now show me that, defend that, celebrate that in your classrooms.*

Then you can stand up and sing about the land of the free(自由的国土)*. I've known Bob Rumson for years. And I've been operating under the assumption that the reason Bob devotes so much time and energy to shouting at the rain*(捕风捉影)*was that he simply didn't get it. Well, I was wrong. Bob's problem isn't that he doesn't get it. Bob's problem is that he can't sell it!*

We have serious problems to solve, and we need serious people to solve them. And whatever your particular problem is, I promise you, Bob Rumson is not the least bit interested in solving it. He is interested in two things, and two things only: making you afraid of it, and telling you who's to blame for it. That, ladies and gentlemen, is how you win elections. You gather a group of middle age, middle class, middle income voters who remember with longing an easier time, and you talk to them about family, and American values and character, and you wave an old photo of the President's girlfriend and you scream about patriotism(爱国主义)*. You tell them she's to blame for their lot in life. You go on television and you call her a whore*(娼妇)*.*

Sydney Ellen Wade has done nothing to you, Bob. She has done nothing but put herself through school, represents the interests of public school teachers, and lobby for the safety of our natural resources. You want a character debate, Bob? You better stick with me, 'cause Sydney Ellen Wade is way out of your league(不够格).

I've loved two women in my life. I lost one to cancer. And I lost the other 'cause I was so busy keeping my job, I forgot to do my job. Well, that ends right now.

Tomorrow morning the White House is sending a bill to Congress for its consideration(审议). *It's White House Resolution*(决议)*455, an energy bill requiring a twenty percent reduction of the emission*(排放)*of fossil fuels*(化石燃料)*over the next ten years. It is by far the most aggressive stride*(激进的一步)*ever taken in the fight to reverse*(扭转)*the effects of global warming. The other piece of legislation*(议案)*is the crime bill. As of today, it no longer exists. I'm throwing it out. I'm throwing it out and writing a law that makes sense. You cannot address crime prevention without getting rid of assault weapons*(攻击性武器)*and hand guns. I consider them a threat to national security, and I will go door to door if I have to, but I'm gonna convince Americans that I'm right, and I'm gonna get the guns.*

We've got serious problems, and we need serious people. And if you want to talk about character, Bob, you better come at me with more than a burning flag and a membership card. If you want to talk about character and American values, fine. Just tell me where and when, and I'll show up. This a time for serious people, Bob, and your fifteen minutes are up.

The president is lashing back at his opponent at this conference. First, by admitting being a member of the CLU, he justifies it as a means of upholding the American constitution of protecting civil rights. Next, he denounces the opponent's groundless accusation and vicious attack on his girlfriend. At last, he makes a vow to devote himself as president of the country to his people, and endeavor to pass the two bills in the congress. The speaker stands behind a podium without much freedom to move his body, but his stern face and sharp eyes work as a strong aid in his speech as well as the pounding of his fist on the podium.

9.9 School Opening & Valedictory Speech

At a school opening ceremony, the speaker to the whole student body is usually the school principal. In a graduation ceremony, there is usually a class-elected speaker representing the whole class to give a farewell speech. This speech is called <u>valedictory</u>, and the speaker is a <u>valedictorian</u>. A valedictorian is an academic title conferred upon the student who delivers the closing or farewell statement at a graduation ceremony. Usually, the valedictorian is the highest ranked student among those graduating from an educational institution. The valedictory address generally is considered a final farewell to classmates, before they disperse to pursue their individual paths after graduating. A valedictory speech is usually persuasive as well as inspiring, focusing on encouragement to the fellow graduates and gratitude to the teachers, combined with warm recalling of the past events in the course of the study. In English culture on this occasion, there is another form of speech called commencement, i.e., a speech made by an invited guest speaker, who, more often than not, is a prominent figure in the field of politics, acting, writing, singing, sports, or a scientist, such as the one Steve Jobs gave at the graduation ceremony of Stanford University in 2005.

1) President of an art college speaking on the school opening day

(*Fame*, 2009)

"*Welcome. This year we received over 10,000 applications for the 200 openings*(名额)*from students all across New York City. And you got in. Congratulations! For the next four years, you have the unique opportunity to immerse*(沉浸)*yourselves in the arts. You can be spontaneous*(自发性), *original*(创造性), *maybe even a little outrageous*(出格). *You got it made, right? Wrong. You're gonna have it twice as hard as everybody else. In the mornings, you're gonna have all your arts classes. After lunch, you will cram*(拼命学习)*in a full day of academics. Drop below a C average and you're out. No exceptions. Now, let me make this very clear. We don't care about your headshot*(头像), *or your dress size, or your dreams of being in OK! Magazine*(杂志名), *on talk shows, on the red carpet. Here you'll learn a discipline. Here you'll come to understand what being a performing artist really means. Here you'll dedicate yourself to your craft*(才艺). *Now, if you're looking for shortcuts, if you want fame, if you want easy rewards, I highly recommend that you get up and leave now. There are many very talented young people who would be thrilled to take your place. So, have a great year.*"

The speaker urges the newcomers to treasure the hard-earned opportunity to work hard in pursuit of art. The speech ends with a good wish.

2) A London high school headmaster giving an opening speech

(*Dead Poets Society*, 1989)

"*Ladies and gentlemen, boys, the Light of Knowledge. One hundred years ago, in 1859, 41 boys sat in this room and were asked the same question that now greets you at the start of each semester. Gentlemen, what are the Four Pillars? (Students stand and chant together: tradition, honor, discipline, excellence)*

In her first year, Welton Academy graduated five students. Last year, we graduated 51. And more than 75% of those went on to the Ivy League（常春藤盟校）. (Claps) This... This kind of accomplishment is the result of fervent（热诚的）dedication to the principles taught here. This is why you parents have been sending us your sons. This is why we are the best preparatory school（预备学校）in the United States.

As you know, our beloved Mr. Portius of the English Department retired last term. You will have the opportunity later to meet his replacement, Mr. John Keating, himself an honoured graduate of this school, and who, for the past several years, has been teaching at the highly regarded（享有盛名的）Chester School in London. (Claps)"

Speaking to the new comers and their parents, the headmaster first touches the glory of the school history, which follows the school motto, and then the achievements they have got. At last, he introduces briefly a new teacher.

3) Elle Woods delivering a valedictory speech at Harvard Law School's 2004 Graduation Ceremony

(*Legally Blonde*, 2001)

"On our very first day at Harvard, a very wise Professor quoted Aristotle: 'The law is reason free from passion.' Well, no offense(得罪) to Aristotle, but in my three years at Harvard I have come to find that passion is a key ingredient(关键因素) to the study and practice of law—and of life. It is with passion, courage of conviction(信念), and strong sense of self that we take our next steps into the world, remembering that first impressions are not always correct. You must always have faith in people. And most importantly, you must always have faith in yourself. Congratulations class of 2004—we did it!"

The speaker showcases what a Harvard graduate looks like: radiant facial expressions, crystal-like voice and a melodious tone. The speech is pleasantly inspiring.

Election Campaign

Running as a candidate for a position, a prize and privilege requires the applicants or candidates to compete against each other in presenting himself/herself and convince the authority for their favor or the supporters for their votes. The occasion comes in various forms and levels, from schools to corporate cultures, from communities to political campaigns. The most striking features of this speech is stirring, agitating and arousing in order to gain support and votes from the audience.

Tracy Flick runs for President of the student body and speaks to the students.

(*Election*, 1999)

"Poet Henry David Thoreau once wrote, 'I cannot make my days longer, so I strive to make them better.' With this election, we here at Carver also have an opportunity to make our high school days better. During this campaign, I've spoken with many of you about your many concerns. I spoke to Eliza Ramirez, a freshman, who said she feels alienated(疏远) from her own homeroom(年级教室). I spoke to a sophomore, Reggie Banks, who said his mother works in the cafeteria and can't afford to buy him enough spiral notebooks for his classes. I care about Carver and I care about each and every one

Chapter 9 Speaking on Special Occasions 特殊场合的演讲

of you. Together we can all make a difference. When you cast your vote for Tracy Flick next week, you won't just be voting for me. You'll be voting for yourself and for every other student here at Carver. Our days might not be any longer but they can sure be better. Thank you."

The speech follows a standard routine: first she takes a pledge, and then shares her experience and feeling, at last, calls for the support.

Inauguration Address

An inauguration is a formal ceremony to mark the beginning of a leader's term of office. An "inaugural address" is the speech given at this ceremony which informs the people of his/her intentions as a leader. Political inaugurations often feature lavish ceremonies, in which the politician publicly takes his or her oath of office in front of a large crowd of spectators. The equivalent ceremony in another jurisdiction may be called a "swearing-in"(宣誓就职). A monarchical inauguration is similar to what in another jurisdiction may be called a coronation(加冕) or enthronement(登基). The speech can also be made by any ordinary person of any working position, who begins routinely with expression of gratitude towards the new employer, and his/her plan or resolve on the new post.

Darcy Maguire address the department colleagues on her first day in the company,

(*What Women Want*, 2000)

"Thank you, Danny. Thank you all for the warm welcome. Let me start off by saying the feeling is mutual. I'm absolutely thrilled to be here. When I first started in this business, it was my dream to work at Sloane Curtis. In fact, I believe I even applied for a job here twice. But it was BBD & O that offered me a home. And what I learned there was that any success I had was a direct result of the team of people that I work with. I know that two heads are better than one. I know that five heads are better than two. And I know that if we put our heads and our hearts into this company, we will

deliver. I know that. Now I love challenges. I love hard work. I look forward to sitting at this very table, tossing ideas(交流思想) around, until what I feel will be the way hours of the morning. But most importantly, I want the work we do to say something, about who we are, how we think, or we feel. So, as our friends in Hollywood say, 'let's cut to the chase'(进入正题), how we get to turn this company around? When Sears decided to go after women in their advertising and said, 'come see the soft side of Sears.' Their revenues(收入) went up 30%. 30%, that's huge. Female driven advertising totaled 40 billion dollars last year. And Sloane Curtis's share of that was...zero. If you want to sell an anti-wrinkle cream(防皱霜) or a Ford Muston(福特野马跑车) to a woman, forgive me, but this is the last place you play your business, and we can't afford to not have a piece of 40 billion dollar pie. So I have put together a little kit for everybody. Nobody panic, this is supposed to be fun. Every product in this box is looking for new representation(推销点子) right now. And they are all made for women. I'm pretty sure all the women here are pretty familiar with those products. So for the men, let's just briefly run through them. Here you go, Nick. Each kit contains anti-wrinkle cream, mascara(睫毛膏), moisturizing lipstick(润唇膏), bath beads(沐浴珠), quick-dry nail polish(速干指甲油), an at-home waxing(脱毛蜡) kit, a more wonderful wonder bra, a home pregnancy test, hair volumizer(头发膨松剂), pore cleansing strips(毛孔清洁贴), Advil(一种止痛药), control top panty hose(连裤袜), and a visa card. Now I want everybody to come up with something... for one product, for two, the whole box... whatever moves you. We'll get together tomorrow; have a little show-and-tell(展示报告) to see where we are. How is 8:30 for everybody? Great. See you at 8:30 tomorrow morning."

Newly appointed Department manager Darcy gives her thanks to her boss for the opportunity and warm welcome, and then produces her ideas and plans by analyzing the present market. An image of a new team leader is shown in the speech.

9.12 Business Presentation

Business is all about selling —a product, topic or concept. When making a business presentation, the most important thing is to know our material. If we do not know everything about what we are selling, it is not likely that the audience will be buying. Keep our audience focused and interested. Making effective business presentations takes practice, but with a few tips at hand, and the help of modern computer technology, we are ready to take on the challenge.

(1) Use key words for our topic. Seasoned presenters use key phrases and include only essential information and make them consistent throughout the delivery.

(2) Use slide layout in PowerPoint. Make our slides easy to follow. Avoid all capital

letters avoid fancy fonts. Choose a font that is simple and easy to read such as Arial, Times New Roman or Verdana.

(3) Limit the number of slides. Keep the number of slides to a minimum, and ensure that the presentation will not become too long and drawn out. It also avoids the problem of continually changing slides during the presentation, which can be a distraction to our audience.

(4) Use photos, charts and graphs. Combining photos, charts and graphs and even embedding digitized videos with text, will add variety and keep our audience interested in the presentation. Avoid having text-only slides.

(5) Avoid excessive use of slide transitions and animations. Too much can distract them from what we are saying. Remember, the slide show is meant to be a visual aid, not the focus of the presentation.

(6) Make sure our presentation can run on any computers. This is very important! Otherwise, all effort is in vain.

At the same time, we should also keep in mind the following guidelines:

(1) We are not an entertainer. A business presentation serves a professional purpose, and the tone of it should reflect that fact. An occasional joke or funny story can add a human touch to an otherwise boring subject, but too much humor is not a good idea. Jokes can often fall flat or, worse, offend the audience. Avoid jokes about sex, age, race, social class or language barriers. It is easy to see attempted humor as a simple way to make an audience interested. But the best way to win an audience over is to deliver a good, memorable presentation on the subject matter.

(2) Get to know the venue. If possible, rehearse our presentation at the venue. This will help build confidence and allow us to get a feel for the size and position of the audience. On the day of the presentation, make sure we set up all necessary equipment in plenty of time. If we'll be using microphones, a laptop, a slide projector or a big-screen TV make sure we test them before the audience arrives.

(3) Offer follow-up contact details. In some situations, such as a sales presentation, it is obvious that the company's contact details will be included on a slide towards the end of the presentation.

1) Marketing executive Kate giving a business presentation to the clients about the new toy product launching, the Big Boss

(BBC Starting Business English)

"*In the next hour or so, I am going to introduce you to a completely new concept in toy manufacture. I shall begin by talking about the market research which led to the development of this product. Then I shall explain the technical developments, the production and our marketing strategy. Finally, I shall outline our recommendations as to how you can make this product a success in your territory. By the end of the hour, you'll be able to see why Bibury Systems are so committed to this new venture*(项目)*, and why we are so confident that we can capture the American market. So let's begin with the background...*

...So to sum up, everything indicated that the market was ready for a hi-tech product, a product that would appeal to both parents and children, a product that lets the user decide the character of the toy.

Ladies and gentlemen, let me introduce a breakthrough in toy technology. Ladies and gentlemen, I give you Big Boss.

...To conclude the presentation, we have seen that Big Boss can succeed in the American market. We have a product that can give the user more than anything else on the market. There is nothing that can touch it(与之抗衡)*. Other competitors cannot deliver the technology. They cannot match our price, and they can't compete with our television campaign. Big Boss is going to be coast to coast at peak hours every day in the New Year.*

And how much are we spending on this campaign? Well, let's have a look at the individual territories."

Introducing the new toy, Marketing executive Kate's speech follows the general agenda: first introducing the main points; then market research, product research and manufacturing, regional marketing strategy; and then price and advertising advantages; and at last, her confidence and prospect for the product.

2) Gordon Gekko Addressing the stockholders

(*Wall Street*, 1987)

"*Well, I... I appreciate the opportunity you're giving me, Mr. Cromwell, as the single large shareholder in Teldar Paper, to speak.* (laughter) *But ladies and* gentlemen, we are not here to indulge in (沉溺于) fantasy, but in political and economic reality. America, America has become a second-rate power. Its trade deficit (贸易赤字) and its fiscal deficit (财政赤字) are at nightmare proportions (比例). On the days of the free market, when our country was a top industrial power, there was accountability (问责制) to the stockholder. The Carnegies, the Mellons, the men that built this great industrial empire, made sure of it, because it was their money at stake (处在危险中). Today, management has no stake in the company! Altogether, these men sitting up here own less than 3% of the company. And where does Mr. Cromwell put his $1,000,000 salary? Not in Teldar Stock. He owns less than 1%. YOU own the company. That's right, YOU, the stockholder. And you are all being royally screwed over (整垮) by these... these bureaucrats, with their... their steak lunches, their hunting and fishing trips, their corporate jets (公司专机) and golden parachutes (黄金降落伞). (Mr. Cromwell: This is an outrage! You're out of line (过分), Gekko!)

Teldar Paper, Mr. Cromwell, Teldar Paper, has 33 different vice presidents, each earning over $200,000 a year. Now I have spent the last two months analyzing what all these guys do. And I still can't figure it out. (laughter) One thing I do know is that our paper company lost $110 million last year. And I'll bet half of that was spent in all the paperwork going back and forth between all these vice presidents! (laughter) The new law of evolution (进化) in corporate America seems to be, survival of the unfittest. Well, in my book you either do it right, or you get eliminated (消灭). In the last seven deals that I've been involved with, there were 2.5 million stockholders who have made a pre-tax profit (税前利润) of $12 billion. (applause) Thank you. I am not a destroyer of companies. I am a liberator (解放者) of them. The point is, ladies and gentlemen, that greed, for lack of a better word, is good. Greed is right. Greed works. Greed clarifies (澄清), cuts through and captures the essence of the evolutionary spirit. Greed, in all of its forms, greed for life, for money, for love, knowledge, has marked the upward surge of mankind. And greed, you mark my words (记住我的话), will not only save Teldar Paper, but that other malfunctioning (功能失调的) corporation called the USA. Thank you very much."

In this speech, Gordon Gekko strikes us as a hero who is slashing at the corrupt and incompetent corporate management, and at the same time justifying himself as the liberator of companies, and advocating his idea about greed: greed is good. The speech is full of bold intimidation, overbearing individualism, and more importantly, shameless ambition and greed. And the language is powerful. With the successful acting of the businessman, Michael Douglas won the Oscar of the best actor in the leading role in 1988.

9.13 Opening & Closing Ceremony

The occasions include competing events, conferences, important social gatherings, ceremonies, performances, celebrations, etc. Typical examples are annual American music and movie award events such as Oscar and Grammy. In England, the annual State Opening of Parliament addressed by the Queen is called the Queen's Speech. Speeches made on these occasions are mostly formal, brief and with appropriate amount of enthusiasm. The main function of an opening speech is official declaring, and formal guiding, and that of a closing speech is usually making a summation, evaluation and an appeal, as it usually signifies the conclusion of an event. And the main feature of an opening (closing) speech is usually conciseness, and the amount of use of daily language depends on the degree of formality of the occasion, combined with an appropriate amount of enthusiasm to inspire, express good wishes and infuse hope and confidence.

Following is the full text of the speech given by Jacques Rogge, President of International Olympic Committee at the 29th Olympics opening ceremony in Beijing on August 8, 2008.

(Jacques Rogge, President of IOC, 2008)

"*Mr. President of the People's Republic of China, Mr. Liu Qi and members of the organizing committee, dear Chinese friends, dear athletes,*

For a long time, China has dreamed of opening its doors and inviting the world's athletes to Beijing for the Olympic Games. Tonight, that dream comes true. Congratulations, Beijing. Through her, Beijing, you have chosen as the theme of these Games, "One World, One Dream". That is what we are tonight. As one world, we grieve (沉痛) *with you for the tragic earthquake in Sichuan Province. We were moved by the* great courage and solidarity (团结) of the Chinese people. As one dream, may these Olympic Games bring you joy, hope and pride. Athletes, the Games were created for you by our founder (奠基者), Pierre de Coubertin. These games belong to you; let them be the athletes' games. Have fun. Remember, however, they are about much more than performance alone; they are about peaceful gathering of two hundred and four national Olympic committees, regardless of athletic origin, gender, religion or political system. Please compete in the spirit of Olympic values, excellence, friendship and respect. Dear athletes, remember that you're role models for the youth of the world. Reject doping (拒绝毒品) and cheating; make us proud of your achievements and your conduct... As we bring... as we bring the Olympic dream to life, our warm thanks go to the Beijing Organizing Committee for its tireless work; our special thanks also go to the thousands of gracious volunteers, without whom, none of this could be possible. Beijing, you're a host to the present, and a gateway to the future. Thank you, gan xie ni!

I now have the honor of asking the President of the People's Republic of China to open the Games of the 29th Olympia of the modern era."

Rogge's opening speech follows the routine of the opening ceremony:

As a formal guidance:

(1) Explaining the meaning of "One World, One Dream", for one world, "we grieve with you for the tragic earthquake in *Sichuan* Province"; for one dream, "may this Olympic Games bring you joy, hope and pride".

(2) Olympic games are peaceful gatherings of unity instead of competition between nations. "... they are about peaceful gathering of two hundred and four national Olympic committees..."

(3) Advising the athletes' to set up a good example, say no to doping and cheating. "... you're role models for the youth of the world. Reject doping and cheating; make us proud of your achievements and your conduct."

(4) Giving thanks to the people involved in the games. "... our warm thanks go to Beijing Organizing Committee for its tireless work; our special thanks also go to the thousands of gracious volunteers..."

As an official declaring:

The speech declares the beginning of the game, "... asking the President of the People's Republic of China to open the Games of the 29th Olympia of the modern era."

(Jacques Rogge, President of IOC, 2008)

Dear Chinese Friends,

Tonight, we come to the end of 16 glorious days which we will cherish forever.

Thank you to the people of China, to all the wonderful volunteers and to BOCOG(北京奥组委)!

Through these Games, the world learned more about China, and China learned more about the world. Athletes from 204 National Olympic Committees came to these dazzling (令人炫目的) venues(场馆) and awed(令人敬畏) us with their talent.

New stars were born. Stars from past Games amazed us again. We shared their joys and their tears, and we marveled at(惊叹于) their ability. We will long remember the achievements we witnessed here.

As we celebrate the success of these Games, let us all together wish the best for the talented athletes who will soon participate in the Paralympic Games(残奥会). They also inspire us.

To the athletes tonight: You were true role models. You have shown us the unifying power of sport. The Olympic spirit lives in the warm embrace of competitors from nations in conflict. Keep that spirit alive when you return home.

These were truly exceptional Games!

...

In the closing speech, Rogge has shown four aspects.

Evaluation: ① Praising the game. "Through these Games, the world learned more about China, and China learned more about the world." ② Praising the venues ("dazzling"). ③ Praising the people involved ("awed us with their talent"). ④ Praising the athletes ("marveled at their ability").

Appealing: ① Giving blessing to the special Olympic athletes ("let us all together wish the best"). ② Olympic spirit is beyond the borders. "... unifying power of sport. The Olympic spirit lives in the warm embrace of competitive rivals from nations in conflict."

③Calling on the athletes to bring back the spirit to their homes. "Keep that spirit alive when you return home."

Summation: "These were truly exceptional Games!"

Announcement: ① The conclusion of the game. "I declare the Games of the XXIX Olympiad closed..." ②Looking forward to the next game. "I call upon the youth of the world to assemble four years from now in London to celebrate the Games of the XXX Olympiad."

(Opening speech at the 55th Grammy Awards)

Welcome to the greatest music show on earth—the Grammy Awards!

What a *spectacular*(壮观的)*performance by Taylor Swift*(泰勒·斯威夫特), *right? Now, I'm happy to see that my friend T-swizzle*(歌迷对 Taylor Swift 的昵称)*has already won a Grammy today, and she is nominated tonight in the "Record of the Year" category*(年度最佳唱片奖项)*for that song. Now Taylor just sang that "We'll Never Ever Gonna Get Back Together", but the truth is that at Grammies, we always get back together, and that's what makes this music the biggest tonight.*

One year ago, I stood on this stage and was honored to host the show for the first time. Right up to the night before, I intended to spend this part of the show properly introducing myself to you, but then in a flash(一瞬间)*, we suffered a loss in our music family. And our show had to change. So this year, I want to take just a moment to tell you why it means so much to me to host the show for you. See, wherever you come from, eventually*(最终)*you have that moment when it hits you*(让你突然领悟)*why the Grammy Award is music's ultimate*(终极的,最高的)*honor. For me that moment came when I first saw Michael Jackson cradling*(紧抱)*all those Grammies in one. Remember this? That magical image inspired me to go after my own dreams. And the same is true for many of us in this great hall tonight. We each experienced a Grammy moment when one of our musical heroes inspired us and set us on a course to get here too. That was true for Justin Timberlake*(贾斯汀·廷伯莱克)*, growing up in Memphis*(孟菲斯,在美国田纳西州)*, for Beyonce*(碧昂斯)*, growing up in Huston*(休斯敦,在美国得克萨斯州)*, for Carrie Underwood*(凯莉·昂德伍德)*in Oklahoma*(俄克拉荷马城,在美国俄克拉荷马州)*, for*

Adele(阿黛尔), in England; for Gotye in Bruges(来自比利时的一位歌手). I hope I pronounced that correctly. And for Rihanna(蕾哈娜) in Barbados(巴巴多斯,加勒比海岛国), coming from all these different places and making all kinds of music. We all somehow dream the same dream, and one way or another, with a little luck and a lot of Grace(上帝的恩惠), we all made it here tonight. And as your host, let me tell you all, we're so happy to see you here.

You see, I'm standing here because music was, is and always will be my first love. For me, the Grammies equals(等于) music. And that, ladies and gentlemen, is an equation (等式) that has been proven true for 55 years. Now, you probably don't know that my father James Nunya was a recording artist(录音师) in his own right(凭自身努力). And the first time I saw one of my father's songs on vinyl(黑胶唱片), it hit me, this dream really could come true. Now so far, and I stress(强调) so far, I've won two Grammies. When I received them, I gave my Grammies to my grammy, my grandmother to look after them, because she always looked after me. And more than anyone, my grandmother told me to dream, dream, dream. When that great lady passed(过世) more than a decade ago, I took those Grammies into my home where my family lives, and I cherish, and polish(擦拭) them regularly. And anytime I look at them, they inspire me to strive for(努力) excellence, just like you kids at home should do. Because when you get right down to it(归根结底), a Grammy isn't just a shiny trophy(奖杯) to hold onto, Grammy is a dream come true. Well, in Adele's case last year, six dreams come true. So I'm proud and humble(谦卑的) to say, those two Grammies are mine, and the show is ours, all of ours. So whether you down here tonight, or whether you up there, or tuning in(收听,收看) us anywhere in the world, this show is yours, too. So are you ready for your show? Are you ready for your show? All right then, let's get back to the music.

The speech opens the ceremony in a unique way in the following: ①borrowing Swift's song, illustrating the theme of the event is that "we'll always get together"; ②remembering Michael Jackson and honoring the nominated singers present at the event; ③telling stories about his father and grandmother in order to share his dream about music, and the dream of all the singers.

9.14 Sermon

In Christianity, a sermon (also known as a homily within some churches) is often delivered in a place of worship, most of which has a pulpit(讲道坛) or ambo(读经坛), an elevated architectural feature. A sermon is an oration by a prophet or member of the clergy. Sermons address a biblical, theological, religious, or moral topic, usually expounding on a type of belief, law or behavior within both past and present contexts.

Elements of preaching include exposition（说明）, exhortation（告诫）and practical application.

The word "sermon" comes from a Middle English word which was derived from an Old French term, which can mean "discourse" or "to join together" and later "conversation", which could mean that early sermons were delivered in the form of question and answer, and that only later did it come to mean a monologue. In modern language, the word "sermon" can also be used pejoratively（轻蔑地、贬义地）in secular terms to describe a lengthy or tedious（乏味的）speech delivered with great passion, by any person, to an uninterested audience.

1) The Sermon on the Mount by Jesus of Nazareth

(*Jesus*, 1979)

"Blessed are you poor—for yours is the Kingdom of God. Blessed are you who hunger now—for you shall be filled. Blessed are you who weep now—for you shall laugh. Blessed are you when men hate you and reject you and insult you and say you are evil, all because of the Son of Man（人子，即耶稣基督）. Be glad when that happens and dance for joy, because a great reward is kept for you in Heaven—for their ancestors did the very same things to the Prophets（预言者）.

How terrible for you who are rich now—you have had your easy life. How terrible for you who laugh now—for you shall mourn and weep. How terrible when all men speak well of you—for their ancestors said the very same things about the false prophets. But I tell you who hear me: love your enemies. Do good to those who hate you. Bless those who curse you. Pray for those who mistreat you. If anyone strikes you on the one cheek, let him hit the other one also. And if someone takes away your coat, let him have your shirt as well. Give to everyone who begs from you. And if someone takes what is yours, do not ask for it back again. Do for others only what you would have others do for you.

If you love only the people who love you, why should you receive a blessing—for even sinners love those who love them. And if you do good to those who do good to you, why should you receive a blessing—even sinners do that.

No, love your enemies and do good to them. And lend expecting nothing back. And then you will have a great reward—for you will be sons of the Most High God. For He is good to the ungrateful and to the wicked(邪恶的).

Be merciful, just as your Father is merciful. Judge not and you will not be judged. Condemn not and you will not be condemned. Forgive and you will be forgiven. Give and it will be given to you—for the measure you give will be the measure you get back. One blind man cannot lead another. If he does, they will both fall into a ditch."

This is the most noted sermon in Christianity, the Sermon on the Mount by Jesus of Nazareth, expanding the meaning of "eight blessings".

2) A church minister giving a sermon

(*Daddy's Little Girls*, 2007)

"*So my assignment today is to encourage your faith by using what Paul*(保罗:耶稣门徒之一) *said. He said,* "*And let us not grow weary*(厌倦)*in well doing.*" *He said,* "*For in due season you shall reap*(收获), *if you faint not.*" *Now what I'm trying to tell you is that God is faithful. And in his faithfulness, he reminds us that in doing good, you shall get weary. There is no sin in getting weary. The sin is giving up, because I'm here to announce to you, you're so close to your due season, you're about to taste it. There's about to be a manifestation*(彰显)*of God in your life. And it's not time to throw in the towel*(放弃)*. It's time to lift up your head because something's about to happen in your life and God's gonna ensure it. The evidence that you're so close to your breakthrough, the evidence that you're so close to your payday and your reward for walking righteous, is that you will feel like... You better hear this. I'm telling something, you will feel like you're about to faint. And when you feel like you're about to faint, don't faint, because that says I'm right there next to my miracle. I'm right there, right at the door of my due season. I'm talking to those that walked into this church today with their head kind of hung down*(垂头丧气), *and just about to give up and about to lose your faith. I'm encouraging you, keep the faith, stay right there, don't faint, hold on. God is about to* bring your due season. And you need to give him praise, you need to bless his name, you need to tell him, "I'm still holding on." God bless you. God bless you. And God bless you."

In this speech, by borrowing Paul's words, the speaker asks people not to give up in doing good even in distress and in despair, for God will reward you in harvest season.

3) A priest's sermon about faith

(*Have a Little Faith*, 2011)

"A man seeks employment on a farm and he hands this letter of recommendation to his employer. The letter reads simply, 'He sleeps in a storm.' Desperate(极度渴望的) for help, the owner hires the man. Several weeks pass and one night, a powerful storm rips(撕扯)through the valley. The howling(嚎叫)wind awakens the owner who calls for his new hired hand, but the man is sleeping soundly(睡得正甜). So the owner leaps out of bed and races to the barn, and sees to his amazement that the animals are secure, the bails(一捆捆)of wheat are bound(捆好)and wrapped, the silo doors are latched(拴好), and the grain is dry. Ah, now he understands, 'He sleeps in a storm.' My friends, if we tend to the things that are important in life, if we arrived with those we love, and behave in line with(符合)our faith, we will never wallow(打滚,沉溺于)in the agony(痛苦)of 'I should have', 'I could have'. No. We could sleep in a storm."

Using an analogy, the priest tells a story to inspire people to have faith, to "sleep in a storm". The story sounds a little flat, but the speaker achieves the effect by telling the story in a sincere and natural way.

9.15 Farewell

In a send-off or farewell party or dinner, the main character in the event is usually expected to give a speech. The theme of the speech is mainly expressing good wishes or gratitude, resolution or hope, amidst a little emotional recalling of past events and reluctant parting.

1) A Chinese woman leaving America for China speaking to her children and friends in the farewell party

(*Dim Sum Funeral*, 2008)

"*Thank you everyone, for coming. For those who came to the house and gave money, Victoria will make sure that you get it all back, but I will keep the dress. <u>This is such a beautiful send-off</u>. You have made this old lady very, very happy. Facing death changes everything, so dragon lady no more. Life is so fragile（脆弱的）. We must cherish each day and all those who have a place in our hearts. Next week, I will leave for China with Mr. Chow Lin. I will die where I was born. But before I do, I hope to take care of some unfinished business. If there is any advice I can give, it is: don't leave things till it's too late. Well, let's dance.*"

The terminally ill old lady is leaving for her motherland to die there, but before she goes, she has a lot to say with only a few words: thanking the guests, giving advice and sharing her future plan.

2) A British official giving a speech on his Chinese colleague's transfer to the United States

(*Rush Hour*, 1998)

"*Forgive me, Consul Han, but I believe we can ill afford*（不能承受）*to lose man of your high character*（德高望重）. *And speaking as a friend, who's fought side by side with you for 15 years, I'll sorely*（痛心地）*miss your unshakable support you've given to Royal Hong Kong police. So, on behalf of all Brits*（英国人）, *who have ever carried the*

Speaking on Special Occasions 特殊场合的演讲

shield(警徽)*of Hong Kong, we shall miss you and wish you nothing but happiness as you take up your new post in the United States. Ladies and gentlemen, Consul Han!*"

The speaker conveys two ideas in his speech, regretting his leaving as an old friend and expressing good wishes.

 Class Speech

A teacher is always giving public speeches in class, despite how the students respond to them. Mostly, the purpose for the speeches is to inform on a certain topic, a term or theory. So the methods are usually explaining, describing and illustrating, except that sometimes, the teacher inspires and motivates the students. On some occasions, the students are also public speakers in a class presentation.

Warren Buffet used to attend Dale Carnegie's public speaking coaching classes, and he once said that improving one's communicative ability can promote his personal value in the future by 50%. In school education, speaking skills are not only necessary for academic purpose, but also for social activities. As part of comprehensive qualities, a student who can present himself/herself in front of his/her classmates usually engages in informative and persuasive purposes. A teacher in class gives more informative speeches than persuasive ones, for the main task in class is to expound some theories, concepts and ideas. In rare cases, a teacher will impose his own opinion on his students, for the fact that a teacher is mainly the guide and organizer in the class.

1) A teacher speaking to the students in the first class

(*Dead Poets Society*, 1989)

"'*O Captain, my Captain.*' *Who knows where that comes from? Anybody? Not a clue? It's from a poem by Walt Whitman*(美国诗人惠特曼)*about Mr. Abraham Lincoln. Now in this class you can either call me Mr. Keating, or, if you're slightly more daring* (大胆的), '*O Captain, my Captain.*' *Now let me dispel*(祛除)*a few rumors so they don't fester*(溃烂)*into facts. Yes, I, too, attended Hell-ton*(学校的名字本来是Welton,

说话者故意篡改) and survived. And, no, at that time, I was not the mental giant you see before you. I was the intellectual equivalent of a 98-pound weakling(弱者). I would go to the beach, and people would kick copies of Byron in my face. Now... Mr. Pitts? That's a rather unfortunate name. Mr. Pitts, where are you? Mr. Pitts, would you open your hymnal(诗集) to page 542, read the first stanza of the poem you find there, 'To the Virgins, to Make Much of Time'(英国诗人赫伯特的诗歌《规劝少女们珍惜时光》)? Yes, that's the one. Somewhat appropriate, isn't it?

(Pitts recites: 'Gather ye (你) rosebuds while ye may, /Old time is still a-flying;/ And this same flower that smiles today / To-morrow will be dying.')

Thank you, Mr. Pitts. 'Gather ye rosebuds while ye may.' The Latin term for that sentiment(情感) is 'Carpe diem'. Who knows what that means?

('Carpe diem.' That's 'Seize the day'.)

Very good, Mr....

(The student replies: Meeks.)

Meeks. Another unusual name. Seize the day. 'Gather ye rosebuds while ye may.' Why does the writer use these lines?

(A student answers: Because he's in a hurry.)

No! Ding! Thank you for playing anyway. Because we are food for worms, lads(小伙子们). Because, believe it or not, each and every one of us in this room is one day going to stop breathing, turn cold and die. I would like you to step forward over here... peruse(细看) some of the faces from the past. You've walked past them many times. I don't think you've really looked at them. They are not that different from you, are they? Same haircuts. Full of hormones(荷尔蒙), just like you. Invincible(无所不能), just like you feel. That world is their oyster(牡蛎). They believe they're destined for great things, just like many of you. Their eyes are full of hope, just like you. Did they wait until it was too late to make from their lives even one iota(微小) of what they were capable? Because, you see, gentlemen, these boys are now fertilizing(施肥) daffodils(水仙花). But if you listen real close, you can hear them whisper their legacy to you. Go on, lean in. Listen. Do you hear it? Carpe. Hear it? Carpe. Carpe diem. Seize the day, boys. Make your lives extraordinary."

On the first day of class, the teacher takes the students out in the hall to inspire them by asking them a series of questions, citing at the same time, poetry by Walt Whitman and George Herbert. To the students, this way of launching the first class is unique, surprising and full of fun.

2) A professor introducing to the students the course of Applied Electrical Engineering

(*Flash of Genius*, 2008)

"Good morning, everybody, welcome you all to the first day of the quarter for Applied Electrical Engineering. My name is Dr. Robert Kearns. I'd like to start by talking to you about ethics(伦理道德). I can't think of a job or a career where the understanding of ethics is more important than engineering. Who designed the artificial aortic heart valve(人工主动脉瓣膜)? An engineer did that. Who designed the gas chambers(毒气室)at Auschwitz(奥斯威辛集中营)? An engineer did that, too. One man was responsible for helping save tens of thousands of lives, another man helped kill millions. Now I don't know what any of you end up doing in your lives, but I can guarantee you that there will come a day where you have a decision to make. And it won't be as easy as deciding between a heart valve and a gas chamber. Everything we do in this classroom ultimately(最终) comes back to that notion(观念). All right? Grades count, too (分数当然也重要)."(*Students laugh*)

The teacher introduces the course by asking a question, making them aware of the importance of this course to their future career.

3) A student in class speaking on the topic of success

(*Fame*, 2009)

"There are some things success is not. It's not fame. It's not money or power. Success is waking up in the morning, so excited about what you have to do that you literally(几乎)fly out the door. It's getting to work with people you love. Success is *connecting with the world and making people feel. It's finding a way to bind*(结合) *together people who have nothing in common but a dream. It's falling asleep at night knowing you did the best job you could. Success is joy and freedom and friendship, and success is love.*"

In this short presentation, the student shares her idea of success by giving a series of analogy of it.

9.17 Court Opening & Summation

A trial court is always a battle field between the representing counsels of two sides: the defendant and the plaintiff. In the jury system, the lawyers' chief purpose and task is not to convince the judge or the gallery, but the jury members or jurors, for they will give the final verdict of whether the defendant is guilty or not guilty. The judge only acts as the regulator and administrator of the trial session. Public speech making happens in every round of the session: opening statement, cross-examination and concluding summary. The speaker, most often, is the counsel on either side, or the defendant, or even the witness, though under the administration of the judge, there is a certain amount of constraint of freedom in speech manners and time limit. Speaking in this premise is always a good textbook for us to learn how to give a skillful persuasive speech.

1) A prosecutor's opening statement

(*Body of Evidence*, 1993)

Judge: *Are the people*(公诉方)*ready to proceed? Mr. Garry?*

Prosecutor: *Yes, your honor.*

Andrew Marsh made, what turned out to be, a fatal mistake: he fell in love. He fell in love with a ruthless(残忍的), *calculating*(诡计多端的)*woman who went after an elderly man with a bad heart and a big bank account. You all can see the defendant Rebecca Carlson. But as this trial proceeds, you will see she is not only the defendant, she is the murder weapon herself. If I hit you and you die, I am the cause of your death, but can I be called a weapon? The answer is yes. And what a deadly weapon Rebecca Carlson has made of it? The state（公诉方）will prove that she seduced Andrew Marsh and manipulated（操纵）his affections until he rewrote his will（修改遗嘱）, leaving her 8 million dollars, that she insisted on increasingly strangling（窒息）sex, knowing he had severe heart condition. And when that didn't work faster enough for her, she secretly doped him with cocaine（可卡因）. His heart couldn't take the combination（并发作用）, and she got what she wanted.*

She is a beautiful woman, but when this trial is over, you will see her no differently than a gun or a knife or any other instrument used as a weapon. She is a killer, and the worst kind, a killer who disguised（伪装）herself as a loving partner.

The prosecutor opens his speech with a metaphor comparing the accused as a murder weapon, recounting the process of the premeditative murder, and then ends with the weapon metaphor. The speech finishes where it begins, with a well-knit structure, concise but precise language, powerful and sonorous words, a stern and decided face.

2) The defending counsel's opening statement

(*Body of Evidence*, 1993)

"Ladies and gentlemen, you were told in jury selection, that the testimony（证词）in this trial will be sexually explicit（性露骨的）. And you may find it offensive（情趣低下的）. You may even be disgusted by what you hear. But I want you to remember that Rebecca Carlson is not on trial for her sexual tastes, she's been tried for murder, and the charge of her with murder is ludicrous（荒唐的）. The state would like you to believe that she somehow fornicated（私通）Andrew Marsh to death. But the state's case is built on fantasy, not fact. And the facts, as they are, are entirely circumstantial（没有确凿证据的）. It's not a crime to be a beautiful woman; it's not a crime to fall in love with an old man. This case should have never come to trial. But since it has, I know you'll listen to the testimony objectively. And when you hear the evidence objectively, you will acquit（无罪释放）Rebecca Carlson, of the charges against her."

Quite different from the prosecutor, the defending counsel opens his speech in a measured and calm way, arguing about the point of the case, laying for the defending ground of the later trial.

9.18 Wedding Hosting

The Bible dictates that "a man will leave his father and mother and be united to his wife, and the two will become one flesh." Characterized with religious colors, wedding ceremonies are based on reference to God, and are frequently embodied into other church ceremonies such as Mass. In the Roman Catholic Church "Holy Matrimony" is considered to be one of the seven sacraments(圣礼), in this case, one that the spouses bestow upon each other in front of a priest and members of the community as witnesses. As all sacraments, it is seen as having been instituted by Jesus himself. In the Eastern Orthodox Church, it is one of the mysteries, and is seen as an ordination and martyrdom.

Most Christian churches give some form of blessing to a marriage; the wedding ceremony typically includes some sort of pledge by the community to support the couple's relationship. A church wedding is a ceremony presided over by a Christian priest or pastor, whose opening speech is worthy of our attention. And he will end the ceremony by pronouncing in this way: By the power(by virtue of the authority) vested in me by the laws of the state of Illinois, now I pronounce you man and wife; (speaking to the bridegroom) you may kiss the bride now.

In the vow-exchange section, there are three prevailing versions:

(1) I, (name of the bride/groom), take you (name of the bride /groom), to be my lawfully wedded husband/wife, to have and to hold from this day forward, for better or for worse, for richer, or poorer, in sickness and in health, to love and to cherish, from this day forward until death do us part(分离).

(2) I, (name), take you (name), to be my lawfully wedded husband/wife, my constant(恒久的) friend, my faithful partner and my love from this day forward. In the presence(见证,在场) of God, our family and friends, I offer you my solemn(神圣的) vow to be your faithful partner in sickness and in health, in good times and in bad, and in joy as well as in sorrow. I promise to love you unconditionally, to support you in your goals, to honor and respect you, to laugh with you and cry with you, and to cherish you for as long as we both shall live.

(3) I, (name), take you (name), to be my husband/wife, my partner in life and my one true love. I will cherish our union(结合) and love you more each day than I did the day before. I will trust you and respect you, laugh with you and cry with you, loving you faithfully through good times and bad, regardless of the obstacles(阻碍) we may face together. I give you my hand, my heart, and my love, from this day forward for as long as

we both shall live.

1) A priest presiding Angus and Nora's wedding

(*Four Weddings and a Funeral*, 1994)

"Dear friends, what a joy it is to welcome you to our church on this wonderful day for Angus and Nora. Before we start the service, let us all join together in the first hymn(赞美诗). Dearly beloved, we are gathered together here in the sight of(见证) God and in the face of this congregation(教友) to join together this man and this woman in holy matrimony, which is an honorable estate, instituted(创立) in the time of man's innocence(混沌初期), therefore, if any man can show any just cause(正当理由) or impediment(阻碍) why they not be lawfully joined together, let him speak now, or forever hold his peace(保持缄默). Do you promise to love her, comfort her, honor and keep her in sickness or in health, and forsaking(不顾) all others, keep thee only onto her for as long as you both shall live?" (Bridegroom and bride: I do.) (Repeating after the priest: To love and to cherish, till death us do part. And thereto(因此) I pledge thee my troth(誓言): with this ring, I thee wed(娶); with my body, I thee worship; and with my all worldly goods(世俗的财产), I thee endow(赠予).)

The typical Christian part of the ceremony features a chorus, a hymn to God for his blessing and grace, and then followed by the wedding proceedings.

2) A priest hosting the wedding of Charles and Lora

(*Four Weddings and a Funeral*, 1994)

"*Dearly beloved, we are gathered together here in sight of God and in the face of this congregation, to join this man and this woman in holy matrimony, which is an honorable estate, instituted of God in the time of man's innocence, signifying onto us this mystic reunion, that is betwixt*（在……之间）*Christ and His church, and therefore, is not by any to be enterprised*（买卖）*, nor taken in hand unadvisedly, lightly*（轻浮地）*, or wantonly*（草率的）*, but reverently*（崇敬地）*, discreetly*（谨慎地）*, and advisedly, soberly*（清醒地）*, and in the fear of God, therefore, if any man can show any just cause why they may not lawfully be joined together, let him speak now, or else, hereafter, forever hold his peace.*"

Different from the last one, this speech focuses on the priest's exhorting, i.e. advising the bride to be sincere and serious in marriage.

In this chapter we have been led through 18 occasions set in typical English cultural background where one could be asked or expected to give a speech as a guest or member of a social group almost anytime during the course of the event. When coming to a close of the chapter, apart from language learning, we have come to understand:

Firstly, that many of these speeches can be spontaneous and unexpected, hence, an amount of colloquialism can be expected. That is understandable and forgivable, as daily conversation and public speaking share some common ground as well as some distinguished differences as is somewhat thoroughly discussed in Chapter 4.

Secondly, that some of these occasions are so unique in English culture, such as sermons, eulogies, weddings and court trials, that understanding these speeches and learning how to prepare one like that goes along with a little reserve of English culture. And vise versa, some cultural knowledge can help us go a long way in understanding these speeches much better.

Thirdly, that Western humor can be found almost everywhere in these speeches as we appreciate them, even in a formal and serious setting. Whereas when humor is too much of a demand for both understanding and using it for a non-native speaker, it is essential for us to get the importance of using humor in a speech. Please find more in Chapter 7 about the charm of humor in speech.

Last but not least, that if we can appreciate and learn how to use some rhetorical devices in speeches in these examples, we deserve to be congratulated, for even a single flash of such use of language can go so far in a speech that we can be highly regarded and appreciated by the audience as a speaker, not just understanding but also creating the beauty of language, such as puns, similes, metaphors, parallel structures and rhetorical questions, and so on and so forth. To find more, please refer to Chapter 4.

Topics for One-Minute Speech Practices

1. How does the fact that condoms are freely distributed on campus relate to moral decay?

2. Should scientists be celebrities?

3. How old would you plan to get married and if you decide to delay your marriage, what would be your advantage?

4. If you are a parent, what values will you teach your child to cherish?

5. Would you still live under your parents' roof when you graduate from college?

6. Can a man and a woman be close friends?

7. How do you comment on celibacy?

8. What do you think of young people living together without getting married?

9. What do you think of college students getting married on campus?

10. How do you look at your family's legacy, and what kind of legacy would you leave to your offspring?

Chapter 10

English Speaking Competitions
英语演讲比赛

Great speakers are not born; they are trained. —Dale Carnegie
伟大的演说家不是天生的,而是训练出来的。□ 戴尔・卡耐基

Success is won by three things: first, effort; second, more effort; third, still more effort. —Thomas Hardy
获得成功的三要素:首先是努力,其次还是努力,第三仍然是努力。□ 托马斯・哈代

●本章要点●

- 介绍国内两大英语演讲比赛的异同点
- 演讲的评价标准
- 比赛中的定题演讲
- 比赛中的即兴演讲
- 比赛中的答问环节
- 比赛中的辩论环节

 10.1 English Speech Evaluation

Increasing globalization and international exchanges has propelled China into a boom of English learning, especially of oral English learning and practicing, and to cater to that need, the most influential media groups in China, e. g. the Foreign Language Teaching and Research Press, CCTV, and *China Daily* etc. have endeavored to organize and sponsor competitions of various forms and levels, producing annually excellent speakers who enjoy the glamour of being broadcast nationwide or sent abroad to participate in speaking competitions, not to mention the prestige of better academic and employment opportunities in their futures. More importantly, these speaking competitions have opened our eyes, stirred our enthusiasm in studying English and provided us great opportunities to learn

English beyond our classroom, campus and involve us on a global stage presenting the image of the nation. Such noted names who rose from these competitions as shining stars as *Liu Xin*, *Rui Chenggang* in the past years, are still the well-reputed anchor and anchoress on CCTV.

10.1.1 Two most prominent public speaking competitions in China

There are two most influential and authoritative public speaking competitions in China: the 21st Century Cup and the CCTV Cup (now it is named "FLTRP Cup English Speaking Contest", a combined event of the former CCTV Cup English Speaking Contest and the CCTV Outlook English Competition since 2010). From their ways of organization and format in recent years, they have their common ground and their differences between them.

1) The common ground

☆ Both are organized and sponsored by the largest media and publishing groups in China, enjoying the greatest prestige and influence.

☆ Both select their candidates from the grass-root level and enjoy full-scale media coverage around China.

☆ Both sponsor the winners and their coaches on study tours abroad. 21st Century Cup awards the winners study tours to England, Australia and China's Hong Kong and Macau; the Speaker with the best potential Award will be sent to England participating the international English speaking competition on behalf of China, and the best impromptu speaker will be granted the opportunity for a short-term internship in BBC in England; FLTRP Cup offers similar prizes, including the English Speaking Union Culture Seminar; Oxford International Relations Seminar, Australasian Intervarsity Debating Championship; All-Asian Intervarsity Debating Championship; and the coaches are also awarded with overseas study tours and seminars.

2) The differences

☆ Organizer and Sponsor: 21st Century Cup (created in 1996) is sponsored by China's largest English newspaper syndication China Daily, and organized by 21st Century newspaper. FLTRP Cup (created in 2002) is organized by CCTV and cosponsored by Foreign Language Teaching and Research Press.

☆ Qualified aspiring candidates: 21st Century Cup recruits candidates from all the current college students around China; FLTRP Cup targets all the current registered students in colleges and universities, including postgraduates but excluding on-the-job postgraduates and those students who entered the finals in the past competitions.

☆ Formats and stages: FLTRP Cup semi finalists and finalists are selected through preliminary and second round elimination in each province or area and then they go to the semi-final and final in Beijing. 21st Century Cup finalists are the winners from 4 areas, namely Southeast China, West China, North China and Central China, and the location of the final competition rotates in a different city each time. And meanwhile, the whole process is accompanied with the English speech writing competition.

☆ Content of the competitions. Besides the common prepared speech, the impromptu speech and Q&A session shared by both of them, the 21st Century Cup only adheres to the traditional three parts: prepared speech, unprepared speech and Q&A session. FLTRP Cup examines the speakers' comprehensive knowledge in the semi-final round by asking the contestants questions, and also the their debating ability in the final round. In the semi-final, the procedures, time limit and points are as follows.

Part Ⅰ: Prepared Speech, 3 minutes, 30 points

Part Ⅱ: Impromptu Speech, 3 minutes (the topic will be given 15 minutes prior to the contestant's performance), 40 points

Part Ⅲ: Q&A Session, 2 minutes (two questions based on the contestant's prepared and impromptu speeches), 30 points

Part Ⅳ: Quiz, 5 seconds for each question (four knowledge-based questions), 0.20 points

In the final:

Part Ⅰ: Prepared Speech, 2 minutes, 15%

Part Ⅱ: Q&A Session, 2 minutes, 15%

Part Ⅲ: Impromptu Speech, 1 minute, 30%

Part Ⅳ: Debating, 3 minutes, 40%

☆ The criteria of evaluation are different.

The criteria of evaluation for the 21st Century Cup final are the following:

Prepared Speech: 30%

Impromptu Speech: 40%

Question and Answer: 30%

The specific rules are:

Part Ⅰ Prepared speech (60%)

1. Language (20%)

2. Content (20%)

3. Impression (20%)

Part Ⅱ Q&A (40%)

1. Understanding the question (10%)

2. Response (10%)

3. Fluency and accuracy (10%)

4. Creativity (10%)

The evaluating criteria and principles for the CCTV Cup final are the following:

	Prepared Speech (15%)	Q&A (15%)	Speaking Impromptu (30%)	Debating (40%)	Total (100%)
Content	5%	5%	10%	10%	
Language	5%	5%	10%	15%	100%
Technique	5%	5%	10%	15%	

To be more specific, the rules and principles of evaluating in the prepared speech round are:

1. Impact (the contestant's ability to hold the audience's attention)
2. Technique
3. General level of English

In the question and answer round:

1. Confidence (in using English)
2. Fluency (in using vocabulary, grammar and idiom)
3. Effectiveness (in addressing issues)

In the impromptu speech round:

1. Conviction (in presenting their arguments)
2. Variety (of vocabulary and idioms)
3. Overall Impression

In the debating round:

1. Substance
2. Style
3. Command of English under pressure
4. Empathy (quickness, humor and persuasiveness)

From the comparison and contrast above, we find the two biggest English speaking competitions not only share common ground but also strike differences. Despite the differences, they both aim to explore the candidates' language proficiency, comprehensive quality and spiritual outlook of the young people in modern China, as well as their keen and global perception of the issues and conflicts between modernity and traditions, between social values & obligations and personal pursuits, between personal development and moral integrity under a greater backdrop of social upheaval in China and the ever-changing world. They both are the front-runners in firing up the passion amongst the Chinese people especially the younger ones in pursuing English study with an international view. With their flourishing campaigns, more and more English speaking competitions of various scales and levels are being staged all over China, in schools, communities as well as business cultures.

10.1.2 Judgment of a speech in a speaking competition

From the two sets of criteria applied in the two most prestigious English competitions in China, we now formulate the basic requirements of a successful speech in a competition in the perspective of content, artistic standard, language and ethic.

1) Content judgment

The content and the viewpoints are the essence of a speech. They are embodied in the following 5 areas:

a. A clear message and purpose

One pitfall for many students in a competition is the tendency to say as much as possible in developing a speech, which is quite wrong. Keep focusing on one single idea, especially in a short speech. A list of undeveloped ideas, whatever grandeur they may sound like, is useless.

b. A unique perspective and viewpoint

The top standard is basically about what to say and from what angle to say it. No matter how common a topic is, a fresh cutting point will always attract attention. For example, on the topic "the greatest invention in my eyes", many people would just talk about such "great" inventions as internet, music, compass, printing, TV, or even i-phone. But a student speaker pops up with "eyeglasses" in his speech in a FLTRP Cup competition:

"In the past few days, I was troubled by a really controversial topic: What is the greatest invention? I did a little survey, and was dazzled by many brilliant ideas such as wheels, paper, clock, language, agriculture, penicillin, and so on. All of them are so great that I can't stop admiring the power of men's innovation. However, I am still quite uncertain what the greatest invention in my eyes.

Then this happened. I woke up late this Friday morning and what's wrong? I couldn't find my glasses! How could I live without them? Eyeglasses are always a part of me: they are the very first thing I put up when I wake up in the morning and the last thing I take off before I go to sleep. I was so terrified at the thought of walking outside of my dorm, bare-eyed. And suddenly, flick. The sparkle came out and I found my answer. The greatest invention in my eyes is the eyeglasses."

No matter how good our English is, if we talk about those great inventions without any original meaning and angle, the speech won't stand out.

c. An insightful view at the issue

Many speakers tend to stay superficially on the surface of the issue and can't go any deeper. A mindful and thoughtful speaker will dig deeper into the issue that we take only for granted. The following is one example:

"Absence of identity is dangerous. Without proper identification in cyber space, we are no longer held responsible for what we have done. A recent survey conducted by China Southwest Normal University shows that 30% of Internet users in the school have aggressively offended other users in BBS; 405 have spread fraud information. And this worsens the lack of trust in cyberspace.

An alarming prospect looms large: when we become obsessed with our online identities, life will eventually be brought to a halt because we tend to forget our real life identities and responsibilities: forgetting their identities, students may not study but devote themselves to online games. Employees may not work but chat the days away. Organizations may not function but set foot on online deceptive transactions.

These situations, if not dealt with properly and will finally throw our society into chaos.

So ladies and gentlemen, you may forget your usernames, but please don't forget your identities. Open your eyes and waken your minds, it is the real world we are living in."

When talking about identity online, the speaker's thoughts do not linger on the seemingly important aspect: consequences, but more serious problem: our responsibility.

d. Relevant, credible and sufficient supporting material

Without supporting materials, our empty reasoning is unconvincing. Using examples, statistics, and testimony can help us reason.

2) Artistic judgment

a. A clear-cut structure

All parts or elements of the speech constitute an organic and harmonious wholeness, and there is special and significant stress on an important idea. The clear structure is like a map so that the audience can follow our route. Usually, the structure requires an introduction, a body and a conclusion. The opening part is the first impression presented to the audience, so it's crucial that the introduction is interesting and appealing; and the body is the most important part, which must be logically and clearly organized to be convincing; and then the conclusion reinforces our topic with power and determination.

b. A clear logical relation

Use good transitions and signposts to ensure a logical flow of words and ideas, such as firstly, secondly, another point, etc.

c. Good vocal presentation

Use natural and effective verbal utterances in pronunciation, articulation, volume, pitch/intonation, tone, rate, pauses, and variety during the delivery.

d. Use natural and effective body language

A good command of facial expressions, eye contact, gestures, and postures is very important.

e. A little humor

A proper, relevant and light-hearted humor will work magic in breaking the ice, livening up the atmosphere, and shortening the gap between the audience and the speaker.

3) Language judgment

a. Correctness, idiomaticity, fluency and appropriateness

b. Clear pronunciation and fine intonation

4) Ethical judgment

Thousands of years ago, the Roman scholar Quintilian said that the ideal of commendable speechmaking is the good person speaking well. He tells us that all public speakers should be truthful and devoted to the common good of society, spreading the right values with a good conscience and sense of right and wrong. For an ethical public speaker, we must observe the following points:

a. Don't waste our audience's time. Be fully prepared for the speech.

b. Be honest in what we have to say.

c. Avoid prejudice, profanity, sexism, ageism and racism. Avoid name-calling and other forms of abusive language.

d. Avoid plagiarism. Identify the sources; give credit to the sources we refer to in our speech.

Topic-Assigned Speech

Usually designated as the first session in a competition, the topic-assigned speech confines the contestants to a topic limit as well as a time limit. It is a most popular and indispensible part in an English speaking competition throughout China, in schools, communities or corporate cultures. Besides the common features and requirements of a good prepared speech, a topic-assigned speech in a speaking competition has other features of its own as follows.

1) Prepare fully

A contestant has sufficient amount of time to prepare for a topic-designated speech, including doing research, collecting data, writing and proof-reading the manuscript, memorizing and rehearsing. Meanwhile, there is lots of opportunity to seek for help from the candidate's teacher, advisor or friends.

2) Don't just speak from memory

Giving a speech from memory of a prepared manuscript can be risky if a speaker doesn't know how to control the rate, pause and intonation, as well as a good eye-contact with the audience. Otherwise, merely blurting out from our memory gives away our poor management of speaking skills.

3) Preparing the questions in advance

The follow-up questions from the judges are usually related to the prepared speech, so it may be wise for the candidate to prepare for the potential questions in advance which might pop up during the competition. But more importantly, the preparation process is good for training the speaker's ability to use the language and think in the language.

4) Look at all the audiences

In a competition, the contestant is not only talking to the audiences, but also the judges. So he/she should move his/her eyes in a way he is talking to everyone among the audience, making even the audience sitting farthest away in the back sense that we're talking to him/her.

5) Prepare for the formal occasion

The occasion is usually more formal than those speeches that happen in daily life. So a formal dress code is required. For a male speaker, it's the traditional three pieces: shirt-tie-suit; for the female speaker, the formal outfits.

6) The Time Limit

The time limit can be tricky, but with good rehearsal, it is controllable.

10.3 Unprepared Speech

Speaking impromptu, as the most baffling and also scary task in day-to-day public speaking as well as in a speaking competition, gives the speaker no time or little time to prepare, practice and polish the speech. In a speaking competition, an impromptu speech tests the speaker's real language competency and all-round qualities. It usually takes up 1—3 minutes of a speaker's whole stage time, and the scores take up about 30%—40% of the total. Therefore, this section really counts if a speaker wants to stand out.

10.3.1 What does this part tell about a speaker?

This session is a test of a speaker's comprehensive qualities, i.e. thinking, reasoning and language using. Without any former preparation, a speaker must have relative ability to analyze the topic in depth and width; organize the speech in good reasoning with unity and coherence, and deliver it with fluency and accuracy of the language.

10.3.2 How to tackle nervousness

The mere thought of standing and speaking in front of a large audience is terrifying enough for many people, let alone giving an unprepared speech. Those excellent speakers all have the same qualities, which can be summed up in the following:
☆ Know that being nervous is normal. There is nothing to be ashamed about it.
☆ Don't distract ourselves by worrying about our appearance. Being stressed over whether the tie is straight or not, the hair is tidy or not, the clothes are neat or not will only panic us even more.

☆ Don't start our speech too quickly. Take our time to think. Start speaking and thinking at the same time, for it is unlikely that we will know nothing at all about the topic.

☆ Look at our audience and the judges. Don't forget eye-contact with them prior to and in the course of our speaking.

10.3.3 What are the strategies?

Speaking impromptu is baffling enough for a native speaker, let alone a nonnative one. The good speakers have provided us some good experience as follows on how to deliver a good impromptu speech.

1) Be prepared

It's not true to say that we can't prepare for an impromptu speech. In a long term view, we must be a proactive thinker, a keen observer and a critical thinker, who concern themselves with the things, issues, phenomena, current affairs that are happening in everyday life. Only when we have a large storage of the knowledge and thoughts on a vast array of issues up our sleeve, can we dispatch them anytime and anywhere we want.

2) Brain storming

In a short term view, in preparing for the on-the-spot, last-minute speech, having a couple of strategies on hand will always pay off. About a certain issue, there are usually some different strategies to help us deal with.

a. We can think of some key words and then talk about each of them in turn;

b. We can compare two views/sides by analyzing the similarities and differences;

c. We can spot the problem and then provide the solutions;

d. We can summarize the pros and cons of an issue and then offer our opinion, and so on.

3) Understand the theme

If the impromptu speech title is a question, don't forget to answer it first. Don't spend a large portion of the time beating around the bush and then end our speech without a specific answer which states our stance on the issue. This is a big no-no to Chinese contestants for the fact that they are deeply influenced by this habitual way of thinking.

If the title is a statement, and needs our attitude of agreeing or not agreeing, we also need to give a precise reply. That is to say: open our speech by stating our opinion clearly. For example in one competition, a title is "if you were the first Chinese astronaut to go to the moon, and you could leave three objects, what would they be?"

We may start our speech by saying, "If I were the first Chinese astronaut to go to the moon, I would take with me the following three items…" or we may start with a story or an anecdote. For example, when one contestant was asked to talk about how surveillance invades our privacy, she opened by saying, "This topic reminds me of a news report that I read recently…"

Chapter 10 English Speaking Competitions 英语演讲比赛

4) Give a good introduction

If possible, grab the audience's attention immediately at the opening, either our remark is interesting, surprising or humorous. For example, a speaker begins his impromptu speech, "I guess most of you have seen the movie Terminator. I want to make a very bad prophecy that human beings will one day be terminated by our own technology."

5) Offer good support

Learn to use personal experience, examples and statistics in our major portion of our speech. Because many impromptu topics ask for a personal opinion on a certain issue, contestants should feel free to draw upon their own experiences in the speech. For example, a speaker explained that she didn't want to become famous because she was shocked and scared by attacks on her appearance and privacy when her photo or rumor was posted online.

6) Leave with a quick conclusion

Use a simple sentence to wrap everything up. For instance: "And that's all. Thank you." Or we can say, "In conclusion, I strongly believe that smoking in public places should be banned."

Remember we are thinking on our feet, so do not overstate our introduction, or the body of the speech, or the ending of the speech. Caution against running out of the time limit, balance the three parts, and limit the body development to two or three ideas. Having too many irons in the fire only confuses both the speaker and the audience.

7) Do it with passion and sincerity

One speaker talked about what he would do if his friend wanted to commit suicide: "Besides being a good counselor, I would even grab him by his ears and arms to stop him!" From here, we can see good speakers put true emotions into their answers. It shows that they believe and at the same time make the audience believe in the words that they've spoken. If a speaker just states the answer mechanically, it won't be as persuasive. Just as Goethe said, you'll never move others heart to heart, unless our speech comes from your heart.

10.3.4 Some impromptu speech titles

Prepare for them shortly and practice in front of our classmates or friends.

(1) Some people think campus love is good for their life in college, some others oppose it. What's your opinion?

(2) Some people maintain that dating on-line has enriched our life, while others are against it. What about you?

(3) If you could land on a planet which is inhabited by aliens and you could take one thing as a present to them as a good will gesture, what would you choose to take?

(4) What advice would you like to give to somebody who is addicted to the Internet?

(5) If you could know the future, what would you choose to know? And why?

(6) Some people believe that in China today women should go back home to be full-time housewives so as to give more opportunities to men. Do you agree? Why?

(7) Some people hold the view that the Earth is being harmed by human activities. Others feel that human activity makes the Earth a better place to live. What is your opinion?

(8) Is marking western holidays a sign of a modern China or of tradition sacrificed to commercial interests?

(9) University education and employment.

(10) Modern technology and our health.

The Q & A Session

The Q & A section is one of the most critical sections of the contest. It's usually where a majority of the points will come from. It tests a speaker's ability to respond, to analyze and above all, to organize language to express.

10.4.1 Prepare before the contest

There are two kinds of preparation: preparing for the topic-designated speech and preparing for the impromptu speech. As we well know, the former is much easier than the latter.

1) Preparing questions for the topic-designated speech

Try to put ourselves in the shoes of those judges and imagine what questions they would raise, and then prepare for those questions; or we can seek help from our friends or teachers who can work out some last minute questions for us to answer on the spot.

2) Preparing questions for the unprepared speech

This part will be much more baffling and complicated, for a speaker's English comprehensive ability and his/her day to day concern with the social topics will count most. As an extension of the unprepared speech, the questions will be closely connected to the unprepared speech, so doing a pre-contest overhaul of the speech and preparing the topics in different categories will make things easier.

10.4.2 Delivery on the stage

The process will be a complicated one, including listening, analyzing and speaking. So how can we do it well?

1) First and foremost, be a good listener

"The highest compliment that you can pay anyone is to listen intently to him" (Isaac

Marcosson). This remark has told us that a good speaker must first of all be a good listener, who is characterized with the following traits: he follows the question all the way attentively, and starts thinking in the course quickly, and analyzes the main point in the question and then begins organizing his response promptly. Therefore, a speaker must first learn how to be a good listener. In daily life, many of us are absent-minded listeners without enough attention, or another extreme is that we listen to the details so hard that we miss the big picture or the main idea, or jump to conclusion too early, or pay too much attention to the speaker's appearance or other distracting factors on the scene. There are some points we must be on guard against in order to listen well on the stage.

a. Don't listen too hard for the details

Focus on the main point of a question. A good listener knows how to grasp the asker's main points among or summoning all the details.

b. Learn to listen well despite the outside interruptions

There is always the possibility of disturbing factors happening in a speaking environment, such as noise, the question asker speaks too fast, or the question is too long, or he/she has an accent that is too hard for you to catch up with, and worse, we're nervous. All these factors will get in the way of our comprehension of the question. Just relax ourselves and focus.

c. It's not a shame not to have understood the question

It's all right to miss a question, but don't hesitate to say "Pardon me?" or "I beg your pardon?" or "Could you repeat that question?" There should be no need to worry that we may be laughed at by the audience or the judges for not having heard the question, for we are engaged conscientiously in a sincere process of communication and the audiences are expecting the speaker to complete the communication so they want us to succeed.

d. Don't pretend to have understood the question

It will cause a disaster to answer a question without understanding it. So in order to confirm our understanding, especially when the question is too long with many distracting details or the speaker is too fast, we can repeat in the words of the speaker or of ourselves what we have heard. This will mean a plus for us, because we have bought some time for ourselves to think of and organize our answer. Here is an example. In a speech contest, a speaker responds to the question from a judge by beginning, "Ok, thank you for your question. If I have understood your question correctly, you meant to ask me to suggest several examples that birds and human beings can co-exist peacefully together. Is that right? OK, umm... I think I have a perfect example here on my hand. And that happens on my campus..."

e. Start speaking only after the judge has finished talking

Respect the judge, and don't start to speak until he/she has finished talking. Some speakers are so anxious and eager to give an answer especially when he/she presumes he/

she has understood the question that they can't wait to start talking before the judge finishes the question. More often than not, the candidate may have just grasped part of the question, or even worse, not even close to half of it, which can cause embarrassment and backfire to the speaker himself/herself, to say nothing of the fact that it is very unwise and impolite to interrupt another speaker.

f. Try answering the question with grace and ease

Don't regard this process as a challenge from the judge, or a question-answer session only, but rather, a communication depending on cooperation on both sides' efforts. A little interaction will always do us credit, with such small talks as "um, that is really a good question." "This question is very much unexpected, and also very personal, but I don't mind sharing my views about that with all of the audiences here." Any rigid, inflexible way of dealing with questions won't go far in this session.

2) Be a good speaker

How to speak well earns the major scores, so the following points are valuable pieces of advice.

a. Answer the question directly

Don't linger on the unimportant facts or details, for you can't afford to waste the limited time you're allowed, which is usually from 30 seconds to 1 minute.

b. Answer the question by hitting the target

Some speakers stand there on the stage and start talking away but they never answer the question or even get close to it. We must show that we have heard the question, understood it and our answer is related to the question. Otherwise, it's only a showoff of good pronunciation, thus there is the so called a "snow job", meaning pretending to be doing something only to mislead and deceive others. It is a death sentence to our speech especially if the judge is a foreigner, for they know the difference, of which we can be sure.

c. Don't engage in empty talk

Some speakers play the flattering games of politicians and use abstract and grandiose language by showing off their proficient English, but such a speech is worthless if there's not a meaning in it. So remember that showing off our flowery language doesn't count.

d. Answer the question within the time limit

If we understand the rules clearly, we will know that there is usually more than one question. And the time limit is so strict that we may be stopped in the middle of talking. If we stall too much time on the first answer, then we are stealing the time from our second answer. Using quotes or statistics or examples may help us convince the audience and judges, but remember we can't spend too much time using them. A direct answer would be just fine if we can organize our thoughts and language well. For example, Question: "*Sex education is not well-established in China. Do you think it is the parents' problem or* the children's?" Answer: "Firstly, parents should be open and willing to share their experience, more like a friend. Secondly, children should realize that asking questions about sex is not something to be ashamed of. Thank you!" From this way of answering by a contestant, we see that a good response doesn't need to be exhaustingly elaborate or extended. A crispy, prompt and determined answer works just fine.

e. Don't forget the eye contact with our audience

Remember that we're not speaking to the judge alone. Many speakers fix their eyes on the judges (or the only judge who presented the question), so they forget eye contact with the audience and other judges at the same time. Keep in mind that the room is full of other people, and they are also part of our communication process.

f. Keep up with our composure when answering questions

When answering the question, some speakers will find themselves, of course unconsciously, hard to stay the way they were when delivering the speech. It's not uncommon to see some of them standing awkwardly, leaning on the desk, tilting head so hard to one side, bending the body, resting the whole body weight on the lectern, fixing the eyes only on one judge, etc. this happens usually because the contestant is nervous about the possibility that he/she can't understand the question, or simply just that he/she is too eager to resume the proper manners and composure.

g. Try adding some ingredient of humor

A little good humor will light up the whole section. In one speaking competition, the judge asked a question, "*How would you persuade your father to give up driving his car for the sake of environment protection?*" and the speaker answered, "*My dad is actually in the audience. Hey dad, it's good to take a walk, and plus you could lose some weight*". We can imagine, with the audiences bursting into light-hearted chuckle, how delighted the speaker has made the whole room feel.

10.5 Debating

10.5.1 The nature of the activity

Interesting but challenging as it may be, debating enables us to develop a keener insight into the social issues, strengthen our ability to think critically, analyze discreetly, respond swiftly, and organizing and expressing our ideas logically. It also challenges our open-mindedness and willingness to accept new ideas.

10.5.2 The guidelines for debating

No matter if it's debating an independent competition, or as part of a speaking competition, the topics are always split into opposite sides for two teams to find each other's loophole and rebut it. The process stresses more on the adequacy and appropriateness of the evidence, the teamwork among the debaters, and the reasoning methods.

1) Note the difference between argument and quarrel

We quarrel with somebody because we feel threatened or wronged and then get emotional or even angry, but we argue because of disagreement on some issue, then we need to rectify our ways of communicating or persuading, or change our views about life, or world views and values. This process requires us to have an open mind, an honest attitude, but not to be hostile to the opposite side and take on them as deadly enemies.

2) Use a solid reasoning mechanism and avoid fallacies

To build a strong argument, we need to use strong evidence to support our claims, and resort to clear and effective reasoning method so as to tie the evidence to support our propositions. By taking these steps, we make our argument persuasive. The most common types of reasoning are: inductive, deductive, analogical and causal. In most cases, we need more than one type to convince others.

a. Inductive reasoning

Reasoning that arrives at a general conclusion from specific instances or examples is known as inductive reasoning. For example, when President Franklin Roosevelt gave a national speech after the Japanese air force launched a surprise attack on the ships in Hawaii:

Yesterday, the Japanese government also launched an attack against Malaya.

Last night Japanese forces attacked Hong Kong.

Last night Japanese forces attacked Guam.

Last night Japanese forces attacked the Philippine Islands.

Last night Japanese forces attacked Wake Island.

This morning the Japanese attacked Midway Island.

<u>Japan has, therefore, undertaken a surprise offensive extending throughout the Pacific area.</u>

The last sentence is the summary of the above details, thus it is an inductive reasoning. In reasoning in this way, the mistake we may make is coming to a *hasty generalization*, for example, "My sister doesn't like sports; my girl friend doesn't like sports either. So all girls don't like sports." Then, a fallacy happens.

b. Deductive reasoning

It's the reasoning where a conclusion is reached by showing how a general premise also applies to a specific case. Thus, with deductive reasoning, we argue from a general principle to reach a conclusion about something specific. A syllogism is often the way of deductive argument, which has three elements: a major premise, a minor premise and a conclusion. For example:

Major premise: All English majors have excellent speaking skills.

Minor premise: Allen, my friend, is an English major.

Conclusion: Allen has excellent speaking skills.

The trick of a sound reasoning of this type lies in the precondition that the major premise must be a commonly agreed or accepted viewpoint. Otherwise, a fallacy will happen.

c. Analogical reasoning

It's a reasoning by comparison which links up two things and claims that what is true for one is therefore also true for the other. This strategy is especially useful when we want to advocate or oppose a viewpoint. For example, the failure of some earlier programs will lead to the conclusion that the similar programs will also fail. When using this strategy, we should be cautious about two key questions: Are the two similarities between the two cases relevant? Are there crucial differences between the two cases? When these two preconditions are violated, a fallacy (*poor analogy*) will happen, for example: "Since you're good at playing tennis, you must be good at playing badminton."

d. Causal reasoning

In this reasoning, there are two directions, either from cause to effect or from effect to cause. In testing whether it is reasoning from cause to effect or from effect to cause, we must ask two questions: first, might there be other causes that have produced the observed effect? Second, is the causation in the direction postulated?

e. Some common causal fallacies

When we claim that because one event follows another, the first event is the cause of the second, we are making a causal fallacy. i. e. Tom had a bath at six o'clock. The shower was broken. So Tom must have broken the shower.

☆ Slippery slope fallacy

It happens when we claim how a particular action will set forth a chain of events that will, inevitably lead to another certain result. For example when we claim that selling condoms on campus will cause more teenage pregnancy in schools and that will lead to moral decay among students; you would be committing a fallacy called *slippery slope fallacy*.

☆ Bandwagon fallacy

When we think most people do something or think so, or everyone does something or thinks so, then we also do it and think so, we're making a bandwagon fallacy. i. e. "Everyone thinks this TV is good, so I think it great too."

☆ Either-or fallacy

When there are other possibilities, but we give only two options to a problem, then we're making an either-or fallacy. i. e. "We'll either have to invest more in this factory or the workers will all get laid-off."

☆ Red herring

This happens when irrelevant facts or arguments are used as distractions, also called smoke screen. i. e. when a politician is accused of irresponsible conduct in protecting environment, he defends himself by saying, "Why are we talking about environment when there are so many people suffering from starvation?" then he is guilty of red herring fallacy.

☆ Ad hominem

This is known as name-calling, involving attacking irrelevant personal characteristics rather than the idea itself. i. e. "Since he has a criminal record, how could he take up such an important responsibility?"

10.5.3　Appreciating an example

This is a debate from the movie *The Great Debaters* (2007)

Wiley College vs. Harvard University

Resolved: Civil Disobedience is a Moral Weapon in the Fight for Justice

Harvard Dean: On this historic occasion, we welcome the distinguished team from Wiley College, our illustrious(优秀的)judges, you, the audience, and through the wonder of radio, the nation. Harvard University celebrates its 300th anniversary this year, and in Franklin Delano Roosevelt, its fifth President of the United States. But no university, no matter how grand or Augustan its history, can afford to live in the past. So, in the spirit of tomorrow(本着放眼未来的精神), I introduce to you, today, the debaters from Wiley College: Samantha Booke and Mr. James Farmer, Jr. Mr. Farmer will argue the first affirmative(正方观点).

James Farmer, Jr: Resolved(辩题): Civil disobedience(非暴力抵抗)is a moral weapon in the fight for justice. But how can disobedience ever be moral? Well I guess that depends on one's definition of the words—word. In 1919, in India, ten thousand people gathered in Amritsar to protest the tyranny(独裁)of British rule. General Reginald Dyer trapped them in a courtyard and ordered his troops to fire into the crowd for ten minutes. Three hundred seventy-nine died—men, women, children, shot down in cold blood. Dyer said he had taught them "a moral lesson". Gandhi and his followers responded not with violence, but

with an organized campaign of noncooperation. Government buildings were occupied. Streets were blocked with people who refused to rise, even when beaten by police. Gandhi was arrested. But the British were soon forced to release him. He called it a "moral victory". The definition of moral: Dyer's "lesson" or Gandhi's victory. You choose.

First Harvard Debater: From 1914 to 1918, for every single minute the world was at war, four men laid down their lives. Just think of it: Two hundred and forty brave young men were hurled into eternity every hour, of every day, of every night, for four long years. Thirty-five thousand hours; eight million, two hundred and eighty-one thousand casualties. Two hundred and forty. Two hundred and forty. Two hundred and forty. Here was a slaughter immeasurably greater than what happened at Amritsar. Can there be anything moral about it? Nothing—except that it stopped Germany from enslaving all of Europe. Civil disobedience isn't moral because it's nonviolent. Fighting for your country with violence can be deeply moral, demanding the greatest sacrifice of all: life itself. Nonviolence is the mask civil disobedience wears to conceal its true face: anarchy(无政府主义).

Samantha Booke: Gandhi believes one must always act with love and respect for one's opponents—even if they are Harvard debaters. Gandhi also believes that law breakers must accept the legal consequences for their actions. Does that sound like anarchy? Civil disobedience is not something for us to fear. It is, after all, an American concept. You see, Gandhi draws his inspiration not from a Hindu scripture(印度教教义), but from Henry David Thoreau, who, I believe, graduated from Harvard and lived by a pond not too far from here.

Second Harvard Debater: My opponent is right about one thing: Thoreau was a Harvard grad; and, like many of us, a bit self-righteous(自以为是). He once said, "Any man more right than his neighbors constitutes a majority of one..." Thoreau the idealist could never know that Adolf Hitler would agree with his words. The beauty and the burden of democracy is this: No idea prevails without the support of the majority. The People decide the moral issues of the day, not "a majority of one".

Samantha Booke: Majorities do not decide what is right or wrong. Your conscience does. So why should a citizen surrender his or her conscience to a legislature(立法)? For we must never, ever kneel down before the tyranny of a majority.

Second Harvard Debater: You can't decide which laws to obey and which to ignore. If we could, I'd never stop for a red light. My father is one of those men that stands between us and chaos: a police officer. I remember the day his partner, his best friend, was gunned down in the line of duty. Most vividly of all, I remember the expression on my dad's face. Nothing that erodes the rule of law can be moral, no matter what name we give it.

James Farmer, Jr: In Texas, they lynch(用私刑)Negroes. My teammates and I saw a

man strung up by his neck—and set on fire. We drove through a lynch mob, pressed our faces against the floorboard(车底板). I looked at my teammates. I saw the fear in their eyes; and worse—the shame. What was this Negro's crime that he should be hung, without trial, in a dark forest filled with fog? Was he a thief? Was he a killer? Or just a Negro? Was he a sharecropper(佃户)? A preacher? Were his children waiting up for him? And who were we to just lie there and do nothing? No matter what he did, the mob was the criminal. But the law did nothing—just left us wondering why. My opponent says, "Nothing that erodes the rule of law can be moral." But there is no rule of law in the Jim Crow South, not when Negroes are denied housing, turned away from schools, hospitals—and not when we are lynched. Saint Augustine said, "An unjust law is no law at all", which means I have a right, even a duty, to resist—with violence or civil disobedience. You should pray I choose the latter.

Topics for One-Minute Speech Practices

1. What does travelling mean to you?
2. What do you want from a job? Satisfaction or money?
3. What do you think of the talent show on TV?
4. How would you donate your money/material to people who need it? Through charity organization or other means?
5. What do you think of beauty contest?

6. What do you think of on-line dating?
7. How do you understand the statement that peace on earth begins at home?
8. What is your view on women playing soccer?
9. Do you think getting married too late will be a problem for you?
10. What qualities do you look for in a boyfriend (girl friend)?

Selected Maxims & Mottos
最好的格言警句精选

Life and Happiness 人生和幸福

The time of life is short, but to spend that shortness basely, it would be too long. —William Shakespeare

人生短暂,但如果卑贱地活着,则很漫长。——莎士比亚

I don't want to earn my living, I want to live. —Oscar Wilde

我不想谋生,我要生活。——王尔德

Nothing in life is to be feared. It is only to be understood. —Marie Curie

人生没有什么可怕的,只有需要去探索的。——居里夫人

Life can only be understood backwards; but it must be lived forwards. —S. Kierkegaard

要理解人生必须向后看,但要更好地活着必须向前看。——克尔凯郭尔

There are only two tragedies in life. One is not to get your heart's desire, and the other is to get it. —G. B. Shaw

人生只有两种悲剧。一种是得不到想要的,另一种是得到了。——萧伯纳

To be without some of the things you want is an indispensable part of happiness. —Betrand Russell

求之而不得是幸福必不可少的条件之一。——罗素

The tragedy of life is not so much what men suffer, but what they miss. —Thomas Carlyle

人生的悲剧并不在于受了多少痛苦,而是错过了多少东西。——卡莱尔

Do not pray for easy lives. Pray to be stronger men. —J. F. kennedy

不要祈祷过舒适的生活,而应该祈祷成为强者。——约翰·肯尼迪

Everyone is a moon, and has a dark side which he never shows to anybody. —Mark Twain

每个人都是月亮,都有一道不为人知的阴影。——马克·吐温

Doing what you like is freedom; liking what you do is happiness. —Frank Tyger

做喜欢做的事情就是自由,喜欢所做的事情就是幸福。——弗兰克·泰格尔

Happiness is a way station between too little and too much. —Channing Pollock

幸福是太多和太少之间的中间站。——波拉克

Happiness is a butterfly, which, when pursued, is always just beyond your grasp, but which, if you will sit down quietly, may alight upon you. —N. Hawthorne
幸福就像一只蝴蝶,当你追逐时总是离你远去;但当你静坐下来,说不定它会停歇在你身上。——霍桑

Most folks are about as happy as they make up their minds to be. —Abraham Lincoln
大多数人的幸福取决于他们想要多少幸福。——林肯

We have no more right to consume happiness without producing it than to consume wealth without producing it. —G. B. Shaw
如果没有创造幸福,我们就没有权利享受幸福;正如我们如果没有创造财富就不能享受财富。——萧伯纳

Happiness is not a goal. It is a by-product. —Eleanor Roosevelt
幸福并不是一个目标,它只是目标的副产品。——罗斯福夫人

Misfortune is a man's touchstone. —Charles Beaumont
不幸是一个人的试金石。——贝蒙

In three words I can sum up everything I've learned about life. It goes on. —Robert Frost
我对人生的真谛这样总结:生命不止,奋斗不息。——弗罗斯特

The secret of being miserable is to have leisure to bother about whether you are happy or not. —G. B. Shaw
不幸的根源在于有闲工夫担心自己是否幸福。——乔治·萧伯纳

A contented mind is the best blessing one can enjoy in this world. —Joseph Addison
心满意足是一个人在世界上获得的最好的福祉。——艾迪生(作家)

We grow neither better nor worse as we grow old, but more like ourselves. —M. L. Becher
随着年龄的增长我们并不会变好或变坏,而是变得更像我们自己。——贝彻

Liberty means responsibility. That is why most people dread it. —G. B. Shaw
自由意味着责任,这就是为什么大多数人害怕它。——萧伯纳

Three grand essentials to happiness in this life are something to do, something to love, and something to hope for. —Joseph Addison
幸福人生的三要素是:有所为、有所爱、有所希望。——约瑟夫·艾迪生

You cannot find peace by avoiding life. —Virginia Woolf
逃避人生不会让你找到安宁。——弗吉尼亚·伍尔芙

Three things help me balance the odds of life: sleep, hope and laugh. —Immanuel Kant
三事助吾抵御人生逆境:睡眠、希望和付诸一笑。——康德

No man is a failure who is enjoying life. —William Feather.
享受生命的人都不是失败者。——威廉·费特

Fear not for the future; weep not for the past. —Percy Bysshe Shelley

未来不足惧，过往不须泣。——珀西·比希·雪莱

As soon as we wish to be happier, we are no longer happy. —Walter Savage Landor
人一旦想要更快乐，就不会再快乐。——沃尔特·萨维奇·兰多

We make a living by what we get; we make a life by what we give. —Winston Churchill
靠获取我们得以生存，靠付出我们活得充实。——温斯顿·丘吉尔

The greatest and most important problems in life are all in a certain sense insoluble. They can never be solved, but only outgrown. —Carl Jung
人生中所有最重大和最重要的问题在某种意义上是无法解决的。我们无法解决它们，只能在成长中超越它们。——卡尔·荣格

We all have our time machines. Some take us back; they're called memories. Some take us forward; they're called dreams. —Jeremy Irons
我们都有自己的时光机。带我们回到过去的，叫回忆；带我们前往未来的，叫梦想。——杰瑞米·艾恩斯

Perseverance is not a long race; it is many short races one after another. —Walter Elliott
坚持不是长跑，而是一个接一个的短跑。——沃尔特·埃利奥特

Hope and Desire 希望和欲求

Don't part with your illusions. When they are gone you may still exist, but you have ceased to live. —Mark Twain
不要放弃梦想。放弃了梦想虽生犹死。——马克·吐温

Hope is a good breakfast, but it is a bad super. —Francis Bacon
希望是一道很美的早餐，却是一道难吃的晚餐。——培根

He who never lives by hope will die by hunger. —Joseph R. Drake
没有希望支撑的人会死于饥饿。——德雷克

He who has never hoped can never despair. —G. B. Shaw
从没有希望的人从不会绝望。——萧伯纳

I have not failed. I've just found 10 000 ways that won't work. —Thomas Edison
我从没有失败过，我只是试过了一万种行不通的方法。——爱迪生（发明家）

It is the eye that makes the horizon. —Ralph Emerson
视野决定了前方的地平线。——爱默生

The best way to realize your dreams is to wake up. —Paul Valery
实现梦想的最好办法是醒过来。——瓦雷里

Man can climb to the highest summit, but he cannot dwell there long. —G. B. Shaw
人类可以爬到最高峰，但不能在那里久住。——萧伯纳

The best way to get rid of a temptation is to yield to it. I can resist everything but temptation. —Oscar Wilde

抗拒诱惑的最好办法是屈服于它。除了诱惑，我什么都能抗拒。——王尔德

A dreamer is one who can only find his way by moonlight, and the only punishment is that he sees the dawn before the rest of the world. —Oscar Wilde

梦想者只能在月光中找到方向，他为此遭受的惩罚是他比所有人提前看到曙光。——王尔德

Two men look out through the same bars: one sees the mud, and the other, the stars. —Frederick Langbridge

两个人向铁窗外望去，一个人看到的是泥泞，另一个人看到的是星辰。——朗布里奇

We can accept finite disappointment, but never lose infinite hope. —Martin Luther King

我们可以暂时失望，但不能永无指望。——马丁·路德·金

Desire is half of life; indifference is half of death. —Khalil Gibran

欲望是生命的一半；冷漠是死亡的一半。——纪伯伦

Life and Death 生和死

The value of life lies not in the length of the days, but in how we make use of them. —Michel de Montaigne

生命的价值不在于长短，而在于我们如何发挥了它的作用。——蒙太古

The dead are only dead when they die in the thoughts of the living. —Jean Anouilh

只有不再活在人们心中的人才是真的死了。——阿罗尔

We would rather die on our feet than live on our knees. —Franklin Roosevelt

宁愿站着死，也不求跪着生。——罗斯福

Life is fine and enjoyable, but you must learn how to enjoy your fine life. —O. Henry

生命如此美好，但你要懂得如何去享受美好的生活。——欧·亨利

A light heart lives long. —William Shakespeare

豁达者长寿。——莎士比亚

Woman and Man 男人和女人

A woman should soften but not weaken a man. —Sigmund Freud

女人应当让男人变得柔情而不是柔弱。——弗洛伊德

There are but two things that chiefly excite us to love a woman: an attractive beauty and unspotted fame. —Miguel de Cervantes

激发我们去爱一个女人的理由不外乎有两个：漂亮的外表和纯洁的美德。——塞万提斯

When a woman marries again, it is because she detests her first husband; when a man marries again, it is because he adores his first wife. —Oscar Wilde

女人再嫁是因为憎恶前夫，男人再娶是因为太爱前妻。——王尔德

A man without a wife is but half a man. —Benjamin Franklin

人无贤妻只能算半个男人。——富兰克林

Men of few words are the best men. —William Shakespeare
寡言少语的男人是最优秀的男人。——莎士比亚

The test of a man or woman's breeding is how they behave in a quarrel. —G. B. Shaw
判断男人和女人教养如何,有效的方法是看他们如何争吵。——萧伯纳

Women are meant to be loved, not to be understood. —Oscar Wilde
女人生来是要被爱的,而不是被理解的。——王尔德

If a woman can't make her mistakes charming, she is only a female. —Oscar Wilde
如果一个女人不能让她的错误变得迷人,那她只能算一个雌性动物。——王尔德

I like the men who have a future and women who have a past. —Oscar Wilde
我看重有未来的男人和有过去的女人。——王尔德

A man's face is his autobiography; a woman's is her work of fiction. —Oscar Wilde
男人的面孔是他的自传,女人的面孔是她的幻想作品。——王尔德

One should never trust a woman who tells her real age. If she tells that, she tells everything. —Oscar Wilde
永远不要相信说出自己真实年龄的女人。如果她把这都说了,她什么都会说。——王尔德

Women are never disarmed by complements. Men always are. That is the difference between two sexes. —Oscar Wilde
恭维话从来不让女人失去戒备,但可以让男人缴械,这就是性别差异。——王尔德

A woman will not hate you when you say you love her, but just friends. —Samuel Johnson
一个女人不会因为你说爱她而恨你,但是会因为你说你们只是朋友而恨你。——约翰逊

Youth and Age 青年和老年

At twenty years of age, the will reigns; at thirty, the wit; and at forty, the judgment. —Benjamin Franklin
20岁支配我们的是意志;30岁时,是智慧;40岁时,是判断力。——富兰克林

When I was young, I admired clever people. Now that I am old, I admire kind people. —Abraham Herschel
年轻时我崇拜聪明人。现在老了,我崇拜善良人。——赫舍尔

Growing old is not upsetting; being perceived old is. —Kenny Rogers
老了并不可怕,可怕的是在他人看来你老了。——罗杰斯

The tragedy of old age is not that one is old, but that one is not young. —Oscar Wilde
老龄的悲剧并不在于变老了,而在于再也不年轻了。——王尔德

I would rather see a young man blush than turn pale. —M. Cato
我宁愿看到年轻人的脸羞红而不愿看到他们脸色苍白。——卡托

Today is the first day of the rest of my life. —John Denver

今天是我余生的第一天。——约翰·丹佛

As I approve of a youth that has something of the old man in him, so I am no less pleased with an old man that has something of the youth. —Marcus Tullius Cicero

我赞赏那些具有老人风度的青年,同样也喜欢那些带有青年气息的老人。——马库斯·图留斯·西塞罗

Love, Marriage and Family 爱情、婚姻和家庭

Love asks for faith, and faith asks for firmness. —George Herbert

爱情要求忠诚,忠诚要求坚定。——赫伯特

First love is only a little foolishness and a lot of curiosity. —G. B. Shaw

初恋不过是少量的愚蠢加上大量的好奇心。——萧伯纳

True love is like ghost, which everybody talks about but few have seen. —La Rochefoucauld

真爱犹如鬼魂,大家都在谈论这东西,但很少人见到过。——罗切福考尔德

Love sought is good, but given unsought is better. —William Shakespeare

找寻得来的爱是美好的,但不经寻找而赋予的爱情是更美好的。——莎士比亚

Love works in miracles every day: such as weakening the strong, and strengthening the weak; making fools of the wise, and wise men of fools. —Marguerite De Valois

爱情很奇妙,它让坚强者懦弱,让懦弱者坚强;让聪明者糊涂,让糊涂者聪明。——玛格丽特皇后

Love is when you take away the feeling, the passion, the romance and you find out you still care for the person. —Alias

爱情应该是这样的:当感觉、激情和浪漫都消失了的时候,你发现你仍然牵挂着对方。——佚名

To marry means to half one's right and double one's duty. —Arthur Schopenhauer

结婚意味着失掉一半的权利,肩负双倍的责任。——叔本华

Where there is marriage without love, there is love without marriage. —Benjamin Franklin

哪里有没有爱情的婚姻,哪里就有没有婚姻的爱情。——富兰克林

Keep your eyes wide open before marriage and half shut afterwards. —Benjamin Franklin

婚前睁大双眼,婚后双眼半闭。——富兰克林

A successful marriage requires falling in love many times, and always with the same person. —Mignon McLaughlin

成功的婚姻需要我们多次陷入爱恋,而且每次都是爱上同一个人。——麦克罗琳

Marriage is the triumph of imagination over intelligence; remarriage is the triumph of hope over experience. —Oscar Wilde

结婚是想象力战胜了理智,再婚是希望战胜了经验。——王尔德

All happy families resemble one another; each unhappy family is unhappy in its own way. —Leo Tolstoy

幸福的家庭是相似的,不幸的家庭各有各的不幸。——托尔斯泰

Wives are young men's mistresses, middle age's companions and old men's nurses. —Francis Bacon

年轻时妻子是情妇;中年时妻子是伴侣;年老时妻子是护士。——培根

Men marry because they are tired, women because they are curious, both are disappointed. —Oscar Wilde

男人娶妻是因为他们疲惫了,女人嫁人是因为她们好奇,结果他们都很失望。——王尔德

Marriage has many pains, but celibacy has no pleasures. —Samuel Johnson

婚姻有很多痛苦,但单身没有任何快乐。——约翰逊

What is the chief cause of divorce? —Marriage. —Oscar Wilde

离婚的主要原因是什么?——结婚。——王尔德

The course of true love never did run smooth. —William Shakespeare

通往真爱的道路从来没有坦途。——莎士比亚

At the touch of love, everyone is a poet. —Plato

在爱情的触发下,每个人都是诗人。——柏拉图

A man in love is easily deceived. —Aesop

恋爱着的人容易受骗。——伊索

Love looks not with the eyes, but with the mind, and therefore is winged Cupid painted blind. —William Shakespeare

爱情不是用眼睛,而是用心灵去看的,所以长翅膀的爱神被画成盲人。——莎士比亚

When one is in love, he always begins by deceiving himself, and ends by deceiving others. This is what calls romance. —Oscar Wilde

恋爱总是以自欺开始,以欺人结束,这就是所谓的浪漫。——王尔德

To love oneself is the beginning of a lifelong romance. —Oscar Wilde

爱自己是终身浪漫的开始。——王尔德

The praise that comes from love does not make us vain, but more humble. —Sir James Matthew Barrie

由爱而生的赞美不会让我们变得自负,只会让我们更加谦卑。——詹姆斯·马修·巴里爵士

Parents and Children 父母和孩子

One father is more than a hundred school masters. —George Herbert

好父亲抵得上一百个教师。——赫伯特

It is a wise father that knows his own child. —William Shakespeare

再聪明的父亲都不见得完全了解自己的儿子。——莎士比亚

I don't know who my grandfather was. I'm more concerned to know what his grandson will be. —Abraham Lincoln

我不知道我有什么样的祖父,我更关心的是他会有什么样的孙子。——林肯

All I am and can be owes to my angel mother. —Abraham Lincoln

我之所以有今天以及将来的一切,皆归功于我天使般的母亲。——林肯

A fond mother spoils a child. —English saying

慈母多败儿。——谚语

A spoiled child is worse than a parentless child. —English saying

被惯坏了的孩子还不如没有父母的孩子。——谚语

I'm not President but a father in front of my son. —Franklin Roosevelt

在孩子面前我不是总统而是父亲。——富兰克林·罗斯福

A father's virtue is the son's best legacy. —Cervantes

父亲的德行是儿子最好的遗产。——塞万提斯

Character and Virtue 性格和品德

Character is what you are in the dark. —Dwight Moody

一个人的品格在黑暗中显现。——穆迪

A man never discloses his character so clearly as when he describes another's. —Jean Richter

一个人在描述别人性格的时候最能暴露自己的性格。——利尔特

A man's character is like a fence—whitewashing cannot strengthen it. —T. Roberson

一个人的性格就像一道篱笆,再怎么粉饰也美化不了。——罗伯森

All men are equal; it's not birth but virtue that makes the difference. —Voltaire

人人都是平等的,使人不平等的是品德而不是身世。——伏尔泰

The only reward of virtue is virtue; the only way to have a friend is to be one. —Ralph Emerson

美德的唯一回报是美德;交上朋友的唯一方式就是成为别人的朋友。——爱默生

The best thought has been done in solitude. —Thomas Edison

最好的思想都是在孤独中产生的。——爱迪生

The whole dignity of man lies in the power of thought. —P. Pascal

人的所有尊严在于思想的力量。——帕斯卡尔

All empty souls tend to extreme opinion. —William Butler Yeats

空洞的思想都会导致极端的言论。——叶芝

Conceit may puff a man up, but it can never prop him up. —John Ruskin

自傲也许能让一个人膨胀起来,但不可能撑住他。——罗斯金

Discretion is the better part of valor. —John Gould Fletcher

谨慎是勇气中更重要的一部分。——弗莱彻

If there is nothing wrong in this world, then there wouldn't be anything for us to do. —G. B. Shaw
如果这个世界没有错,那我们就无事可做了。——萧伯纳

The man who has never made a mistake will never make anything. —G. B. Shaw
一个从不犯错误的人只会一事无成。——萧伯纳

The greatest of faults is to be conscious of none. —Thomas Carlyle
最大的错误是没有意识到犯了错误。——卡莱尔

Confidence in the goodness of another is good proof of one's own goodness. —Michel de Montaigne
相信别人善良正是证明了自己善良。——蒙田

It's not the fine coat that makes a gentleman. —Thomas Fuller
漂亮的西装并不能使人成为绅士。——福勒

He who praises everybody praises nobody. —Samuel Johnson
对每个人都赞美的人对任何人都没有赞美。——约翰逊

If I'm not better, at least I'm different. —Jean Jacques Rousseau
我不一定比别人出色,但起码要有自己的个性。——让·雅克·卢梭

A cynic is one who knows the price of everything but the value of nothing. —Oscar Wilde
愤世嫉俗的人知道所有东西的价格,但不知道任何东西的价值。——王尔德

A true friend is one who overlooks your failures and tolerates your successes. —Doug Larson
真正的朋友不追究你的过错,也不嫉妒你的成功。——拉森

Conscience and cowardice are really the same things. —Oscar Wilde
良心和懦弱实际上是一回事。——王尔德

To really understand a man, we must judge him in misfortune. —Napoleon Bonaparte
要真正了解一个人,我们须在不幸中考查他。——拿破仑

A great man is the man who makes every man feel great. —G. K. Chesterton
一个真正的伟人能让身边的每个人都感觉自己伟大。——查尔斯顿

The highest compliment that you can pay anyone is to listen intently to him. —Isaac Marcosson
你对他人最好的恭维就是倾听他说话。——马科森

All the beautiful sentiment in this world weighs less than a single act. —James Lowell
世上再美的情感也不如一次行动重要。——罗威尔

Blessed are the poor in spirit, for theirs is the kingdom of heaven. —Matthew 5:3
虚心的人有福了,因为天国是他们的。——《马太福音》5:3

We are what we repeatedly do. —Aristotle
我们日复一日做的事情就构成了我们自己。——亚里士多德

The best audience for the practice of virtue is the approval of one's own conscience. —

Cicero

德行最好的见证者是我们自己的良心。——西塞罗

Treat other people as you hope they treat you. —Aesop

你希望别人如何对待你,你就应该如何对待别人。——伊索

A liar will not be believed, even when he speaks the truth. —Aesop

撒谎者即使讲真话也没人相信。——伊索

Modesty is the kind of pride that is least likely to offend. —Jules Renard

谦逊是一种最不易得罪人的骄傲。——朱耳斯·勒纳尔

Only the shallow know themselves. —Oscar Wilde

只有浅薄的人才会了解自己。——王尔德

One learns people through the heart, not the eyes or the intellect. —Mark Twain

要用心去了解一个人,而不是凭眼睛或智力。——马克·吐温

Courage is the ladder on which all the other virtues mount. —Clare Luce

勇气是所有其他品德借以攀登的梯子。——克莱尔·露丝

Better keep yourself clean and bright; you are the window through which you must see the world. —G. B. Shaw

我们透过自身这扇窗看世界,因此最好让它保持干净明亮。——萧伯纳

Kindness is the language which the deaf can hear and the blind can see. —Mark Twain

善良是一种聋人听得见,盲人看得见的语言。——马克·吐温

There is nothing noble in being superior to your fellow men. True nobility is being superior to your former self. —Ernest Hemingway

比你的同伴优秀没有什么可高贵的,真正的高贵之处是比过去的自己优秀。——海明威

Violet leaves the fragrance onto the feet that crash it; this is forgiving. —Mark Twain

紫罗兰把芳香留在了踩踏它的双脚上,这就是宽恕。——马克·吐温

Only the brave one can forgive. A coward will never forgive. —Anonymous

只有勇敢的人才会宽恕他人,懦夫是不会懂得宽恕的。——佚名

A great man has two hearts. One is bleeding, and the other is forgiving. —Khalil Gibran

伟人有两颗心。一颗心在流血,另一颗心却在宽恕。——纪伯伦

I don't know the secret to success, but I know the key to failure is to please everyone. —Anonymous

我不知道成功的秘密,但我知道失败的原因是试图满足所有人。——佚名

Truth is beautiful, without doubt; but so are lies. —Ralph Waldo Emerson

真相是美的,但是谎言无疑也是美的。——拉尔夫·爱默生

Be yourself, everyone else is already taken. —Oscar Wilde

做你自己,别的角色都已有人扮演了。——奥斯卡·王尔德

Confidence in the goodness of another is proof of one's own goodness. —Michel de

Montaigne

相信别人的善良也就证明了自己的善良。——蒙田

Like a welcome summer rain, humor may suddenly cleanse and cool the earth, the air and you. —Langston Hughes

幽默就像一场酣畅的夏日之雨,骤然把土地、空气和你浇个畅快清凉。——兰斯顿·休斯

Whenever you feel like criticizing anyone, just remember that all the people in this world haven't had the advantages that you've had. —F. Scott Fitzgerald

每当你想要批评别人的时候,要记住,这个世界上并非所有人都有你拥有的那些优越条件。——F·司各特·菲茨杰拉德

Watch your thoughts, for they become words. Watch your words, for they become actions. Watch your actions, for they become habits. Watch your habits, for they become your character. And watch your character, for it becomes your destiny. —Margaret Thatcher

注意你的思想,因为它们将变成言辞;注意你的言辞,因为它们将变成行为;注意你的行为,因为它们将变成习惯;注意你的习惯,因为它们将变成性格;注意你的性格,因为它将决定你的命运。——撒切尔夫人

I'd rather be myself. Myself and nasty. Not somebody else, however jolly. —Aldous Huxley

我宁可做自己,一个讨人嫌的自己,也不当别人,无论他多么快活。——阿道司·赫胥黎

Be not angry that you cannot make others as you wish them to be, since you cannot make yourself as you wish to be. —Thomas Kempis

当你无法让别人按照你的想法行事时,别生气,因为你自己也做不到。——托马斯·坎皮斯

If I am not better, at least I am different. —Jean Jacques Rousseau

即便不是更加出色,至少我与众不同。——让·雅克·卢梭

Have patience with all things, but, first of all with yourself. —Saint Francis de Sales

对所有的事情都要有耐心,但首先对自己要有耐心。——圣·弗朗西斯·沙雷

For their soul's good, man should do each day two things they disliked. —William Somerset Maugham

人每天都该做一两件自己不喜欢的事情,以求心灵平静。——威廉·萨默塞特·毛姆

Be nice to people on your way up, because you will meet them on your way down. —Wilson Mizner

上坡时,对别人好一点,因为下坡时,你们还会相遇。——威尔逊·米茨纳

I choose my friends for their good looks, my acquaintances for their good characters, and my enemies for their intellects. —Oscar Wilde

我按照外表来选择朋友,按照人品来选择熟人,按照智商来选择敌人。——奥斯卡·王尔德

Cause and Career 事业和职业

Nothing is impossible to a willing heart. —Thomas Heywood
有坚强的意志,无所不往。——海伍德

20 years later, we'll more regret what we didn't do than we did. —Mark Twain
20年后,我们更后悔的不是做了什么,而是没有做什么。——马克·吐温

There are no shortcuts to any place worth going. —Beverly Sills
任何值得去的地方都是没有捷径的。——希尔斯

The dictionary is the only place where success comes before work. —Arthur Brisbane
只有在字典里,成功排在劳作之前。——布里斯班

There are many different ways to go wrong, but only one way to go right, so that's why it's easy to fail and difficult to succeed. —Aristotle
犯错有很多方式,但做对只有一种,这就是为什么失败容易成功难。——亚里士多德

Many of life's failures are experienced by men who haven't realized how close they were to success when they gave up. —Thomas Edison
很多人失败是因为没有意识到,在他们放弃的时候离成功如此接近。——爱迪生

In just two days, tomorrow will be yesterday. —Johann W. Goethe
再过两天,明天就成了昨天。——歌德

All is well that ends well. —William Shakespeare
结果好一切都好。——莎士比亚

I am a slow walker, but I don't walk backward. —Abraham Lincoln
我走路很慢,但从不后退。——林肯

Don't try to be better than your contemporaries or predecessors, just be better than yourself. —William Faulkner
不要试图超越同时代的人或前人,你只需要超越你自己。——福克纳

The landscape belongs to the man who looks at it. —Ralph Waldo Emerson
风景属于看风景的人。——拉尔夫·爱默生

Believe those who are seeking the truth. Doubt those who find it. —Andre Gide
相信那些寻求真理的人;怀疑那些找到真理的人。——安德烈·纪德

Education and Knowledge Pursuit 教育和求知

The roots of education are bitter, but the fruits are sweet. —Aristotle
教育的根是苦的,但结出的果实是甜的。——亚里士多德

There are three good ingredients in life: learning, earning and yearning. —Christopher Morley
美好人生的三个要素:学习、收获和期望。——莫里

Education is a gradual progress of discovering one's ignorance. —Anonymous
教育是让我们意识到自己无知的一个循序渐进的过程。——佚名

What we want is to see the child in pursuit of knowledge, and not knowledge in pursuit of the child. —G. B. Shaw

我们应该让孩子追求知识,而不是让知识穷追孩子。——萧伯纳

Imagination is more important than books. —Albert Einstein

想象力比书本更重要。——爱因斯坦

The good life is one inspired by love and guided by knowledge. —Bertrand Russell

美好的生活由爱激励,由知识引导。——罗素

A good book is the purest essence of a human soul. —T. Carlyle

一本好书是作者灵魂的精华。——卡莱尔

If you have a garden and a library, you have everything you need. —Cicero

如果你有一座花园和一间书房,你便有了一切。——西塞罗

Wherever they burn books they will also, in the end, burn human beings. —Heinrich Heine

在焚烧书籍的地方,最终也会焚烧人类。——海涅

A little learning is a dangerous thing. —Alexander Pope

一知半解是很危险的事情。——蒲伯

Reading makes a full man, conference a ready man and writing, an exact man. —Francis Bacon

阅读使人充实,交谈使人机智,写作使人精确。——培根

There are two motives for reading a book: one that you enjoy it; the other that you can boast about it. —Bertrand Russell

阅读的目的无外乎两个:一个是出于兴趣,另一个是用来炫耀。——罗素

Reading is to the mind what exercise is to the body. —Richard Steel

阅读之于大脑正如锻炼之与身体。——斯梯尔

Wisdom is in the head not in the beard. —Aesop

智慧不在年高,而在大脑。——伊索

Everybody is ignorant, only on different subjects. —Will Rogers

每人都有无知的一面,只不过是在不同的领域罢了。——罗杰斯

Knowing others is intelligence; knowing yourself is true wisdom. Mastering others is strength; mastering yourself is true power. —Anonymous

理解别人是聪明;理解自己才是真正的智慧。控制别人是强力;控制自己才是真正的力量。——佚名

The difference between school and life: in school, you're taught a lesson and then given a test. In life, you're given a test that teaches you a lesson. —Anonymous

学校和人生的区别是:在学校你先上完一课然后再测验,而人生是你先接受测验,从而学到一课。——佚名

To be ignorant of one's ignorance is the malady of the ignorant. —A. Alcott

意识不到自己的无知是最大的无知。——阿尔克特

Wise men talk because they have something to say; fools, because they have to say something. —Plato
聪明的人说话是因为有话要说,愚蠢的人说话是因为要说些话。——柏拉图

Be wise worldly, not worldly wise. —Ed Howe
做一个聪明的世俗人,不要做一个世俗的聪明人。——豪伊

Fools and wise men are equally harmless. It is the half fools and half-wise men that are dangerous. —Wolfgang Goethe
愚蠢的人和聪明的人都无害于他人,危险的是那些半聪明半愚蠢的人。——歌德

If the only tool you have is a hammer, you tend to see every problem as a nail. —Abraham Maslow
如果你只有锤子这个工具,你会把每个问题都看作是钉子。——马斯洛

Life has taught me to think, but thinking has not taught me to live. —Alexander Herzen
生活教会了我思考,但思考并没有教会我如何生活。——赫尔岑

Whenever you find yourself on the side of the majority, it is time for you to pause and reflect. —Mark Twain
每当你发现自己站在大多数人这一边,就要停下来好好反省。——马克·吐温

Education is not filling a pail, but lighting a fire. —Butler Yeats
教育不是装满一桶水,而是点燃一团火焰。——叶芝

The best way to pay for a lovely moment is to enjoy it. —Richard Bach
回报一个美好时刻的最好方式就是去享受它。——巴赫

Experience without learning is better than learning without experience. —Bertrand Russell
没有知识的经验强于没有经验的知识。——罗素

Talkers are no good doers. —William Shakespeare
夸夸其谈者不是实干家。——莎士比亚

Let any man speak long enough, he will get believers. —Robert Stevenson
给人足够的时间去讲话,就会有人相信他。——斯蒂文森

He who can, does, he who cannot, teaches. —G. B. Shaw
会动手的做事,不会动手的教人。——萧伯纳

It is better to travel hopefully than arrive. —Robert Stevenson
满怀希望地旅行比到达目的地更快乐。——斯蒂文森

The greatest and most important problems in life in a certain sense can never be solved, but only outgrown. —Carl Jung
在某种意义上,生活中最重大和最重要的问题是无法解决的,我们只能超越它们。——卡尔·荣格

Education is not preparation for life; education is life itself. —John Dewey
教育不是为了人生做准备,教育本身就是人生。——杜威

Live each day as if you're going to die tomorrow and learn each day as if you're going to live forever. —Mohandas Gandhi
每天好好活着,就当自己明天就要死去;每天好好学习,就当自己长生不死。——甘地

The end of all our exploring will be to arrive where we started and get to know the place for the first time. —T. S. Eliot
我们探索的终点是回到出发的原点,并开始首次了解它。——艾略特

The best remedy for excessive admiration is to acquire knowledge of many things. —Rene Descartes
对过度崇拜最好的治疗方法是去获取众多事物的知识。——笛卡尔

Reading is to the mind what exercise is to the body. —Joseph Addison
阅读之于心智正如锻炼之于身体。——约瑟夫·艾迪生

Emotions and Feelings 情绪和情感

A friend is a present we give ourselves. —Robert Stevenson
交一个朋友就是送给自己一份礼物。——斯蒂文森

The only thing worse than being talked about is not being talked about. —Oscar Wilde
世界上只有一件事比被人议论更糟糕,那就是没人议论你。——王尔德

A true friend stabs you in the front. —Wilde
真正的朋友才会当面指责你。——王尔德

Anybody can become angry—that is easy; but to be angry with the right person, and to the right degree, and at the right time, and for the right purpose, and in the right way—that is not within everybody's power and is not easy. —Aristotle
人人都有发火的时候,这很容易。但对一个恰当的人,在恰当的场合,在恰当的时间,出于恰当的原因,用恰当的方式发火,这却不是人人能轻易做到的。——亚里士多德

The pessimist complains about the wind; the optimist expects it to change; the realist adjusts the sail. —William Ward
悲观者抱怨起风,乐观者期待风转向,现实主义者调整风帆。——沃德

To be angry is to avenge others' faults on ourselves. —Anonymous
生气是拿他人的错误来惩罚自己。——佚名

Love, friendship and respect do not unite people as much as a common hatred for something. —Anton Chekhov
爱、友谊和尊重都不能像某种共同的仇恨那样把人们团结在一起。——契诃夫

Hatred is blind, so is love. —Oscar Wilde
恨是盲目的,爱也是。——王尔德

Always forgive your enemies, nothing annoys them so much. —Oscar Wilde
永远宽恕你的敌人,没有什么比这个更能令他们恼怒的了。——王尔德

Bitter words may hurt feelings, but silence breaks the heart. —Anonymous
尖刻的话可能会伤人情感,但是沉默会让一颗心破碎。——佚名

Work and Leisure 工作和休息

The best preparation for good work tomorrow is to do good work today. —Elbert Hubbard

为明天最好的准备是做好今天的工作。——哈伯特

The world is a book, and those who do not travel read only one page. —St. Augustine

世界是一本书,那些没有旅行的人只翻开了一页。——奥古斯丁

Travel, in the younger sort, is a part of education; in the elder a part of experience. —Francis Bacon

旅行,对年轻人来说是一种教育,对年长者来说是一种经历。——培根

The man is richest whose pleasure is the cheapest. —Henry D. Thoreau

谁的取悦方式最廉价,谁就是最富有的。(或:能处处寻找快乐的人才是最富有的。)——梭罗

To do nothing at all is the most difficult thing in the world, the most difficult and intelligent. —Oscar Wilde

什么也不做是世上最难的事情,最难也最具智慧。——王尔德

All work without play makes Jack a dull boy. —English saying

只干活不玩耍,聪明的孩子会变傻。——谚语

That man is the richest whose pleasure is the cheapest. —H. D. Thoreau

谁的取悦方式最廉价,谁就是最富有的。——梭罗

I enjoy living among pedestrians who have an instinctive and habitual realization that there is more to a journey than the mere fact of arrival. —E. B. White

我喜欢与步行者为伍,因为他们有一种本能的、习惯性的意识:行走的意义不只在于到达。——E·B·怀特

Weekends are a bit like rainbows; they look good from a distance but disappear when you get up close to them. —John Shirley

周末有点像彩虹,远远看上去很美丽,而一旦走近便消失不见了。——约翰·谢利

Wealth and Money 财富和金钱

Money can buy a pretty dog, but it won't buy the wag of its tail. —Josh Billings

钱可以买来一只名犬,但买不来它摇尾巴。——比林斯

Industry is fortune's right hand, and frugality her left. —John Ray

勤奋是财富的右手,节俭是其左手。——约翰瑞

Take care of the pence, and the pounds will take care of themselves. —Chesterfield

攒下每一分钱,日积月累就会富有起来。——切斯特菲尔德

A penny saved is a penny earned. —T. Fuller

节约一分钱就是赚了一分钱。——福勒

You can't have what you like until you like what you have. —Johann W. Goethe

一个不喜欢自己所拥有的人不会拥有自己所喜欢的。——歌德

The most beautiful things in the world have nothing to do with money. —Anonymous
世界上最美好的东西与金钱无关。——佚名

When money begins to talk, truth will shut its mouth. —Proverb
当金钱开始说话时,真理就会闭上嘴巴。——谚语

Money is a good servant, but a bad master. —Francis Bacon
金钱是很好的奴仆,但却是很坏的主人。——培根

Greed is the root of all evils. —New Testament
贪婪是罪恶之源。——《新约》

Miscellaneous 其他

No one can be perfectly free till all are free; no one can be perfectly moral till all are moral; no one can be perfectly happy till all are happy. —Hebert Spencer
没有人能完全自由,除非每个人都获得自由;没有人能完全讲究道德,除非每个人都讲究道德;没有人能完全幸福,除非每个人都得到幸福。——斯宾塞

Most of the trouble in the world is caused by people wanting to be important. —T. S. Eliot
世上大多数苦难是由雄心勃勃的人造成的。——艾略特

I disapprove of what you say, but I will defend to the death your right to say it. —Voltaire
我不同意你说的话,但我誓死捍卫你说话的权利。——伏尔泰

In the end, we don't remember the words of enemy, but the silence of our friends. —Martin Luther King
最终,我们不记得敌人对我们的辱骂,只记住了朋友们的沉默。——马丁·路德·金

An eye for eye makes the whole world blind. —Mohandas Gandhi
以牙还牙使得人世间充满黑暗。——甘地

He who has no enemies will not be liked by his friends. —Oscar Wilde
没有敌人的人,他的朋友也不喜欢他。——王尔德

Two things fill the mind with ever increasing wonder and awe: the more often and more intensely the mind of thought is drawn to them, the starry heaven above me and the moral law within me. —Immanuel Kant
有两件事物我愈思考愈觉神奇,心中也充满敬畏,那就是我头上的星空与心中的道德准则。——康德

Every saint has a past and every sinner has a future. —Oscar Wilde
每一个圣人都有过去,每一个罪人都有将来。——王尔德

Whenever people agree with me, I feel I must be wrong. —Oscar Wilde
每当人们赞美我的时候,我想我一定错了。——王尔德

One of the most time-consuming things is to have an enemy. —E. B. White

最费时间的事情是树立一个敌人。——E·B·怀特

The biggest devil is me. I'm either my best friend or my worst enemy. —Whitney Huston

最大的魔鬼是我自己。我既是自己最好的朋友,也是自己最坏的敌人。——惠特尼·休斯敦

We can't all be heroes. Somebody has to sit on the curb and clap as they go by. —Will Rogers

并不是每个人都能当上英雄,当有英雄走过的时候,总要有人坐在路边为他们鼓掌。——罗杰斯

It's better to know some of the questions than all of the answers. —James Thurber

弄清楚一些问题比得到所有的答案要好。——詹姆斯·瑟伯

Your wealth is measured by how much is left when you have lost everything. —Anonymous

你的财富是你失去一切以后剩下的东西。——佚名

Motivation is what gets you started; habit is what keeps you going. —Anonymous

动机使你开始行动,而习惯让你继续下去。——佚名

Everyone wants to be on the right side of truth, but not sincerely on the right side of truth. —Anonymous

每个人都想站在真理的一边,但不是每个人都真诚地站在这边。——佚名

The art of being wise is knowing when and what to overlook. —Anonymous

智慧的艺术是知道何时忽略哪些事情。——佚名

Shallow men believe in luck and strong men believe in cause and effect. —Ralph Waldo Emerson

浅薄的人信运气,坚强之士信因果。——爱默生

When life does not find a singer to sing her heart, she produces a philosopher to speak her mind. —Khalil Gibran

当生活找不到一个歌手唱出她的心声的时候,就产生一个哲学家来说出她的心思。——纪伯伦

Love of beauty is taste. The creation of beauty is art. —Ralph Waldo Emerson

爱美是一种品味,而创造美则是艺术。——爱默生

History repeats itself, first as tragedy, then as farce. —Hegel

历史这样重复自己:第一次是个悲剧,再一次就是个闹剧。——黑格尔

As a general rule, people ask for advice only in order not to follow it; or if they do follow it, in order to have someone to blame for giving it. —Alexandre Dumas

通常来说,人们征求意见只是为了不采纳它;就算真的采纳了,也是为了能找个人来当替罪羊。——大仲马

You have enemies? Good. That means you've stood up for something, sometime in your life. —Winston Churchill

你有敌人？很好。这意味着在你一生中的某个时刻,曾有过自己的立场。——温斯顿·丘吉尔

We read the world wrong and say that it deceives us. —Rabindranath Tagore

我们把世界理解错了,却说它欺骗了我们。——泰戈尔

Look at everything always as though you were seeing it either for the first or last time; thus is your time on earth filled with glory. —Betty Smith

看待一切事物,都要像第一次或最后一次看到那样,这样在世间活着才会充满荣耀。——贝蒂·史密斯

The eyes of others are our prisons; their thoughts our cages. —Virginia Woolf

他人的眼光是我们的监狱,他人的看法是我们的牢笼。——弗吉尼亚·伍尔芙

Don't ever wrestle with a pig. You'll both get dirty, but the pig will enjoy it. —Cale Yarborough

永远别和猪摔跤。你们都会弄得浑身是泥,但猪却将乐在其中。——卡尔·雅伯罗

There is one thing alone that stands the brunt of life throughout its course: a quiet conscience. —Euripides

只有一样东西能经受住生活的冲击:一颗坦然的心。——欧里庇得斯

References

[1] BILLIG M. Laughter and Ridicule: Towards a Social Critique of Humor[M]. London: Sage, 2005.

[2] BORG J. Body Language: 7 Easy Lessons to Master the Silent Language[M]. Jersey: FT Press, 2010.

[3] BRUMBERGER E R. Visual Rhetoric in the Curriculum: Pedagogy for a Multimodal Workplace[J]. Business Communication Quarterly, 2005, 68(3): 318-333.

[4] CLARK D L. Rhetoric in Greco-Roman Education[M]. New York: Columbia University Press, 1957.

[5] CRANE D L. Powerful Public Speaking: How to Capitalize on Your Personal Style[M]. Michigan: Brain Research Press, 2000.

[6] ENGLEBERG I N, Wynn D R. Working in Groups: Communication Principles and Strategies[M]. 4th ed. Boston: Allyn & Bacon, 2007.

[7] XU Q G. The Use of Eloquence: The Confucian Perspective[C]// CAROL S L, ROBERTA A B. Rhetoric Before and Beyond the Greeks. New York: State University of New York Press, 2004.

[8] Zimmerman G I, SEIBERT D R, Owen J L. Speech Communication: A Contemporary Introduction[M]. St. Paul, MN: West Publishing Co., 1986.

[9] HARIMAN R. Political Style: The Artistry of Power[M]. Chicago: University of Chicago Press, 1995.

[10] ROUX J L. Effective Educators Are Culturally Competent Communicators[J]. Intercultural Education, 2002, 13(1): 37-48.

[11] LASKOWSKI L. Overcoming Speaking Anxiety in Meetings & Presentations, 1996. http://www.ljlseminars.com/anxiety.htm.

[12] LUCAS S E. The Art of Public Speaking[M]. 8th ed. New York: McGraw-Hill Humanities/Social Sciences/Languages, 2007.

[13] LUCAS S E. The Art of Public Speaking[M]. 10th ed. 北京: 外语教学与研究出版社, 2010.

[14] McARTHUR T. The Oxford Companion to the English Language[M]. New York：Oxford，1992.

[15] MOORE P J，SCEVAK J J. Learning from Texts and Visual Aids：A Developmental Perspective[J]. Journal of Research in Reading，2010，20(3)：205-223.

[16] SPRAGUE J，STUART D. The Speaker's Handbook[M]. 6th ed. Belmont，CA：Wadsworth/Thomson，2003.

[17] WOOD J T. Communication Theories in Action：An Introduction[M]. 3rd ed. Belmont，CA：Wadsworth/Thomson，2003.

[18] Kay S. Practical Presentations[M]. Beijing：Foreign Language Teaching and Research Press，2008.

[19] GIBSON C. 英语演讲实训指南[M]. 北京：外语教学与研究出版社，2008.

[20] 崔林琳，林立. 大学英语演讲教程[M]. 北京：外文出版社，2004.

[21] 丁往道，吴冰，钟美荪，等. 英语写作手册(修订本)[M]. 北京：外语教学与研究出版社，1999.

[22] 高瑛，孙利民，仇云龙. 英语演讲教程[M]. 上海：复旦大学出版社，2010.

[23] 胡曙中. 英语修辞学[M]. 上海：上海外语教育出版社，2002.

[24] 胡曙中. 现代英语修辞学[M]. 上海：上海外语教育出版社，2004.

[25] 康苏珊，金利民，樊葳葳. 英语演讲选评100篇[M]. 北京：外语教学与研究出版社，2008.

[26] 刘亚猛. 追求象征的力量：关于西方修辞思想的思考[M]. 北京：三联书店，2004.

[27] 卢天贶，刘寒辉，萧美玲，等. 英汉对照外国名言录[M]. 上海：上海人民出版社，1997.

[28] 宿玉荣，王帆，范悦. 英语演讲比赛参赛指南[M]. 北京：外语教学与研究出版社，2006.